T0342552

The Economics of Sovereign
Debt and Default

CREI Lectures in Macroeconomics

Jordi Galí, Series Editor
Editorial Advisory Board: Fernando Broner, Gino Gancia,
Alberto Martín, Giacomo Ponzetto, and Jaume Ventura

The Economics of Sovereign Debt and Default

MARK AGUIAR

MANUEL AMADOR

PRINCETON UNIVERSITY PRESS

PRINCETON & OXFORD

Published by Princeton University Press
41 William Street, Princeton, New Jersey 08540
6 Oxford Street, Woodstock, Oxfordshire OX20 1TR

press.princeton.edu

All Rights Reserved

ISBN 978-0-691-176819
ISBN (e-book) 978-0-691-189246

British Library Cataloging-in-Publication Data is available

Editorial: Hannah Paul and Josh Drake
Production Editorial: Brigitte Pelner
Production: Erin Suydam
Publicity: Kate Hensley (US), Kathryn Stevens (UK)

This book has been composed in Arno

Printed on acid-free paper ∞

Printed in the United States of America

10 9 8 7 6 5 4 3 2 1

To our families

CONTENTS

LIST OF FIGURES

LIST OF TABLES

ACKNOWLEDGMENTS

This book began as a series of lectures delivered by one of us (Mark) in 2016 as part of the *CREi Lectures in Macroeconomics* series. We are indebted to Jordi Galí and Jaume Ventura for inviting us to talk about our work. We are also grateful for the comments received during the event from the faculty and students of CREi and Universitat Pompeu Fabra.

Princeton University Press was kind enough to publish the lectures. We thank Sara Caro, Hannah Paul, and Josh Drake for shepherding the manuscript through publication and showing extreme patience during the writing process. We also thank two anonymous referees for excellent comments on an earlier draft. Pol Antras gave us useful advice on how to turn the lectures into a manuscript.

Some of the work presented in this book benefited and grew from joint work with a number of co-authors and collaborators. We thank Satyajit Chatterjee, Hal Cole, Emmanuel Farhi, Stelios Fourakis, Hugo Hopenhayn, Chris Phelan, Zach Stangebye, and Iván Werning. A particular debt is owed to Gita Gopinath, an early and frequent co-author and the one who encouraged Mark to work on sovereign debt nearly twenty years ago.

We thank Laura Lukas Mann, Castillo-Martinez, and Haonan Zhao for reading the manuscript and catching several typos and mistakes, as well as for making many excellent suggestions for improving the presentation. Graduate students at Stanford, Rochester, and Gerzensee saw early versions of the work contained in this book, and students at Minnesota and Princeton read manuscript drafts. The interactions with our students were instrumental in developing the economics and in sharpening the presentation of what follows. A special thanks to Stelios Fourakis for writing the programs for the quantitative models.

Both of us benefited from the hospitality of the Federal Reserve Bank of Minneapolis, Manuel as an employee and Mark as a visiting scholar. We highlight that the views expressed herein are those of the authors and not necessarily those of the Federal Reserve Bank of Minneapolis or the Federal Reserve System.

Manuel also acknowledges the previous support from the National Science Foundation through grants 0647875 and 0952816 (1446974).

Finally, our largest debt is to our spouses and children. We dedicate this book to them.

The Economics of Sovereign
Debt and Default

1

Introduction

1.1 Overview

Sovereign debt markets are prone to frequent and serial defaults involving prolonged and costly periods of restructuring, interspersed with tranquil periods in which countries accumulate more debt as prelude to the next debt crisis. This pattern is most prominent in low-income and emerging markets, but, as the euro-area's crisis in the 2010s demonstrated, extends to developed countries as well.

Conceptually, the distinguishing feature of sovereign debt markets is the limited ability for creditors to enforce contracts. Seminal papers such as Eaton and Gersovitz (1981) and Bulow and Rogoff (1989a) are concerned with why governments repay external debt at all. However, lack of commitment to contracts is only the first of many frictions, a partial list of which includes: (i) no or limited state contingency in debt contracts; (ii) an incentive to "dilute" legacy creditors arising from the inability to contract/commit to future debt policies; (iii) large deadweight costs to default and lengthy renegotiations; (iv) vulnerability to self-fulfilling crises; (v) currency mismatch; and (vi) political economy distortions that drive a wedge between the welfare of the citizenry and the objectives of the political incumbents. In the subsequent chapters, we explore the connection between these underlying frictions and the observed behavior of sovereign debt markets. In particular, we emphasize how these frictions influence the government's *equilibrium choices*, including whether to save or borrow, default or repay, dilute, repurchase, or restructure existing bonds, and whether to issue short-term or long-term bonds. We also show how these choices mitigate or exacerbate the inefficiencies stemming from the underlying frictions.

The approach we take emphasizes analytical clarity as a prelude to quantitative implementation. For each topic, we begin with tractable analytical models that isolate the core friction of interest. To the extent possible, we characterize the equilibria of a model by showing an equivalence to an optimization problem, despite the fact that the equilibria may not be constrained efficient. These pseudo-planning problems avoid the need to analyze a complicated fixed point, and instead allow us to study the much more transparent problem of choosing an allocation subject to constraints. After analyzing the simple analytical environments, we turn to the richer quantitative models used in the literature, leveraging the insights of the analytical models to illuminate the "black box" that encloses the quantitative models.

Chapter 2 begins with the core friction of limited commitment. In particular, we study the canonical model of a risk-neutral representative lender insuring a risk-averse government, subject to the constraint that the government can always renege on promised payments. To isolate the role of limited commitment, the contract can be state contingent. The punishment for deviation is allowed to be quite general, and we show how to nest both the canonical punishment of financial autarky, as in Eaton and Gersovitz (1981), as well as the ability to save but not borrow, as in Bulow and Rogoff (1989a). Lack of commitment limits the extent of insurance, but also provides an incentive for the government to save (or reduce debt). In terms of allocations, lack of commitment tilts the path of consumption in favor of delaying consumption into the future, the well-known "backloading" of incentives.

While Chapter 2 focuses on using financial markets for risk sharing and inter-temporal substitution, another important role for international financial flows is to fund investment. This is the focus of Chapter 3. That chapter is motivated by a fact documented in Gourinchas and Jeanne (2013) and Aguiar and Amador (2011) that high-growth emerging markets have net *outflows* of capital, a pattern generated by private net inflows that are more than offset by public outflows. Chapter 3 uses a production economy overseen by a government that lacks commitment to both debt payments and capital taxation/expropriation. This economy is vulnerable to "debt overhang." Specifically, a heavily indebted government has a greater incentive to default and expropriate capital. This, in turn, depresses private investment. Thus public debt and private investment move in opposite directions, generating the empirical pattern described above.

Government policy is set by political incumbents that are present biased and rotate in and out of power stochastically. The political economy frictions are shown to be the key determinant of both public capital flows and the speed at which the economy converges to the frontier. The deeper the political frictions, the less political incumbents are willing to reduce debt, and the slower the pace of private capital accumulation. Through the lens of the model, the heterogeneity in rates of economic convergence seen in the data is driven by the heterogeneous severity of political myopia.

Chapters 2 and 3 focus on the core friction of limited commitment, abstracting from other restrictions on financial markets. This baseline provides a useful starting point, as the remaining frictions have clear implications for whether the incentive to save is enhanced or diminished. The introduction of market incompleteness is a good case in point.

In Chapter 4, we show that market incompleteness provides an additional incentive to save. We initially do this in an environment in which consumption is deterministic (absent default), highlighting that more than precautionary savings is at work. The source of uninsurable risk is the severity of punishment in the case of default, with the costs of default following a simple *iid* process. As markets are incomplete, the government may decide to default in equilibrium. In doing so, there is a deadweight loss, as ideally the government and creditor would like to contract on a state-contingent payment rather than default. This loss succinctly proxies for disruption of economic activity, both real and financial, that often coincides with default status. We show that the larger is this deadweight cost, the greater the incentive for the government to reduce debt.

Why this is the case provides a useful guide to some additional results. The government can always opt not to default at a given point in time—that is, default is *strategic* rather than due to an inability to pay. At the moment of default, despite the deadweight costs, the government strictly prefers default to repayment. So why avoid a situation in which it gets to choose the best of two options? The answer is in how bonds are priced. Competitive bond markets ensure the lenders break even in expectation. Thus, contracted payments include compensation for the entirety of lenders' expected losses; however, if there are deadweight costs of default, the government captures only a fraction of lenders' losses when it defaults. The expected wedge between what the government pays to the lenders absent default and what it gains in default varies with the probability of default, and thus, as we show, varies with the level of debt. The deadweight costs of default, via the equilibrium bond price schedule, provide the government with the incentive to save above and beyond that provided by limited commitment in a complete-markets environment.

This raises the question of whether the equilibrium incentive to save is "strong enough." That is, would a planner (or the lenders) prefer an alternative fiscal policy. We show that short-term bonds ensure the government and lenders agree on the government's debt policy. That is, it does not matter whether debt issuance (conditional on strategic default) is chosen by the government, the lenders, or a planner maximizing the weighted sum of the respective utilities.

In Chapter 5 we show how to extend this result to the richer environments with consumption risk used in the early one-period-bond quantitative models of Aguiar and Gopinath (2006) and Arellano (2008). Along the way, we establish that the competitive equilibria in the one-period bond model can be computed using a pseudo-planning problem. Importantly, the planning problem includes an "implementability constraint" that ensures the planner's chosen allocation respects the absence of state-contingent contracts in the competitive equilibrium. In fact, the planning problem can be computed by iterating on a Bellman operator that is a contraction, establishing existence and uniqueness of equilibrium in the one-period bond model.

While the canonical one-period model is a useful starting point, the efficiency properties described above and in Chapters 4 and 5 make it ill suited to address two other frictions that appear to be empirically relevant; namely, self-fulfilling debt crises and debt dilution. We take up the first of these in Chapter 6. Following Cole and Kehoe (2000), we show that relaxing an implicit assumption in the literature building on Eaton and Gersovitz (1981)—that the government commits to repayment of existing bonds before auctioning new debt—opens the door to self-fulfilling debt crises. Chapter 6 discusses how and when the canonical Cole-Kehoe model can generate a failed auction and induce a self-fulfilling default. Building on Aguiar, Chatterjee, Cole, and Stangebye (2019b), the chapter also discusses that the environment admits several other plausible self-fulfilling scenarios, including sudden stops and overborrowing during a crisis.

Debt dilution is the focus of Chapter 7, which explores debt dynamics in an Eaton-Gersovitz model with long-term bonds. Again, the anlaysis begins with a stripped-down analytical model before moving on to the richer environments used for quantitative analysis. The chapter sheds light on why equilibrium prices fail to provide strong incentives to avoid the costs of default when bonds are rolled over infrequently. In equilibrium, this manifests itself as inefficiently high levels of new borrowing when the government has long-term bonds outstanding.

We also show that the same force can lead to multiplicity, what we term "self-fulfilling debt dilution." This multiplicity is distinct from the rollover crises analyzed in Chapter 6. The latter is static in nature; that is, multiplicity arises even when holding future equilibrium behavior fixed. Self-fulfilling debt dilution is inherently dynamic. Creditor beliefs about future borrowing generate a long-term-bond price schedule that induces a fiscal policy that validates those beliefs. There may be a "borrowing" equilibrium that features high debt and likely default as well as a "saving" equilibrium in which the government deleverages over time to reduce the probability of default. Which equilibrium is realized depends on self-fulfilling beliefs.

The inefficiency generated by the presence of legacy debt raises the question of whether the government should repurchase long-term bonds in equilibrium. We show that this is never optimal for the government to do via arms-length market transactions. However, a coordinated restructuring that avoids holdouts can be Pareto improving.

With these analytical results in hand, we turn to the quantitative models with long-term debt popular in the literature, such as those proposed by Chatterjee and Eyigungor (2012b) and Hatchondo and Martinez (2009). The combination of stochastic deadweight costs of default and the incentive for debt dilution combine to generate patterns that match key empirical moments.

1.2   Empirical Landscape

Before delving into analytical and quantitative models, it is useful to survey the empirical landscape. This will establish what the theory is trying to explain, as well as clarify what is included and what is left out of the models.

Incomplete Contracts. The vast majority of sovereign debt contracts promise fixed, non-contingent payments. There are some examples of payments linked to GDP or commodity prices. For example, Argentina's 2005 restructuring included warrants linked to GDP growth. The Brady plan included bonds with payments linked to oil revenues or GDP, as well. Nevertheless, these are the exceptions rather than the rule.

However, the process of default and renegotiation makes sovereign debt implicitly state contingent. Grossman and Van Huyck (1988) model de facto state-contingent contracts by distinguishing "excusable default" from debt repudiation. Bulow and Rogoff (1989b) introduce a post-default bargaining protocol to generate ex post state-contingent payments.

Sovereign debt contracts also do not typically make promises regarding future fiscal policy or have rates that vary with changes in default probabilities. This leaves bondholders vulnerable to risk induced by future government decisions. Hall and Sargent (2020) discuss US Liberty Bonds that allowed holders to exchange their initial bonds for those with a higher coupon if the Treasury auctioned additional debt in the future at more favorable terms. The same authors also characterize various put and call options that have been included in US bonds to insure bondholders or the US Treasury against future price changes. Such clauses are not typical in sovereign debt markets.

Sovereign bonds are also issued on a "pari passu" (Latin for equal footing) basis. While open to interpretation, this means there is no explicit seniority across bond issuances (Wright, 2014). This makes selective default—that is, defaulting on bond series A while repaying series B—difficult if not impossible for bonds issued in the same jurisdiction (Schumacher, Trebesch, and Enderlein 2012).

Sovereigns rely on a variety of instruments and intermediaries to tap global financial markets. Using World Bank data, Schlegl, Trebesch, and Wright (2019) document the mix of official and private lending to emerging and developing economies since 1980. A large fraction of credit is extended by governments or multilateral institutions, such as the World Bank and International Monetary Fund. Private sector lending was primarily bank loans in the 1970s and 1980s, but the Brady Plan, and the associated "Brady bonds" introduced in 1989 to resolve the Latin American debt crisis of the 1980s, helped spur a switch toward bond finance. More precisely, it was a return to bond finance, which had been relatively common in the nineteenth and the first half of the twentieth centuries (see Meyer, Reinhart, and Trebesch 2019).

For the most part, the models of this book involve bonds traded in competitive markets. To the extent banking relationships are competitive and non-exclusive, the insights carry over to bank lending as well. We do not consider models of non-competitive lending, such as government-to-government or multilateral agency loans, or long-term exclusive relationships.

Legal Enforcement and Reputation. Sovereign debt can be governed by domestic law or foreign law. For example, Argentine bonds issued in New York are subject to US courts, while those issued in Buenos Aires are governed by Argentine law. If the consequences of default were purely reputational, the location of issuance should not be a major factor. However, it is well documented that it matters for pricing and payment under whose jurisdiction a bond is issued. For example, at the time of its restructuring in 2012, Greece had bonds issued under local law as well as English law.[1] The behavior of yields leading up to the restructuring as well as the treatment of creditors ex post differed depending on whether foreign or domestic law was operative (Choi, Gulati, and Posner 2011; Zettelmeyer, Trebesch, and Gulati 2013). Schumacher et al. (2012) review how foreign courts enforce sovereign debt contracts. Sovereign immunity limits the scope for punishment or restitution available to creditors in the event of default. In some cases, foreign courts have frozen export revenue or assets on behalf of creditors. However, the main threat is to disrupt issuance or payments of new bonds until an agreement is reached with existing bondholders.

While legal considerations play a role in sovereign debt markets, there is evidence that reputation (as captured, for example, by the previous history of default) matters as well. Cruces and Trebesch (2011) document how the history of default and repayment is correlated with future spreads.[2] Related to this, George Hall and Thomas Sargent have a body of work that documents how the United States built up its reputation as a reliable debtor in order to establish deep and reliable markets for government bonds.[3]

In the models described in the remaining chapters, any notion of "reputation" is captured by a default state variable, which potentially involves direct costs as well as financial autarky. But richer notions of reputation exist in the literature. Such notions rely on the financial market's belief about a hidden government type. Naturally, this market belief (which corresponds to the country's reputation) evolves over time and is affected by the country's history of default and repayment. The papers by Cole, Dow, and English (1995), Alfaro and Kanczuk (2005), D'Erasmo (2011), Egorov and Fabinger (2016), Perez (2017), and Amador and Phelan (2020) studied models where the market has imperfect information about the government's type and learns from the government's equilibrium actions. There is a related work that focuses on the market's asymmetric information and learning about a hidden productivity state of the country. For examples of these, see Sandleris (2008), Phan (2017), and Dovis (2019).

---

1. For more on the data and modeling of selective default between domestic and foreign-issued bonds, see Erce and Mallucci (2018).

2. See also Meyer et al. (2019) and Asonuma (2016).

3. See, for example, Hall and Sargent (2014, 2019, 2020).

Currency. As a rule of thumb, sovereign bonds issued in financial centers like New York or London are typically issued in global currencies, such as dollars, pounds, or euros. Conversely, bonds issued in domestic financial markets are typically denominated in domestic currency, although there are notable exceptions of domestically issued bonds paying out in foreign currency.[4] The fact that external borrowing by developing countries is denominated in foreign currency was famously explored by Eichengreen and Hausmann (1999). Recently, there is a growing trend toward more foreign participation in domestic sovereign bond markets in emerging markets.[5]

Debt Intolerance. In a world in which many developed economies have public debt-to-GDP ratios that often exceed 100%, it is striking how low external debt-to-income ratios are for emerging markets at the time of default. For example, Argentina's 2001 default occurred when public debt was roughly 50% of annual GDP. Reinhart, Rogoff, and Savastano (2003) document that many debt crises occur at relatively low debt levels, coining the term "debt intolerence" to describe this phenomenon.

Maturity. Broner, Lorenzoni, and Schmukler (2013) and Arellano and Ramanarayanan (2012) document maturity choice for emerging market governments. In the Broner et al. (2013) sample, which covers the majority of external, US-dollar-denominated debt issuances for a sample of eleven emerging markets between 1993 and 2009, debt issuances ranged between one-year and thirty-year maturities, with the 75th percentile centered around ten years. For the same period, they report the 75th percentile of US Treasury issuances of five years. Based on Broner et al. (2013), Chatterjee and Eyigungor (2012a) calibrate their model to a maturity of five years to match the median issuance of Argentina. Arellano and Ramanarayanan (2012) document that the average maturity of issuances for Argentina, Brazil, Mexico, and Russia ranged between nine and twelve years for roughly the same years.[6]

Both Broner et al. (2013) and Arellano and Ramanarayanan (2012) document that as spreads increase, governments shorten the maturity of issuances relative to issuance in relatively tranquil times. A similar pattern of issuances

---

4. For example, both Argentina and Russia issued domestic-law US dollar bonds as part of their restructurings. See Chamon, Schumacher, and Trebesch (2018).

5. See Burger and Warnock (2007); Arslanalp and Tsudo (2014), and Du and Schreger (2016a).

6. See the respective papers for details, including how defaults and restructuring are handled.

can be observed for the affected countries during the 2011–2012 European sovereign debt crisis (Bocola, Bornstein, and Dovis 2019). Broner et al. (2013) attribute this behavior to an increase in the risk premium charged to longer-maturity bonds during crises, while Arellano and Ramanarayanan (2012) appeal to the balance between hedging and incentives related to the discussion in Chapter 7.

Default. Tomz and Wright (2007, 2013) construct a database of 176 sovereign entities spanning 1820 to 2012. They document that the unconditional probability of default is 1.8% per year. Excluding 1945–1980, a period with little external borrowing, the probability rises to 2.2% per year.

Meyer et al. (2019) collect data on ninety-one countries with debt issued in London or New York over the period 1815–2016. They identify 313 defaults or distressed restructurings, defined as exchanges of debt at a loss. Reinhart and Rogoff (2004) document that countries tend to default more than once (so-called serial defaulters). Moreover, the nineteenth and twentieth centuries contain a number of defaults by rich countries, indicating that default has not been exclusively a phenomenon of poor or developing economies.

The canonical models of default predict countries' default during recessions. Tomz and Wright (2007) find modest evidence in this regard. Roughly two-thirds of defaults begin when output is below trend. Average deviation of output from trend at the start of default is a modest -1.6%. The cross-sectional correlation between output and default status is only -0.08. While output is typically above trend in periods of non-default, there are many instances of sharp recessions without default.

Reinhart and Rogoff (2004) document that many debt crises are preceded by or coincide with banking crises. Bailouts as well as the drop in revenue associated with financial crises strain fiscal authorities. A notable example of this mechanism is Ireland's debt crisis after the global financial crisis of 2008. Ireland's debt-to-annual GDP was less than 25% in 2007. By the end of 2010, the crisis accompanied by a large banking system bailout had forced Ireland to seek assistance from the EU. Debt-to-GDP peaked at over 130% by 2013. More broadly, Reinhart and Rogoff (2009) document that government debt increases 86% in the three years following systemic financial crisis.

Restructuring and Haircuts. Once a country has defaulted on external creditors, they remain in default status until a settlement is reached with creditors. Tomz and Wright (2007) document in their sample that the mean length of default is 9.9 years and the median length is 6.5 years. There is substantial heterogeneity in the duration between initial default and settlement; the standard deviation of duration of default is 10.5 years. Debtors spend roughly 19% of the sample period in default status.

In most cases, the defaulting government and creditors come to an agreement in which creditors accept restructured bonds with different payment terms and maturities than the original bonds. That is, from the creditors' perspective, a default implies a loss due to delay, negotiation costs, and a potential write-down of debt obligations—the so-called haircut.

There are different methods of computing haircuts. The task is complicated by the need to assess the impact of maturity changes as well as changes in face value. The canonical approach was pioneered in Sturzenegger and Zettelmeyer (2008). Their method takes the implied yield, r, using the secondary market prices of the restructured bonds at the time of settlement. The haircut is then the present discounted value of the promised sequence of payments in the restructured bonds divided by the present value of the original bonds, both discounted at the rate r. By construction, the numerator is the secondary market price of a restructured bond. The denominator is the counterfactual market value of an original bond priced using the same yield as the new bonds. Thus, this ratio captures the loss (if any) due to the bond exchange relative to hypothetically keeping the original bonds to sell in the post-default market.

Cruces and Trebesch (2013) document in a sample of 180 restructurings spanning sixty-eight countries and the period 1978–2010 a mean haircut of 37% with a standard deviation of 27%. They find larger haircuts (mean 87%) in the subsample of highly indebted poor countries. They also find that longer default durations are associated with larger haircuts. Interestingly, Benjamin and Wright (2008) find that the size of haircut and length of default are uncorrelated with initial debt levels. However, Benjamin and Wright (2008) and Trebesch and Zabel (2017) document that a more severe decline in output post-default is associated with a larger haircut.

While default typically involves haircuts for creditors, it is not the case that default necessarily lowers the face value of debt. This reflects that restructured bonds tend to be longer maturity, and the losses are imposed by delaying payment into the future rather than reducing the face value of payments. Benjamin and Wright (2008) document that the median and average post-default debt-to-GDP ratio is 5% and 25% higher, respectively, than at the time of default. In the Cruces and Trebesch sample, only 57 of 180 cases involved reduction in face value.

As noted above, while in default status, governments are excluded from debt markets. Even after coming to a resolution with creditors, governments do not immediately access primary debt markets. Cruces and Trebesch (2013) look at the duration between default resolution and first loan or bond issuance (or new credit to public sector). They find that the average duration is 2.3 years when haircuts were less than 30%, but 6.1 years on average when haircuts were greater than 30%. Moreover, the spreads on newly issued bonds after re-entry are increasing in the size of the haircut imposed on the defaulted bonds.

Interest Rate Spreads. Sovereign bonds from emerging economies as well as some developed economies have yields greater than comparable bonds from the United States or Germany. This "spread" can be quite large; for example, at the height of the euro-area debt crisis in the summer of 2012, Spanish 10-year bonds had a yield of close to 7%, compared to German 10-year bonds, which had a yield of less than 2%. The spreads for emerging market bonds like those of Argentina can be even greater; based on data from the Emerging Market Bond Index (EMBI) for Argentina in the 1990s, Chatterjee and Eyigungor (2012b) target an average spread over three-month US T-bills of roughly 8%.

The high spreads compensate creditors for the risk of default. However, even including the losses due to the default, sovereign bonds return more on average than comparable US bonds (a "risk premium" or "excess return").[7] Meyer et al. (2019) document that between 1815 and 2016, a sample of sovereign bonds from sixty "serial defaulters"[8] had an annualized realized (including defaults and restructurings) mean return of 7%, or 4% more than comparable US or UK bonds.[9] For the modern period 1995–2016, investors in the bonds of serial defaulters earned a mean annual return of 9.3%, or 5.2 percentage points more than investors in US bonds.

Returns on sovereign bonds are also volatile. Meyer et al. (2019) document that the annual standard deviation of real returns in their 1815–2016 sample is 14%, more than double the volatility of US equities. The ratio of average spreads to standard deviation (the Sharpe ratio) is 0.37 for this

7. For sovereign debt models featuring risk premia, see Borri and Verdelhan (2011), Lizarazo (2013), Pouzo and Presno (2016), and Tourre (2017).

8. Serial defaulters are countries that defaulted at least twice in the sample period or that spent 20% of the years since 1815 (or independence) in default status.

9. Spreads prior to 1918 use 10-year UK bonds as a benchmark, and 10-year US bonds for the subsequent 100 years.

sample, compared to 0.32 for US equities, suggesting that as an asset class, the risk-return tradeoff is relatively favorable for sovereign bonds, despite the frequent defaults.

Sovereign bond spreads are correlated with major international global risk factors. For example, Longstaff et al. (2011) look at spreads on credit default swaps (CDS) for twenty-six countries spanning October 2000 to January 2010.[10] The spreads are correlated across countries: The first principal component explains 64% of the variation. Moreover, sovereign CDS spreads are more related to the US stock and high-yield markets than they are to local economic measures. The first principal component of spreads has a correlation with the US Stock Market of 0.61 and the VIX -0.75. Longstaff, Pan, Pedersen, and Singleton (2011) regress spreads on local variables as well as a number of global indicators. Local variables explain roughly 40% of total explained variation (R^2) in CDS spreads, with the remaining 60% accounted for by global factors.[11]

1.3 Goals

The literature on sovereign debt has exploded since Eaton and Gersovitz (1981). The repeated waves of debt crises since the early 1980s have driven much of this interest, as each crisis allows us to evaluate existing models in a new light as well as point out directions for future research. Coinciding with the theoretical and quantitative research has been a boom in empirical research, both on modern crises as well as historical episodes, only a fraction of which is outlined in the previous section.[12] The interplay of empirics and theory has been a tremendous strength of this literature.

10. Credit default swaps are insurance contracts that pay out if and when a debtor defaults or restructures at unfavorable terms. Thus, the premiums (or "CDS spreads") reflect the probability of default plus any risk premium. CDS spreads are correlated with, but not identical to, the spreads on the underlying bonds. Although we do not discuss them in this book, see Salomao (2017) for an analysis of the role CDS contracts played during the Greek debt crisis.

11. After documenting the negative covariance between spreads and output, Neumeyer and Perri (2005) build a model in which exogenous shocks to a country's borrowing rate partially drive the business cycle. Uribe and Yue (2006) provide a methodology to measure the relative impact of foreign versus domestic shocks in driving emerging market interest rates, as well as the subsequent feedback between foreign interest rate shocks and domestic output.

12. For surveys, see the handbook chapters Eaton and Fernandez (1995); Aguiar and Amador (2014); Aguiar et al. (2016). See also the textbook treatment in Chapter 13 of Uribe and Schmitt-Grohé (2017).

A number of books on sovereign debt have been published in recent years.[13] The bulk of this work has been focused on documenting empirical patterns and analyzing key historical episodes. There has been less focus on the theoretical modeling of debt and default, and we hope this work at least partially fills this gap. The book has elements of both a textbook and a monograph. The focus is what we have learned in our own research on sovereign debt. But, we do not work in a vacuum. We build on the large body of work that precedes us, and, perhaps more important, have benefited from a strong cohort of contemporaneous researchers. Our own research includes work on debt overhang, growth under limited commitment and political economy frictions, constrained (in)efficiency of debt markets, debt dilution, debt buybacks, indeterminacy of equilibrium and self-fulfilling crises, and maturity choice. These contributions constitute the bulk of the book, but, to the extent possible, we include results from other researchers that speak directly to or have inspired our own contributions.

A unifying thread throughout is a tractable analytical framework that isolates the theoretical mechanisms at work, after which, when relevant, we discuss how the analytical models help us understand the richer, quantitative models that have become popular in the literature. These latter models are useful to understand to what extent our models can quantitatively match key empirical moments, but often operate as a "black box." A primary goal is to bridge the gap between simple models and the quantitative literature.

The book can thus serve as an introduction to these themes, a companion work to those interested in quantitative sovereign debt research, and a synthesis of our own work. While the analysis is geared to the level of a graduate student, each chapter begins and ends with a non-technical overview of the key questions and core results. When appropriate, the concluding sections also summarize the policy implications of the respective chapter.

13. A partial list includes Sturzenegger and Zettelmeyer (2007); Tomz (2007); Reinhart and Rogoff (2009); Drelichman and Voth (2011) and Abbas, Pienkowski, and Rogoff (2019).

2

Limited Commitment

2.1 Introduction

This chapter explores how limited commitment impacts insurance and the evolution of consumption and debt. We study a simple insurance problem in which risk-neutral foreigners insure a risk-averse Small Open Economy (SOE) that faces a stochastic endowment and lacks commitment. We look for equilibria that are supported by the threat of permanent exclusion from international financial markets. This is the canonical reputational punishment of Eaton and Gersovitz (1981), but in an environment with complete markets. We also discuss the important critique of reputational models put forward by Bulow and Rogoff (1989a).

In this chapter and throughout the book, the main tool for analysis will be constrained planning problems. In particular, we look for constrained efficient allocations that maximize the joint surplus of a representative foreign lender and the government of the small open economy. Planning problems provide a tractable and transparent method of understanding the associated competitive equilibria.

2.2 Environment

Consider a discrete-time SOE environment. The economy is subject to exogenous shocks, which we denote by a general state index, $s_t \in \mathbb{S}$, where $\mathbb{S}$ is a discrete set with $N < \infty$ elements. Denote histories up to period t by $s^t = (s_0, s_1, \ldots, s_t) \in \mathbb{S}^t$. Let $\pi(s^{t+k}|s^t)$ denote the probability of history s^{t+k} conditional on s^t. We assume s_t follows a first-order Markov process, and will therefore use $\pi(s^{t+k}|s^t)$ and $\pi(s^{t+k}|s_t)$ interchangeably. For convenience, we write the period-0 probability of history s^t as $\pi(s^t)$ rather than $\pi(s^t|s_0)$.

Consumption savings decisions in the SOE are made by the *government*, a term we will use synonymously with the *sovereign*. The government has preferences over consumption streams. For notation, let c denote a sequence of consumption at each history, $c = \{c(s^t)\}_{t \geq 0, s^t \in \mathbb{S}^t}$. We assume that preferences are defined over consumption streams that are bounded with values in $\mathbb{R}_+$, a set we denote $\mathbf{C}$. The sovereign's preferences $U : \mathbf{C} \to \mathbb{R}$ are given by:

$$U(c) = \sum_{t=0}^{\infty} \beta^t \sum_{s^t \in \mathbb{S}^t} \pi(s^t)u(c(s^t)). \tag{2.1}$$

We assume $\beta \in (0, 1)$. We also make the usual assumptions on the felicity function: $u' > 0$, $u'' < 0$, and $\lim_{c \to \infty} u'(c) = 0$. Note that by defining U over sequences in $\mathbb{R}_+$ we assume that $u(0)$ is well defined, although it may be arbitrarily low.

Foreign lenders are risk-neutral and discount at $R^{-1} = (1 + r^\star)^{-1} \in [\beta, 1)$. We restrict the foreign lenders to be weakly more patient than the sovereign to avoid scenarios in which the sovereign accumulates an unbounded asset position. The assumption of risk neutrality is usually justified on the grounds that the debtor country is small in world financial markets plus an assumption that the domestic economy's endowment is uncorrelated with the rest of the world. Standard diversification arguments then imply that the country's endowment risk is priced at the risk-free rate. However, empirically there is evidence that sovereign bonds pay a premium over the risk-free rate, and so this assumption is made more for tractability than realism.

The problem we consider involves a government that wishes to use foreign financial markets to smooth endowment fluctuations.[1] Specifically, the SOE receives a random endowment $y(s_t)$ indexed by the state s_t. The endowment is drawn from a discrete set of N elements, has maximal element $\bar{y} < \infty$, and a minimal element $\underline{y} > 0$.

---

1. The usual assumption in the literature, which we maintain in what follows, is that the government has enough instruments to control the private sector's decisions, and thus the analysis can be done in a consolidated manner. For a different approach and an exploration of the issues that arise when the government and the private sector cannot be consolidated, see Jeske (2006).

2.3   First-Best Risk Sharing

Before discussing risk sharing under limited commitment, a useful benchmark is the full-commitment risk-sharing arrangement. In particular, we characterize allocations that are on the Pareto frontier between the sovereign and the representative lender.

For a given allocation c, the payoff to the government is $U(c)$. The associated payoff to the lender is:

$$P(c) = \sum_{t=0}^{\infty} R^{-t} \sum_{s^t \in \mathbb{S}^t} \pi(s^t) \left[y(s_t) - c(s^t) \right]. \tag{2.2}$$

Note that P is the present discounted value of net payments to the lender. Hence, $P(c)$ is the market value of the government's net liability position associated with the allocation c. We refer to Pareto-optimal allocations as efficient:

Definition 1 *An allocation c is **efficient** if there is no alternative allocation $\tilde{c} \in C$ such that $P(\tilde{c}) \geq P(c)$ and $U(\tilde{c}) \geq U(c)$, with one inequality strict.*

Let $\mathbb{V}$ denote the feasible values for the government:

$$\mathbb{V} \equiv \left\{ v \,\middle|\, \frac{u(0)}{1-\beta} \leq v < \lim_{c \to \infty} \frac{u(c)}{1-\beta} \right\}.$$

Efficient allocations solve the following problem:[2]

$$\sup_{c \in C} P(c) \text{ subject to } U(c) \geq v, \tag{FB}$$

for $v \in \mathbb{V}$. In recursive formulations of this problem, the constraint is typically referred to as the "promise keeping" constraint; this constraint ensures that the chosen allocation delivers (at least) the promised utility to the government.

Problem (FB) has a linear objective function with a strictly convex constraint set that has a non-empty interior. If $v = \frac{u(0)}{1-\beta}$, then $c = \{c(s^t) = 0\}$ is the efficient allocation; otherwise, the optimal allocation features at least one

---

2. We characterize Pareto-efficient allocations by exploring planning problems directly. The equivalence of these allocations and a competitive equilibrium with a complete set of Arrow-Debreu securities follows from standard welfare theorems.

state with interior consumption. Let μ_{FB} be the Lagrange multiplier on the constraint $U(c) \geq v$. The first-order condition for interior $c(s^t)$ is:[3]

$$\beta^t R^t u' \left(c(s^t) \right) = \frac{1}{\mu_{FB}}.$$

This condition implies that consumption is a deterministic function of time and independent of the realizations of the endowment. Consumption declines over time if $\beta R < 1$ and remains constant if $\beta R = 1$. Given that lenders are risk-neutral, the efficient allocation has all risk borne by the lenders.

2.4 Limited Commitment

We now consider the environment in which the sovereign can renege on its financial commitments. Our environment closely resembles that of Worrall (1990), which builds on the work of Thomas and Worrall (1988).[4]

We assume that if the sovereign reneges on its financial commitments at some history s^t, its deviation value is $V^D(s_t)$, where the value depends on the current shock realization $s_t \in s^t$. The canonical deviation value of Eaton and Gersovitz (1981) assumes the government loses access to financial markets and simply consumes its endowment every period. This is usually referred to as a *deviation to autarky*. Denote the autarky payoff to the government at history s^t by:

$$V^A(s_t) \equiv u(y(s_t))) + \mathbb{E}_{s_t} \sum_{k=1}^{\infty} \beta^k u(y(s_{t+k})),$$

where $\mathbb{E}_{s_t}$ denotes expectation conditional on state s_t. Note that the notation $V^D(s_t)$ can easily generalize to include additional Markovian shocks beyond y that shift the deviation value. For example, losses to the endowment or utility costs of deviation can be easily accommodated.

---

3. If $u'(0)$ is finite and $\beta R < 1$, the allocation may call for consumption to be zero after some finite number of periods. At that point, the multiplier on the constraint $c(s^t) \geq 0$ ensures the first-order condition holds at $c(s^t) = 0$.

4. See also the related work by Harris and Holmstrom (1982), Kehoe and Levine (1993), Kocherlakota (1996), and Alvarez and Jermann (2000), which also focuses on the implications of self-enforcing constraints in environments with risk sharing. For an early application of this contractual approach to international capital flows that also incorporate a moral hazard component, see Atkeson (1991). For a more recent paper, see Muller, Storesletten, and Zilibotti (2019).

As before, we consider risk-sharing arrangements between a representative foreign lender and the sovereign. Under limited commitment, we must ensure that this arrangement is voluntarily adhered to by the sovereign. We are therefore interested in self-enforcing allocations:

Definition 2 *An allocation c is **self-enforcing** if at every history s^t, the government prefers to continue rather than deviate to autarky; that is, for all t and s^t:*

$$u(c(s^t)) + \mathbb{E}_{s^t} \sum_{k=1}^{\infty} \beta^k u(c(s^{t+k})) \geq V^D(s_t). \tag{SE}$$

One interpretation of constraint (SE) is contract-theoretic. It restricts the type of contracts that can be written between a principal (the representative lender) and the agent (the government). Without an additional enforcement mechanism, a contracted allocation that violates this condition cannot be implemented, as the government can achieve higher welfare by deviating at some history.

Another interpretation of constraint (SE) is game theoretic. In particular, following Kletzer and Wright (2000), consider a repeated game in which during each stage nature draws y_t, the sovereign makes a transfer $a \in [0, y_t]$, and the foreign lender makes a transfer $a^* \geq 0$. Consumption of the sovereign will be $c_t = y_t - a_t + a_t^*$, and the net payment to the lender will be $y_t - c_t$. The history of the game through time t is $h^t = (y^t, a^t, a^{*t})$, where $a^t = (a_0, a_1, \ldots, a_t)$ is the history of sovereign transfers, and similarly for the foreign lender, a^{*t}.

We can construct subgame perfect equilibria (SPE) as follows. Note that $a = a^* = 0$ in every period is a Nash equilibrium of the stage game between the foreign lender and sovereign. Moreover, it is straightforward that this equilibrium generates the lowest payoff to the sovereign among all SPE, and hence serves as the "grim trigger" that sustains the sovereign's equilibrium strategy. Following Abreu (1988), to verify whether an allocation c can be supported as an SPE, we simply need to check whether the sovereign has an incentive to deviate at any history h^t, with a deviation followed by reversion to the SPE that yields the lowest payoff to the sovereign.[5] This is constraint (SE) with

---

5. See the work on sustainable plans by Chari and Kehoe (1990) and Chari and Kehoe (1993) that analyze the implications of this reversion to the worst outcome in a competitive equilibrium model with a government that lacks commitment.

$V^D = V^A$. Thus, any allocation that is self-enforcing can be implemented as a SPE of the repeated game between government and lender.[6]

2.5 Constrained Efficient Allocations

We now study *constrained efficient* allocations:

Definition 3 *An allocation c is **constrained efficient** if there is no other self-enforcing allocation $\tilde{c} \in C$ such that $P(\tilde{c}) \geq P(c)$ and $U(\tilde{c}) \geq U(c)$, with one inequality strict.*

For $v_0 \in \mathbb{V}$, constrained efficient allocations solve the following problem:[7]

$$P^{CM}(v_0, s_0) = \sup_{c \in C} P(c) \text{ subject to } U(c) \geq v_0, \tag{P}$$

$$\text{and (SE) for all } t \geq 0, s^t \in \mathbb{S}^t.$$

The "CM" superscript represents complete markets, to be contrasted in the next section with a more restrictive contracting space. Problem (P) has a linear objective and a strictly convex constraint set. P^{CM} is decreasing and concave in v_0. It is strictly decreasing and strictly concave on the domain $v_0 \geq V^D(s_0)$, which is the relevant domain for our analysis. If $v_0 < V^D(s_0)$ the sovereign either deviates or the lender must deliver $V^D(s_0)$ and receive $P^{CM}(V^D(s_0), s_0)$, which is akin to debt forgiveness.

To simplify notation, let the N possible deviations values be denoted $\{v_n^D\}_{n=0}^N$. That is, for each $s_t \in \mathbb{S}$, there is an n such that $V^D(s_t) = v_n^D$. Without loss, we can order the set such that $v_1^D < v_2^D < \ldots < v_N^D$.

To ensure an interior allocation, we make the following assumption:

Assumption 1 $u(0) + \beta v < v_1^D$ *for all $v \in \mathbb{V}$.*

This assumption states that regardless of continuation value and deviation value (as $v_1^D \leq v_n^D$ for all n), the government strictly prefers to deviate rather

---

6. The preceding game-theoretic interpretation left a loose end. We did not check whether the lender has an incentive to deviate from the equilibrium allocation; this reflects the assumption that the lender can commit. Implicit in this statement is that the lender can also commit to the punishment equilibrium. See Wright (2002) and Kletzer and Wright (2000) for discussion. The latter paper also discusses how self-enforcing allocations are renegotiation-proof.

7. As before, we consider a planning problem. Constrained efficient allocations in the current environment can be decentralized with a complete set of Arrow-Debreu securities subject to restrictions on the government's net indebtedness in any state. See Alvarez and Jermann (2000) for a full discussion of a closely related environment.

than consume zero today. Hence, self-enforcing allocations always deliver strictly positive consumption at all histories.

While problem (P) can be solved recursively, attacking the sequence problem directly has some nice expositional properties. We do so by forming the Lagrangian.[8] Let $\mu \geq 0$ be the multiplier on the promise-keeping constraint $U(c) \geq v$, and let $\lambda(s^t)\pi(s^t)\beta^t \geq 0$ be the multiplier on the self-enforcing constraint (SE) at history s^t. We scale the multiplier by $\pi(s^t)\beta^t > 0$ to simplify later expressions. The Lagrangian is:

$$\mathcal{L} = \sum_{t=0}^{\infty} R^{-t} \sum_{s^t \in \mathcal{S}^t} \pi(s^t)\left[y(s^t) - c(s^t)\right] \tag{L}$$

$$+ \mu \left[\sum_{t=0}^{\infty} \beta^t \sum_{s^t \in \mathcal{S}^t} \pi(s^t)u\left(c(s^t)\right) - v \right]$$

$$+ \sum_{t=0}^{\infty} \beta^t \sum_{s^t \in \mathcal{S}^t} \pi(s^t)\lambda(s^t)\left[\sum_{k=0}^{\infty} \beta^k \sum_{s^{t+k} \in \mathbb{S}^{t+k}} \pi(s^{t+k}|s^t)u\left(c(s^{t+k})\right) - V^D(s^t) \right].$$

Given the convexity of the problem, the optimum is characterized by the first-order conditions for $\{c(s^t)\}$ and the complementary slackness conditions. In evaluating the first-order condition for $c(s^t)$, note that $u(c(s^t))$ appears in all self-enforcing constraints leading up to s^t. The first-order condition for $c(s^t)$ is:

---

8. There are many technical assumptions that lie behind the validity of Lagrangian techniques in infinite-dimensional spaces. Given the infinite sequence of participation constraints, a natural environment is to assume that the set of participation constraints maps allocations into the space of bounded sequences (ℓ_∞). This requires that utility is bounded, where the difficulty usually lies in ensuring utility is bounded below at zero. The natural space for multipliers is the space of summable sequences, ℓ_1. However, the dual of ℓ_∞ is larger than ℓ_1. Fortunately, for many environments of economic interest, it can be shown that the Lagrange multipliers are indeed elements of ℓ_1. See Dechert (1982) and Rustichini (1998) for details. A final requirement is that the participation constraint set includes an interior feasible allocation (if the constraint set is convex and we are characterizing a global optimum), or satisfies a local regularity condition (similar to the full-rank Jacobian condition in finite dimensions) if necessary conditions for an interior optimum are the object of interest. The standard reference is Luenberger (1969).

$$R^{-t}\pi(s^t) = \mu\beta^t u'(c(s^t))\pi(s^t)$$
$$+\lambda(s^0)\left[\beta^t\pi(s^t)u'(c(s^t))\right]$$
$$+\beta\pi(s^1)\lambda(s^1)\left[\beta^{t-1}\pi(s^t|s^1)u'(c(s^t))\right]$$
$$+\beta^2\pi(s^2)\lambda(s^2)\left[\beta^{t-2}\pi(s^t|s^2)u'(c(s^t))\right]$$
$$\vdots$$
$$+\beta^t\pi(s^t)\lambda(s^t)\left[u'(c(s^t))\right],$$

where s^j, $j = 0, 1, .., t$, are histories leading up to s^t; that is, $\pi(s^t|s^j) > 0$ for all $j \leq t$. Using the fact that $\pi(s^t|s^j)\pi(s^j) = \pi(s^t)$, we can rewrite the first-order condition as:

$$1 = \beta^t R^t u'(c(s^t))\left[\mu + \sum_{s^j \in s^t}\lambda(s^j)\right], \qquad (2.3)$$

where $s^j \in s^t$ denotes that s^j is history s^t truncated at period $j \leq t$ (and hence $\pi(s^t|s^j) > 0$).

The summation in brackets on the right of (2.3) represents the difference between constrained efficient allocations and the unconstrained first-best characterized by (FB). Note that via this summation of multipliers, the history of shocks now becomes relevant for current consumption. To isolate the consumption dynamics due to this efficiency wedge, we set $\beta R = 1$.

2.5.1   The Case of $\beta R = 1$

When $\beta R = 1$, the representative lender and sovereign have the same discount factor. With $\beta R = 1$, the first-order condition (2.3) can be rewritten:

$$\frac{1}{u'(c(s^t))} = \mu + \sum_{s^j \in s^t}\lambda(s^j). \qquad (2.4)$$

As μ is constant and $\lambda(s^t) \geq 0$, the right-hand side is weakly increasing over time, and strictly whenever $\lambda(s^t) > 0$. Given strict concavity of u, this implies that $c(s^t)$ is weakly increasing over time, and strictly so whenever $\lambda(s^t) > 0$. The increase in consumption is required to ensure that utility along the equilibrium path is high enough to sustain continued participation. The desire to smooth consumption results in consumption never declining. That is, it would be inefficient for consumption to increase in period t and decrease in period $t + 1$. The increase in period t was needed to satisfy the forward-looking self-enforcing constraint; concavity of u implies the constraint could be satisfied using less resources by a constant level of consumption over t and $t + 1$.

Promising future increases in consumption represents the "backloading" of incentives. Given the forward-looking constraint, pushing consumption into the future relaxes all previous constraints as well. It is therefore efficient to postpone consumption at the margin. This of course assumes commitment on the other side of the arrangement. One sees such arrangements in many contracts. For example, when workers are free to quit and move to another firm, it is optimal for an employer to offer a generous retirement package to employees who remain for an extended period (Holmstrom, 1983).

Another feature of the weakly increasing sum of multipliers is that eventually the self-enforcing constraints no longer bind when $\beta R = 1$. To see this, note that μ is finite. If the terms in the sum of multipliers did not converge to zero, then the left-hand side would diverge, implying $u'(c) \to 0$. However, this implies infinitely large consumption (and for an infinite number of periods, as consumption never falls), which would imply the self-enforcing constraint is slack as well.

More concretely, for any constrained efficient allocation $\tilde{c} = \{\tilde{c}(s^t)\}$, let $\tilde{v}(s^t)$ denote the government's value from history s^t onward implied by that allocation. Standard dynamic programming arguments imply that for any $\tau > 0$ and constrained efficient $\tilde{c}$, we have:

$$P^{CM}(v_0, s_0) = \sum_{t=0}^{\tau} \beta^t \sum_{s^t} \pi(s^t) u(\tilde{c}(s^t))$$
$$+ \beta^{\tau+1} \sum_{s^{\tau+1}} \pi(s^{\tau+1}) P^{CM}(\tilde{v}(s^{\tau+1}), s_{\tau+1}).$$

Now suppose the promised utility at some s^t is $v = \tilde{v}(s^t) \geq v_N^D$, which will be the case if $v_0 \geq v_N^D$ or if v_N^D has been realized along the history s^t. Keeping v (and c) constant thereafter is therefore self-enforcing and fully insures the government. Specifically, the constrained efficient allocation that delivers $v \geq v_N^D$ has $c = c^{ss}(v)$ for all future periods, where $c^{ss}(v) = u^{-1}((1 - \beta)v)$ is the constant consumption level that delivers value v.

The fact that the allocation eventually achieves perfect risk sharing is a common feature in repeated relationships with one-sided limited commitment (see Ray, 2002). Note, however, that $\lim_{t\to\infty} c_t$ is not necessarily the first-best level of consumption at the start of time $c^{FB} = c^{ss}(v_0)$. The fact that consumption is less than first-best at $t = 0$ implies, via the promise-keeping constraint, that consumption is higher than c^{FB} as $t \to \infty$.

We summarize these results in the following proposition:

Proposition 1 *If $\beta R = 1$, consumption in a constrained efficient allocation is weakly increasing over time and converges to a constant level in finite time.*

To obtain a better sense of the dynamics, we make the following simplifying assumption:

Assumption 2 *Let s be an iid process.*

Let $C^{CM} : \mathbb{V} \to \mathbb{R}_+$ denote the constrained efficient consumption policy function associated with P^{CM}; that is, $C^{CM}(v)$ is the efficient consumption chosen for the initial period in problem (2.2) given $v_0 = v$.

We can construct efficient consumption sequences as follows. If $v \geq v_N^D$, first-best risk sharing is self-enforcing from the start. Consumption in this case, as discussed above, is $C^{CM}(v) = c^{ss}(v)$.

Now suppose $v < v_N^D$. Specifically, suppose $v \in [v_n^D, v_{n+1}^D)$ for some $n < N$. Then initial consumption satisfies:

$$v = u(C^{CM}(v)) + \beta v + \beta \sum_{j>n} p_j \left(v_j^D - v \right), \qquad (2.5)$$

where p_j, $j = 1, \ldots, N$, is the probability of state j. The efficient allocation delivers value v by setting initial consumption to $C^{CM}(v)$, and then, if, next period, $v_j^D \leq v$, consumption remains at the initial level, while if $v_j^D > v$ is realized, then the government's value is reset upward to v_j^D. Note that after the first adjustment of consumption, continuation values are always restricted to the N-element set $\{v_n^D\}_{n=1}^N$. Using $v = v_n^D$ in (2.5), we can define $c_n \equiv C^{CM}(v_n^D)$. The path of consumption, after its first upward adjustment, is always among the set $\{c_n\}_{n=1}^N$.

The fact that the government's consumption never falls, but occasionally increases, reflects the partial insurance delivered by a constrained efficient allocation. In exchange, the lender receives $y - c$, which corresponds to the SOE's net exports in this environment. We can establish that $y_n \geq c_n$, with strict inequality for $n > 1$. In particular,

$$v_n^D = u(y_n) + \beta \sum_{j=1}^N p_j v_j^D$$

$$= u(c_n) + \beta v_n^D + \beta \sum_{j \geq n+1}^N p_j \left(v_j^D - v_n^D \right),$$

where the first line is by definition of the deviation value and the second line is by definition of c_n. Differencing, we have:

$$u(y_n) - u(c_n) = \beta \left(1 - \sum_{j \geq n+1}^N p_j \right) v_n^D - \beta \sum_{j=1}^n p_j v_j^D$$

$$= \beta \sum_{j=1}^n p_j \left(v_n^D - v_j^D \right) \geq 0,$$

with equality if $n = 1$ and strict inequality otherwise. As u is strictly increasing, this implies $y_n \geq c_n$, with equality if and only if $n = 1$.

Thus, if $v = v_1^D$, the government consumes its endowment until $V^D > v_1^D$. At that point, the government makes a payment and, in exchange, receives a higher level of consumption going forward with better insurance against future low endowment realizations. Each time consumption increases, the government makes a net payment and receives a higher-valued insurance product going forward. This implies that the government is indebted at $v = v_1^D$; that is $P^{CM}(v_1^D, \cdot) > 0$.

If $v < v_N^D$, then initial consumption $C^{CM}(v)$ is strictly below the first-best consumption level $c^{ss}(v)$. To see this, suppose $v \in [v_n^D, v_{n+1}^D)$ for $n < N$. We have:

$$v = \frac{u(c^{ss}(v))}{1 - \beta} = u(C^{CM}(v)) + \beta v + \beta \sum_{j > n} p_j \left(v_j^D - v \right).$$

Replacing v on the right-hand side with $u(c^{ss}(v))/(1 - \beta)$ and moving it to the left yields:

$$u(c^{ss}(v)) = u(C^{CM}(v)) + \beta \sum_{j > n} p_j \left(v_j^D - v \right) > u(C^{CM}(v)).$$

Hence, initial consumption is below the first-best level, but eventually rises above it (as $c_N > c^*(v)$ if $v < v_N^D$).

We can characterize the associated lenders' value P^{CM} as follows. Denote the N elements of the state space $S = \{e_1, e_2, \ldots, e_N\}$, such that $V^D(e_n) = v_n^D$ and $y(e_n) = y_n$. The payoff $P^{CM}(v, e_n)$ for $v \geq v_N^D$ is $R(y - C^{CM}(v))/r$. For $v < v_N^D$, we can define P^{CM} recursively by:

$$P^{CM}(v, e_n) =$$

$$\begin{cases} P^{CM}(v_n^D, e_n) & \text{if } v_n^D > v; \\ y_n - C^{CM}(v) + R^{-1}P^{CM}(v, e_n) & +R^{-1}\sum_{j>n} p_j \\ & \qquad \left[P^{CM}(v_j^D, e_j) - P^{CM}(v, e_n) \right], \\ & \text{otherwise.} \end{cases}$$

Note that this is already defined for $n = N$ as the first-best payoff. The full function can be defined by recursively working down from $v = v_N^D$, as at each v, $P^{CM}(v, .)$ depends only on how the function is defined for $v' \geq v$.

A hypothetical sample path of a constrained efficient allocation is depicted in Figure 2.1. Panel (a) depicts the consumption dynamics and panel (b) the initial constrained efficient Pareto frontier, $P^{CM}(v, s)$. Specifically, panel (b) depicts $\tilde{P}^{CM}(v) \equiv P^{CM}(v, e_1) - y_n$. Setting the state to e_1 implies that the self-enforcing constraint is not binding for $v \geq v_1^D$. Subtracting y_n implies that the lender's value is independent of the current endowment realization, allowing us to depict a modified frontier that does not shift along the sample path.

The sample path begins with an initial state (v_0, e_1), with $v_0 \in (v_1^D, v_2^D)$. The next realization of V_n^D for $n \neq 1$ along the hypothetical path is v_2^D. At this point, consumption jumps to c_2 and the value jumps to v_2^D to satisfy the self-enforcing constraint. This is depicted in panel (b) by the jump along the constrained efficient frontier. Suppose the next realization of a deviation value greater than v_2^D is v_5^D, then, at that point, consumption jumps to c_5 and the government's value to v_5^D. Thereafter, suppose the deviation value remains less than or equal to v_5^D until the highest realization v_N^D is realized. Once that is realized, consumption remains constant at c_N thereafter.

In panel (a) we also depict the first-best consumption profile, $c^{FB}(v_0) = c^{ss}(v_0)$, for reference. As noted above, the economy starts at a level of consumption below $c^{FB}(v_0) > C^{CM}(v_0)$, but increases at each point where the

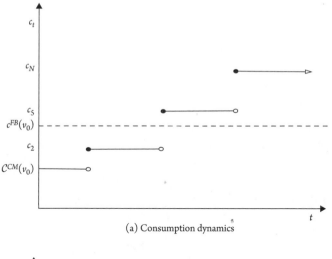

(a) Consumption dynamics

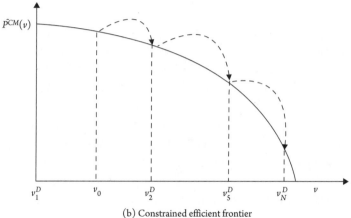

(b) Constrained efficient frontier

FIGURE 2.1. Constrained Efficient Dynamics $(\beta R = 1)$

Note: Panel (a) depicts a hypothetical sample path of consumption in the constrained efficient allocation. The initial consumption corresponds to $v_0 \in (v_1^D, v_2^D)$. The hypothetical path begins with a period of $V^D = v_1^D$, after which v_2^D is realized; which is followed by a period of $V^D \le v_2^D$, after which v_5^D is realized; which is followed by a period of $V^D \le v_5^D$, after which v_N^D is realized. $c^{FB}(v_0)$ depicts as reference the first-best (full-commitment) consumption. Panel (b) depicts a modified constrained efficient frontier: $\tilde{p}^{CM}(v) \equiv p^{CM}(v, e_1) - y_n$, which is invariant to the exogenous state s. We overlay the dynamics of v given the realizations of V^D associated with panel (a).

self-enforcing constraint binds. Eventually, the level of consumption is higher than $c^{FB}(v_0)$.[9] The fact that consumption is higher in later periods would normally provide an incentive to borrow. The self-enforcing constraint prevents this, as repayment would not be credible. Thus, limited commitment naturally places a limit on the amount of debt an economy can accumulate.

The fact that partial risk sharing is feasible implies that deviation never occurs along the equilibrium path. Given the ability to transfer resources across states, there is no benefit in allowing the government to deviate and lose the gains from trade. The ability to lower payments in that state (or raise transfers) to the point where the government is indifferent (and raising payments in other states to keep the foreign payoff the same) is always preferable. Kletzer and Wright (2000) show that constrained efficient allocations can be achieved even under the threat of renegotiation after a deviation. While autarky is an ex post inefficient allocation, the same value can be delivered to the government under a constrained efficient allocation in which the lender captures all the gains from trade. Thus, punishments for deviations can be implemented without inefficiencies.

The self-enforcing constraints bind as higher deviation values are realized, pushing up consumption and continuation values. For a weakly persistent endowment process, a high deviation value occurs when the endowment is relatively high. The fact that the sovereign is tempted to deviate when it is asked to make payments, rather than receive payments, is intuitive and will be a feature of all the models considered in this book. It is important to not conclude that this is a counterfactual feature of the model. While default, as typically defined in the data, often occurs during recessions, it is a misreading of the model to equate empirical defaults to a binding self-enforcing constraint. Recall that deviation never occurs in equilibrium in the current environment, and so cannot be directly compared to something that occurs in the data. Deviation is a never-exercised option that nevertheless weakens the ability to provide insurance. The more useful interpretation of the binding self-enforcing constraints is that they prevent bringing consumption "forward" to low-endowment states to smooth consumption. This is explicit in (2.3). It also is intuitive—the possibility of not repaying debt when times are good tends to restrict the amount that can be borrowed when times are bad.

---

9. We have formally established that $c^{FB}(v_0) < c_N$ if $v_0 < v_N^D$. The fact that we depict $c^{FB}(v_0) \in (c_2, c_5)$ is purely heuristic.

2.5.2 An Impatient Sovereign

If $\beta R < 1$ then (2.3) implies that consumption is not weakly increasing. If the self-enforcing constraint is slack ($\lambda(s^t) = 0$), then (2.3) implies that $c(s^{t-1}) > c(s^t)$. However, an indefinitely decreasing path of consumption cannot be self-enforcing. At some point, the continuation value falls below the deviation value. When the self-enforcing constraint binds, $\lambda(s^t) > 0$ and consumption's fall is mitigated or reversed. In fact, as in the patient case, consumption is set so that the continuation value is exactly equal to $V^D(s_t)$. As before, let c^n denote the level of consumption that is delivered when the self-enforcing constraint binds at $V^D = v_n^D$, $n = 1, \ldots, N$.

Thus the dynamics of consumption are driven by two competing forces—impatience and limited commitment. Consumption converges to an ergodic distribution, bounded above by c^N and below by c^1, the levels of consumption that occur when the highest and lowest deviation values are realized, respectively. Consumption falls when unconstrained to satisfy the sovereign's impatience. When the self-enforcing constraint binds, consumption is adjusted accordingly. This process repeats. Thus, perfect insurance is never attained due to the sovereign's impatience.

2.6 The Bulow-Rogoff Critique

Bulow and Rogoff (1989a), henceforth BR, contains an influential critique of the effectiveness of reputational considerations to sustain debt repayment. Rather than follow Eaton and Gersovitz (1981) and assume financial autarky subsequent to a deviation, BR assume the sovereign is only cut off from future borrowing. That is, the sovereign can save, but not borrow, once it has failed to make a contracted payment.[10]

Suppose the government deviates at history s^t. Let $\{\tilde{c}(s^{t+k})\}$ for $k \geq 0$ denote a candidate post-deviation allocation. In the period of deviation, the government reneges on its promised debt payments, and starts with zero assets. A zero-debt, zero-asset allocation satisfies:

$$\mathbb{E}_{s^t} \sum_{k=0}^{\infty} R^{-k} \left[y(s^{t+k}) - \tilde{c}(s^{t+k}) \right] = 0. \tag{2.6}$$

---

10. For an analysis of the implicit role that secondary markets play in this argument, see the interesting take by Broner, Martin, and Ventura (2010). Some of these ideas came into play during the European sovereign debt crisis, a phenomenon referred to as "renationalization" of the public debt (see Broner, Erce, Martin, and Ventura 2014).

That is, the government's post-deviation consumption must be self-financed in present value.

In periods subsequent to deviation, the government can save but not be a net debtor. Define the government's liability position by:

$$\tilde{b}(s^{t+k}) \equiv \mathbb{E}_{s^{t+k}} \sum_{j=0}^{\infty} R^{-j} \left[y(s^{t+k+j}) - \tilde{c}(s^{t+k+j}) \right].$$

That is, $\tilde{b}(s^{t+k})$ is the implied present value of net payments to the representative lender starting from history s^{t+k}. Note that $\tilde{b}(\cdot) > 0$ implies that there is a promise to make net payments to the lender, and $\tilde{b}(\cdot) < 0$ implies that the government has a net foreign asset position. The Bulow-Rogoff deviation requires that $\tilde{b}(s^{t+k}) \le 0$ for $k \ge 1$.

Thus, after deviation in the Bulow-Rogoff environment, the government's value is given by:[11]

$$V_{BR}^{D}(s^t) \equiv \sup_{\{\tilde{c}(s^{t+k})\}} \sum_{k=0}^{\infty} \beta^k \sum_{s^{t+k}} \pi(s^{t+k}|s^t) u(\tilde{c}(s^{t+k})) \qquad \text{(BR)}$$

subject to

$$\mathbb{E}_{s^t} \sum_{k=0}^{\infty} R^{-k} \left[y(s^{t+k}) - \tilde{c}(s^{t+k}) \right] \ge 0$$

$$\tilde{b}(s^{t+k}) \le 0, \text{ all } k \ge 1, s^{t+k} \text{ such that } \pi(s^{t+k}|s^t) > 0.$$

Definition 4 *An allocation c is **BR self-enforcing** if at every history s^t we have:*

$$u(c(s^t)) + \mathbb{E}_{s^t} \sum_{k=1}^{\infty} \beta^k u(c(s^{t+k})) \ge V_{BR}^{D}(s^t). \qquad \text{(SE')}$$

As $\tilde{c}(s^t) = y(s^t)$ is feasible after deviation, we have that $V_{BR}^{D} \ge V^A$, where V^A is the Eaton-Gersovitz deviation to autarky value.

As mentioned above, autarky is the worst subgame perfect equilibrium in the game between the government and lenders. Hence, using autarky as the punishment for deviation supports the highest values that can be obtained in equilibrium. Using a weaker punishment, that is, a higher deviation value,

---

11. The first constraint is a relaxation of equation (2.6). This is without loss, as the government will never "partially default" and choose to make strictly positive net payments after a deviation.

shrinks the gains from trade between lenders and the government. The BR punishment is weaker than autarky, giving the government a greater incentive to deviate and reducing the government's willingness to repay. Anticipating this, the lenders restrict the liability position of the government in equilibrium. In fact, the BR result states that *zero* debt can be supported in equilibrium when V_{BR}^D is the punishment for deviation:

Proposition 2 *If an allocation **c** is BR self-enforcing, then at all s^t we have:*

$$b(s^t) \equiv \mathbb{E}_{s^t} \sum_{k=0}^{\infty} R^{-k}[y(s^{t+k}) - c(s^{t+k})] \le 0.$$

That is, the BR self-enforcing allocation never features a net liability position for the government.

Proof. Consider the set of *BR self-enforcing* allocations. For each element of that set, c, there is an implied sequence of $b(s^t) = \mathbb{E}_{s^t} \sum_{k \ge 0} R^{-k}[y(s^{t+k}) - c(s^{t+k})]$. Let $\bar{b}$ denote a finite upper bound such that $b(s^t) \le \bar{b}$ for all t, s^t and all BR self-enforcing allocations. Note that for all allocations, $b(s^t)$ is bounded above by setting consumption to zero at all future dates (the natural borrowing limit); that is, $b(s^t) \le \mathbb{E}_{s^t} \sum_{k \ge 0} R^{-k} y(s^{t+k}) \le R\bar{y}/r < \infty$, so there exists a finite bound $\bar{b}$. In particular, define $\bar{b}$ to be the smallest possible non-negative bound:

$$\bar{b} \equiv \inf\{b_{max} \big| b(s^t) \le b_{max}, \forall t, \forall s^t\}.$$

Our task is to prove $\bar{b} > 0$ is not consistent with a *BR self-enforcing* allocation. In the following, we assume that there exists an $\bar{s}^t$ such that $b(\bar{s}^t) = \bar{b}$—that is, the infimum is achieved at some history—but the proof is easily modified to handle the scenario where this is not the case.[12]

Now suppose for a candidate *BR self-enforcing* allocation at arbitrary history s^t the government's net liability position is b. The government's value at that history is bounded above by $W(b; s^t)$, which is defined by the following problem:

---

12. Specifically, for all $\epsilon > 0$, there is a history such that $b(\bar{s}^t) > \bar{b} - \epsilon$. The same proof establishes that, for $\epsilon > 0$, $\bar{b} > \epsilon$ is not consistent with an allocation being *BR self-enforcing*. To see this, replace $\bar{b}$ with $\bar{b} - \epsilon > 0$ in the definition of $\hat{y}$ below and evaluate W at $b = \bar{b} - \epsilon$. As ϵ is arbitrary, this establishes that $b(s^t) \le 0$ is a requirement.

$$W(b; s^t) = \sup_{\{c(s^{t+k})\}} \mathbb{E}_{s^t} \sum_{k \geq 0} \beta^k u(c(s^{t+k})) \tag{2.7}$$

subject to:

$$\mathbb{E}_{s^t} \sum_{k=0}^{\infty} R^{-k} \left[y(s^{t+k}) - c(s^{t+k}) \right] \geq b$$

$$V(s^{t+k}) \geq V_{BR}^D(s^{t+k}) \text{ for all } k > 0, s^{t+k} \geq s^t \tag{2.8}$$

$$b(s^{t+k}) \leq \bar{b} \text{ for all } k > 0, s^{t+k} \geq s^t,$$

where $V(s^{t+k})$ is the continuation value and $b(s^{t+k})$ the net position vis-à-vis the lender implied by allocation $\{c(s^{t+k})\}$ at history s^{t+k}. The first constraint ensures that the government pays b in present value to the lender. The second constraint ensures that the chosen allocation is *BR self-enforcing* at all future histories. It does not change the value of W to add the constraint $b(s^{t+k}) \leq \bar{b}$, as this is satisfied by the definition of $\bar{b}$. Hence, $W(b; s^t)$ is the maximum value attainable from any *BR self-enforcing* allocation that promises payment b. For the allocation to be *BR self-enforcing*, we require $W(b(s^t), s^t) \geq V_{BR}^D(s^t)$ for all t, s^t. We now check whether this is true at $\bar{s}^t$, at which $b(\bar{s}^t) = \bar{b}$.

Define $\hat{y}(s^t) \equiv y(s^t) - \frac{r}{R}\bar{b}$ for all s^t. Let

$$\hat{b}(s^t) \equiv b(s^t) - \bar{b}$$

$$= \mathbb{E}_{s^t} \sum_{k=0}^{\infty} R^{-k} \left[y(s^{t+k}) - c(s^{t+k}) \right] - \bar{b}$$

$$= \mathbb{E}_{s^t} \sum_{k=0}^{\infty} R^{-k} \left[\hat{y}(s^{t+k}) - c(s^{t+k}) \right].$$

We can rewrite the government's problem (2.7) as:

$$W(b; s^t) = \sup_{\{c(s^{t+k})\}} \mathbb{E}_{s^t} \sum_{k=0}^{\infty} \beta^k u(c(s^{t+k}))$$

subject to:

$$\mathbb{E}_{s^t} \sum_{k=0}^{\infty} R^{-k} \left[\hat{y}(s^{t+k}) - c(s^{t+k}) \right] \geq b - \bar{b}$$

$$V(s^{t+k}) \geq V_{BR}^{D}(s^{t+k}) \text{ for all } k > 0, s^{t+k} \geq s^{t}$$

$$\hat{b}(s^{t+k}) \leq 0 \text{ for all } k > 0, s^{t+k} \geq s^{t}.$$

Evaluated at $s^{t} = \bar{s}^{t}$ and $b = \bar{b}$, this problem is identical to (BR), but with a lower endowment sequence $\hat{y}(s^{t}) \leq y(s^{t})$, with a strict inequality if $\bar{b} > 0$. Thus, $W(\bar{b}; \bar{s}^{t}) \leq V_{BR}^{D}(\bar{s}^{t})$, with a strict inequality if $\bar{b} > 0$. An allocation with a net liability position of $\bar{b} > 0$ at some history is therefore not BR self-enforcing.   □

The proof provides a useful intuition for this striking result. The sovereign's problem when it reaches its maximal debt level is identical to the deviation problem, but with a strictly lower endowment. Thus, the sovereign will always deviate at the maximal debt level as long as it is strictly greater than zero. The key idea is that once the government reaches a strictly positive debt limit, the sovereign is making net payments in present value. This can be mapped into a new "net" endowment stream that is strictly lower than the true endowment. Thus the government is better off deviating and saving those additional payments in its own accounts. The original Bulow and Rogoff (1989a) proof is constructive in that it shows how to implement a series of savings contracts at each history after deviation. Our approach to the proof uses a planning problem with a modified punishment for easy comparison to our analysis of constrained efficient allocations.

The assumption of complete markets is not crucial to the result, as shown in Bloise, Polemarchakis, and Vailakis (2016), Auclert and Rognlie (2016), and Aguiar and Amador (2019), as long as the span of assets does not change after deviation. That is, the sovereign does not lose insurance, only the ability to have negative net positions.[13]

The Bulow-Rogoff critique has spawned a large literature that explores additional punishments for deviation beyond financial autarky. See Eaton and Fernandez (1995) and Aguiar and Amador (2014) for some references.

---

13. Bloise, Polemarchakis, and Vailakis (2018) establishes an interesting counter-example to the Bulow-Rogoff critique under incomplete markets. In their environment, interest rates fluctuate and occasionally fall below the growth rate of the endowment. With incomplete markets, the possibility of a sequence of low interest rates makes retaining access to debt markets through repayment more attractive than deviation.

2.7   Conclusion

In this chapter we have explored risk sharing under one-sided limited commitment. We showed that the risk-neutral foreign lender's ability to bear risk is restricted by the sovereign's lack of commitment to repay when deviation is attractive. Backloading consumption mitigates the limited commitment friction, and if $\beta R = 1$, then eventually the sovereign is perfectly insured. There is no "default" in this environment—the completeness of markets and the gains from trade ensure that the option to deviate is never exercised. While the sovereign may receive the deviation value in equilibrium, it does not receive the deviation allocation (autarky). Finally, a deviation value that allows the sovereign to save but not borrow is not a strong enough punishment to sustain debt in equilibrium.

3

Growth under Limited Commitment

3.1 Introduction

The analysis in the preceding chapter focused on external borrowing for insurance and intertemporal substitution. Another prominent reason for international borrowing and lending is to finance investment. In this chapter, we explore how the government's lack of commitment affects growth and capital flows. The analysis will show that limited commitment distorts investment below the efficient level of capital. We will also show that this provides an incentive for net capital *outflows*; in particular, a force for the government to increase public net foreign assets to sustain private capital inflows.

Interestingly, a striking empirical pattern is that emerging economies that display greater than average growth are net capital exporters. This fact was first documented by Gourinchas and Jeanne (2013). Aguiar and Amador (2011) document that these capital outflows are driven by public saving; specifically, growth is accompanied by government's paying down debt or accumulating reserves, while at the same time attracting net private capital inflows. As we shall see, this will be a prediction of the model. The analysis of this chapter builds on Thomas and Worrall (1994), Marcet and Marimon (1992), Alburquerque and Hopenhayn (2004), Aguiar, Amador, and Gopinath (2009), and Aguiar and Amador (2011).[1]

---

1. Another strand of the literature has instead focused on the business cycle implications; see the work of Kehoe and Perri (2002, 2004).

3.2 Environment

To focus on limited commitment, we extend the environment of Chapter 2 to a production economy. In particular, the economy has access to a neo-classical production technology characterized by the production function $F(s, K, N)$, where the exogenous state s indexes productivity, K is physical capital, and N is labor. F is constant returns to scale in K and N and strictly concave.

Domestic agents provide labor inelastically, and, without loss, we can normalize the workforce to one. Let $k \equiv K/N$ and $f(s, k) \equiv F(s, K, N)/N$. Let $c = \{c(s^t)\}$ denote a consumption allocation consumed by the representative worker and we let $\mathbf{C}$ denote the set of such allocations with $c(s^t) \geq 0$. The government's preferences are the same as (2.1). In a subsequent section, we introduce explicit political economy frictions.

The timing of the economy works as follows. After history s^{t-1}, the economy enters period t with $k(s^{t-1})$ units of capital. At the start of period t, s_t is realized, and we update the history to $s^t = (s^{t-1}, s_t)$. Labor is allocated and the economy produces $f(s, k)$. After production, output is divided between domestic consumption, $c(s^t)$, net investment $k(s^t) - (1-\delta)k(s^{t-1})$, where δ is the depreciation rate, and payments to the risk-neutral lender. There are no intertemporal adjustment costs to capital, so capital can be freely adjusted at the end of a period before the next shock is realized (but once invested, capital remains in place for a full period). Let $\mathbf{k} = \{k(s^{t-1})\}$ denote a sequence of capital stocks, starting from an initial capital stock $k(s^{-1})$.

For expositional purposes, we begin by considering an efficient contract between a risk-neutral lender and the government. To parallel the endowment economy analysis, we redefine $P(c, k)$ to denote the payments to the lender given the allocation $\{c, k\}$:

$$P(c, k) = \mathbb{E} \sum_{t=0}^{\infty} R^{-t} \left[f(s_t, k(s^{t-1})) - c(s^t) - k(s^t) + (1-\delta)k(s^{t-1}) \right]$$

$$= Rk(s^{-1}) + \mathbb{E} \sum_{t=0}^{\infty} R^{-t} \left[f(s_t, k(s^{t-1})) - c(s^t) - (r+\delta)k(s^{t-1}) \right].$$

$$(3.1)$$

The right-hand side term in the first line is the present value of net exports; that is, output minus the sum of consumption and investment. The second line rearranges the first and provides an alternative view of the net payments, which is the end of period-0 value of the initial capital stock plus the present value of output minus the sum of consumption and the implied rental rate of capital. National income accounting implies that the term in brackets in the first line is net exports at history s^t, and thus P represents net foreign liabilities as of time zero. Thus $Rk(s^{-1}) - P(c, k)$ represents the total initial wealth of the economy.

3.3   Full Commitment Allocation

We first study the full commitment allocation. The first-best allocation chooses sequences of consumption and capital to maximize $P(c, k)$ subject to $U(c) \geq v$. Let μ_{FB} denote the multiplier on the promise-keeping constraint. The first-order conditions for consumption and capital are, respectively:

$$\beta^t R^t u'(c(s^t)) = \frac{1}{\mu_{FB}}$$

$$\mathbb{E}_{s^t} f_k(s_{t+1}, k(s^t)) = r + \delta,$$

for all $t \geq 0$ and s^t. The first-best allocation provides full insurance for consumption. It also equates the expected return on capital to the rental rate.

3.4   Limited Commitment

We now relax the assumption of full commitment. The government may decide to deviate and renege on the contract. If it does so, it loses access to risk sharing, as was the case in the previous analysis. However, it retains the capital installed in the economy. Let $V^D(s, k)$ denote the deviation value conditional on exogenous state $s = s_t$ and the amount of capital present in the economy at the time of deviation, $k = k(s^{t-1})$. The fact that the deviation value depends on k will be a crucial feature that distinguishes the present analysis from that of the endowment economy.

A natural benchmark is that after deviation, the economy operates as in a closed-economy neoclassical growth model with initial state k. We leave V^D as a general function, making the following assumption:

Assumption 1 *The deviation value $V^D(s, k)$ is differentiable and strictly increasing in k: $V_k^D(s, k) > 0$ for all $s \in S$.*

The fact that the deviation value is increasing in capital is a natural one, but plays an important role in capital and debt dynamics. We define:

Definition 1 *An allocation $\{c, k\}$ is **self-enforcing** if at every history s^t, the government prefers to continue rather than deviate; that is,*

$$V^D(s^t, k(s^{t-1})) \leq \mathbb{E}_{s^t} \sum_{k=0}^{\infty} \beta^k u(c(s^{t+k})), \qquad (3.2)$$

for all histories $t \geq 0$ and $s^t \in \mathbb{S}^t$.

Analogous to the endowment economy, we define $P^{CM}(v)$ to denote the constrained efficient payment to the representative lender given government utility v:[2]

$$P^{CM}(v) = \sup_{c \in C, k} P(c, k) \text{ subject to } U(c) \geq v, \text{ and (3.2) for all } t \geq 0, s^t \in \mathbb{S}^t.$$

$$(3.3)$$

Let μ denote the multiplier on the promise-keeping constraint and $\lambda(s^t)\pi(s^t)R^{-t}$ denote the sequence of multipliers on the self-enforcing constraint. The first-order condition for consumption is:

$$\beta^t R^t u'(c(s^t)) \left[\mu + \sum_{s^j \in s^t} \lambda(s^j) \right] = 1. \qquad (3.4)$$

This first-order condition has the same form as the endowment economy. As before, the summation of multipliers on the self-enforcing constraint provide an incentive to backload consumption to improve risk sharing.

The first-order condition for capital is:

$$\mathbb{E}_{s^t} f_k(s_{t+1}, k(s^t)) = r + \delta + \mathbb{E}_{s^t} \lambda(s^{t+1}) V_k^D(s_{t+1}, k(s^t)). \qquad (3.5)$$

We see that the self-enforcing constraint induces a wedge in the optimal level of capital. As $\lambda(s^{t+1})V_k^D \geq 0$ and f_k is decreasing in k, capital is

---

2. We implicitly assume that there are weakly positive gains from trade and thus it is efficient to keep government from deviating.

always weakly below the first-best level, and strictly so if $\lambda(s^{t+1}) > 0$. A larger capital stock raises the deviation value. Hence, there is an incentive to reduce capital in order to ensure the government complies with the optimal contract.[3]

As before, if $\beta R = 1$, the consumption first-order condition implies that consumption is weakly increasing over time, $\lambda(s^t)$ converges to zero, and full risk sharing is eventually attained. From (3.5), we see that this also implies that capital eventually achieves the first-best level. If $\beta R < 1$, impatience prevents the economy from achieving full insurance and an efficient capital level. Rather, both consumption and capital fluctuate indefinitely in the ergodic distribution. Aguiar et al. (2009) use this feature to explain why economies may exhibit persistent boom-bust swings in investment and output, even when productivity displays no persistence.

Consider the case of $\beta R = 1$. For this parameterization, consumption is weakly increasing over time. This implies that the government's promised utility v is weakly increasing, and we trace out the Pareto frontier. To finance the promised v, from (3.1) the country's total wealth position must also increase; that is, $Rk - P$ trends up over time. Simultaneously, k is increasing until it reaches the first-best level, $k^\star$.

To address public versus private capital flows, we need to divide total wealth between public (government) and private. For example, suppose that new investment (after the initial period) is externally financed, whether through private borrowing or FDI. Then the increase in k is mirrored by an equivalent increase in the private component of external liabilities. So that domestic private wealth is constant as k increases. Then any increase in the total wealth of the country, $Rk - P$, represents a net increase in public foreign assets, or, equivalently, a decrease in the government's external net liability position. Thus, we have government liabilities falling and capital increasing (financed by private capital inflows), reminiscent of the pattern observed in the data.

The preceding analysis suggests a paradigm for understanding growth in emerging economies. The fact that limited commitment deters investment is one example of "debt overhang"; that is, the phenomenon that inherited liabilities depress economic activity below its efficient level.

---

3. In a decentralization of the efficient allocation, such a wedge between the marginal product of capital and the user cost would be implemented by a capital tax. For more discussion on the role of labor and capital taxes, see Aguiar and Amador (2016).

3.5   Growth with Political Economy Frictions

The preceding analysis delivered growth through capital accumulation coinciding with a declining value of government debt. A vast body of empirical work suggests that countries have markedly heterogeneous growth trajectories. Moreover, debt overhang appears to be a more severe problem in many developing economies compared to developed countries, a phenomenon dubbed "debt intolerance" by Reinhart, Rogoff, and Savastano (2003). We now extend the model to understand why, under limited commitment, some countries flourish while others stagnate.

As in Aguiar and Amador (2011), which builds on Amador (2003), we consider an environment in which political parties rotate in and out of power according to a Markov process. That is, rather than one government with a stable set of time-consistent preferences, there exists a sequence of political incumbents that vary over time.

Motivated by Persson and Svensson (1989) and Alesina and Tabellini (1990), participants in the political process prefer consumption during their incumbency. Given per capita consumption c, a political party has flow utility $\tilde{\theta}u(c)$ if in power and $u(c)$ if out of power. The wedge $\tilde{\theta} \geq 1$ captures the extent to which parties prefer consumption to coincide with incumbency.[4]

To focus on political economy frictions, we assume productivity is deterministic. Hence, the only source of uncertainty in the model is due to political turnover. Let $p_{t,t+j}$ denote the probability that the incumbent in period t is also in power in $t+j$. The preferences of the incumbent at period t are:

$$\tilde{W}_t = \tilde{\theta}u(c_t) + \sum_{\tau > t} \beta^{\tau-t} \left(p_{t,\tau}\tilde{\theta} + 1 - p_{t,\tau} \right) u(c_\tau).$$

A particularly tractable case is when $p_{t,t+j} = p$ for all $j > 0$, which assumes political turnover is *iid* across potential incumbents. Aguiar and Amador (2011) discuss how to extend this to the case when incumbents have an

---

4. Another justification for this parameter $\tilde{\theta}$ is as follows. Suppose that when in power, a party receives a higher share ϕ of total government consumption c. Then, the marginal utility when in power is $u'(\phi c)\phi$. The requirement that $\tilde{\theta} \geq 1$ is equivalent to imposing that this marginal utility be increasing in ϕ. (For a general analysis, see Pancrazi and Prosperi, 2020.) Battaglini and Coate (2008) present a political economy model of pork-barrel spending that ends up with a similar specification but where $\tilde{\theta}$ is in addition a function of the state of the economy.

advantage or disadvantage in retaining power. In the *iid* case, incumbent utility becomes:

$$W_t \equiv \frac{\tilde{W}_t}{p\tilde{\theta} + 1 - p} = \theta u(c_t) + \sum_{\tau > t} \beta^{\tau - t} u(c_\tau)$$

$$= \theta u(c_t) + \beta V_{t+1},$$

where $\theta \equiv \frac{\tilde{\theta}}{p\tilde{\theta} + 1 - p}$, V_{t+1} is the utility of private agents in the economy, and W is a renormalization of $\tilde{W}$.

The political economy distortions are summarized by $\theta \geq 1$. If $\theta > 1$, the incumbent strictly prefers consumption today relative to private agents. The current incumbent discounts between two future periods at β, the private sector discount factor. In this way, the incumbent has hyperbolic or quasi-geometric preferences, as in Laibson (1994). The fact that the current incumbent discounts in a non-geometric fashion is a natural consequence of stochastic political turnover; for the incumbent, the current period is special because it is in power with probability one. Any future period must be downweighted by the probability that the current incumbent will lose office in the interim, but also reflect the fact that it may return to power as well.

The current political incumbent is the decision maker regarding deviation. Let $W^D(k)$ denote the deviation utility conditional on capital stock k. As in the prior analysis, we assume W^D is differentiable and strictly increasing in k.[5] The self-enforcing constraint becomes:

$$W_t \geq W^D(k_{t-1}), \forall t \geq 0. \tag{3.6}$$

A useful special case of the deviation utility assumes that in the period of deviation the government keeps all output for current consumption, reneging on debt payments and rental payments to capital owners. Subsequently, capital falls to $\underline{k}$, and consumption is $\underline{c} \equiv f(\underline{k}) - (r + \delta)\underline{k}$. Aguiar and Amador (2011) show how this can be rationalized as an equilibrium of a game between investors and the government as the tax-setting authority. The deviation utility for the party in power is therefore:

$$W^D(k) = \theta u(f(k)) + \beta \underline{W}, \tag{3.7}$$

where $\underline{W} \equiv \frac{1}{1-\beta} u(\underline{c})$.

---

5. We also implicitly use the concavity assumption that $(f'(k) - r - \delta)/W_k^D(k)$ is declining in k. This is satisfied, for example, by a broad class of deviation value functions in the neighborhood of the first-best capital.

We consider constrained efficient allocations that maximize the joint surplus of the representative lender and the private households subject to the sequence of incumbent politicians' self-enforcing constraints. In particular, we consider allocations that solve the following planning problem:

$$\sup_{c \in C, k} P(c, k) \text{ subject to } U(c) \geq v, \text{ and } (3.6) \text{ for all } t \geq 0, s^t \in S^t. \qquad (3.8)$$

Let μ denote the multiplier on the $U(c) \geq v$ constraint and $\beta^t \lambda_t$ the multiplier on the period-t self-enforcing constraint.[6] The first-order conditions for capital and consumption, respectively, are:

$$f_k(k_{t-1}) = r + \delta + \beta^t R^t \lambda_t W_k^D(k_{t-1}) \qquad (3.9)$$

$$\beta^t R^t u'(c_t) \left[\mu + \sum \lambda_{t-j} + (\theta - 1)\lambda_t \right] = 1. \qquad (3.10)$$

The first-order condition for capital is the same as (3.5), but with W^D replacing V^D. In particular, a binding self-enforcing constraint distorts investment below the first-best level.

The first-order condition for consumption also is similar to (3.4), but with an additional term $(\theta - 1)\lambda_t$. When $\theta > 1$, the political economy distortions require additional consumption in the current period to ensure the current incumbent does not deviate. As political incumbents are present-biased relative to the private agents, this is an efficient way to ensure political compliance with the optimal plan. Note that if $\beta R = 1$, we still have $\lim_{t \to \infty} \lambda_t = 0$. Thus, political economy distortions on their own do not prevent convergence to the first-best capital and constant consumption. However, the frictions do affect the speed of convergence.

To get a better sense of dynamics, we explore a special case:

Assumption 2 *Let $\beta R = 1$ and $u(c) = c$.*

This assumption states that the representative private agent discounts at the risk-free interest rate, implying that the only disagreement between the lender and the government is due to political economy frictions. The linear utility allows a transparent analytical treatment of dynamics.[7]

---

6. For convenience, in this case we scale the multiplier on the self-enforcing constraint by β^t rather than R^{-t}. This simplifies the algebra that follows.

7. For a characterization of the dynamics under concave utility, see the online appendix of Aguiar and Amador (2011), where we show how to represent the dynamics using a two-dimensional phase diagram.

Under Assumption 2, the first-order condition for consumption becomes:

$$\lambda_{t+1} = \left(1 - \frac{1}{\theta}\right)\lambda_t. \tag{3.11}$$

Thus, λ_t converges to zero at a rate governed by θ. As θ becomes large, the speed of convergence declines. Political distortions therefore slow the pace at which the economy saves and hence the speed of capital accumulation.

To map this into output growth, we make the following assumption:

Assumption 3 *Assume* $f(k) = k^\alpha$, *for* $\alpha \in (0, 1)$ *and* $W_k^D = \theta f(k) + \underline{W}$.

The first statement assumes technology is Cobb-Douglas, with a capital share parameter α. The second statement assumes that after deviation, consumption equals output, with a continuation value independent of initial capital, as in (3.7).

Under these assumptions, the first-order conditon for capital can be re-written as:

$$\lambda_t = \frac{f_k - (r+\delta)}{W_k^D} \tag{3.12}$$

$$= \frac{1}{\theta} - \frac{r+\delta}{\theta f_k} \tag{3.13}$$

$$= \frac{1}{\theta}\left(1 - (r+\delta)k_t^{1-\alpha}\right). \tag{3.14}$$

The efficient level of capital, $k^\star$, satisfies $f_k(k^\star) = r + \delta$. Substituting in and rearranging, we have:

$$\left(\frac{k_t}{k^\star}\right)^{1-\alpha} = 1 - \theta\lambda_t. \tag{3.15}$$

Taking logs, and approximating $\ln(1 - \theta\lambda) \approx -\theta\lambda$ near the steady-state value $\lambda_\infty = 0$, we have:

$$(1-\alpha)\ln\left(\frac{k_t}{k^\star}\right) \approx -\theta\lambda_t. \tag{3.16}$$

From (3.11), we have $-\theta\lambda_t = -(\theta - 1)\lambda_{t-1}$. Using this, and evaluating (3.16) at $t - 1$, we obtain:

$$\ln\left(\frac{k_t}{k^\star}\right) \approx \left(1 - \frac{1}{\theta}\right)\ln\left(\frac{k_{t-1}}{k^\star}\right).$$

As $\ln y = \alpha \ln k$, the same statement can be made about output. In particular, we can rewrite the above in "growth regression" form:

$$\ln \left(\frac{y_t}{y_{t-1}} \right) \approx \frac{1}{\theta} \ln \left(\frac{y^\star}{y_{t-1}} \right), \tag{3.17}$$

where $y^\star = f(k^\star)$. This equation relates the growth rate between period $t-1$ and t to the distance from the steady-state output at $t-1$. The speed of convergence to the steady-state output is thus inversely related to θ.

Equation (3.17) suggests why economies with different degrees of political economy frictions grow at different speeds. A large empirical literature, starting with Mankiw, Romer, and Weil (1992), has found that typical parameterizations of the closed-economy neoclassical growth model imply counterfactually fast rates of convergence. The predicted rate of convergence is even faster in an open economy absent frictions. However, the open-economy model with limited commitment and political economy frictions suggests slow rates of convergence for countries with high degrees of political distortions.

While the fact that debt depresses investment is a general feature of this framework, the sensitivity depends on θ. To see this, consider the steady state. For $\beta R = 1$, $k \to k^\star$ for all values of θ. Using the special case (3.7), the self-enforcing constraint at $k^\star$ requires:

$$\left(\theta + \frac{\beta}{1-\beta} \right) c_{ss} = \theta f(k^\star) + \frac{\beta}{1-\beta} \underline{c}, \tag{3.18}$$

where c_{ss} is the steady-state consumption level. As $\underline{c} < f(k^\star)$, we have $c_{ss} < f(k^\star)$. Differentiating (3.18) with respect to θ then implies that $dc_{ss}/d\theta > 0$. That is, to sustain the same level of capital, $k^\star$, higher distortions require higher consumption. This in turn is associated with lower payments to lenders in the steady state. Thus, to sustain the first-best level of investment, a more politically distorted economy requires lower debt. In this way, a given level of debt overhang becomes a greater problem as θ increases.

Let us briefly discuss the role of two policies in this context: debt forgiveness and unconditional aid. As noted above, the economy grows by paying down debt. Thus, debt forgiveness speeds the process of convergence. What about unconditional transfers? As with debt forgiveness, transfers relax the budget set. However, if transfers are not conditional on debt repayment, they also increase the deviation value, W^D. This exacerbates the limited commitment friction, slowing growth. Debt forgiveness is not valuable if the government deviates, relaxing the self-enforcing constraint. Hence, it is possible to show that debt forgiveness dominates an unconditional transfer of the same magnitude.[8]

3.6   Conclusion

This chapter explored how sovereign debt distorts investment and growth. In particular, it discussed how sovereign debt overhang depresses new investment. Both empirically and in the conceptual model outlined above, growth is driven by a combination of private investment and reduction in public debt. Limited commitment predicts that public debt and investment move in opposite directions. In addition, by distorting fiscal policy, political economy frictions ultimately distort the pace of growth, suggesting a common source to the cross-sectional heterogeneity in convergence rates, debt dynamics, and the extent of debt "intolerance" seen in the data.

8. See Proposition 5 in Aguiar and Amador (2011) for a formal statement of this result.

4

Incomplete Markets

4.1 Introduction

In the preceding two chapters, we explored how limited commitment disrupted investment and first-best risk sharing, despite the presence of complete markets. The constrained efficient allocations featured limited risk sharing and "backloading." The postponement of consumption eventually allows the lenders and sovereign to more fully exploit the gains from trade. If the sovereign discounts at the same rate as the lenders, then eventually the allocation achieves first-best risk sharing.

We now revisit Chapter 2's environment, but relax the complete markets assumption by exogenously restricting the ability of lenders to provide insurance. In particular, we assume that the government can only trade a non-contingent bond. As we shall see, the lack of state contingency generates default in equilibrium. This is the environment considered in the classic Eaton and Gersovitz (1981) and the subsequent quantitative literature initiated by Aguiar and Gopinath (2006), Arellano (2008), and Hamann (2002). In this chapter, we present a stylized tractable model that transparently highlights how default affects debt dynamics and consumption smoothing. This will set the stage for the richer models used in the quantitative literature discussed in the next chapter.

While the environment analyzed below differs in many important respects from the complete markets benchmark, the core friction—lack of commitment—remains. Correspondingly, we shall see that the incentive to backload consumption (that is, save) remains as well. In the complete markets environment, the incentive to save was provided by improved insurance. In the current environment, the incentive will be to avoid the deadweight costs of default. In the complete-markets-benchmark decentralization, the incentive to save was reflected in endogenous borrowing constraints. In the non-contingent bond model, the incentive will be reflected in the sensitivity of bond yields to the level of indebtedness.

The chapter proceeds as follows. After presenting the environment, we solve a series of planning problems. We then show how the competitive equilibrium with a defaultable non-contingent bond decentralizes the constrained efficient allocation. The latter exercise will allow us to explore how market interest rates provide the "correct" incentives to reduce the probability of default.

4.2   Environment

As in the preceding chapters, consider a small open economy managed by a government that trades financial claims with risk-neutral lenders. To focus on the novel aspect introduced by default, we assume the economy receives a constant endowment y. Hence, there is no need to insure against endowment fluctuations. We shall introduce endowment risk in the next chapter.

It is useful to work in continuous time; we present the discrete-time model in the next chapter. Let ρ denote the government's discount rate and, as in Chapter 2, let $u(c)$ denote the government's flow utility given consumption c.

The government cannot commit to financial contracts. If it decides to default on a promised payment, it is punished by a loss of endowment as well as permanent exclusion. In the absence of endowment risk, exclusion on its own is not an effective punishment. The additional loss of endowment captures disruption to trade, domestic financial markets, etc., that may accompany default. Moreover, as we shall discuss when we turn to quantitative models, it plays an important role in achieving empirically realistic levels of debt in equilibrium. We assume in addition that if the government defaults, the lenders receive zero.

Specifically, suppose the government defaults at time t. Let $\tau_t \in [0, 1)$ denote the fraction of the endowment lost due to default for time-t defaults. The value of default is

$$V_t^D = \int_t^\infty e^{-\rho(s-t)} u\left((1 - \tau_t)y\right) ds = \frac{u\left((1 - \tau_t)y\right)}{\rho}.$$

Note that the subscript t in τ_t indexes the date of default, not the current date going forward; hence, in the above integral, s indexes future dates, but τ_t remains a constant.[1]

We assume that τ_t follows a stochastic process. In particular, the government typically faces a harsh default penalty, $\overline{\tau}$. If it defaults while this punishment is in effect, its default value is $V^D = \underline{V} \equiv u\left((1-\overline{\tau})y\right)/\rho$. However, with Poisson arrival λ, the government has the option to default at a lenient penalty, $\underline{\tau} < \overline{\tau}$, with associated value $V^D = \overline{V} = u\left((1-\underline{\tau})y\right)/\rho > \underline{V}$. If it does not default on the arrival of $\underline{\tau}$, the punishment reverts to the harsh value and the Poisson process is restarted. The variation in default punishments is the only source of uncertainty in the environment. We shall work directly with realized default values: $V_t^D \in \{\underline{V}, \overline{V}\}$, as this is the quantity directly relevant for the default decision.

We shall see that the lenient default state is particularly interesting. If $\underline{\tau} > 0$, there is a deadweight cost of default in this state (as $\overline{\tau} > \underline{\tau} \geq 0$, there is always a loss in the harsh regime). How the size of the gap between $\underline{\tau}$ and zero affects allocations will be the key focus of the analysis. In terms of utility, a value of $\underline{\tau} > 0$ implies a default value $\overline{V}$ that is less than the value of having zero debt and consuming the endowment forever, $u(y)/\rho$. As the lenders are indifferent between default and the latter outcome (both generate zero payments to the lenders), the gap between $\overline{V}$ and $u(y)/\rho$ represents a net loss to the lender-borrower relationship.

As before, the government faces atomistic risk-neutral lenders that discount at rate $r^\star$. We shall assume $r^\star = \rho$, so there is no disagreement between lenders and government about time preferences:

Assumption 6 $\rho = r^\star$.

In Chapter 7 we discuss a relatively impatient government.

4.3   Complete Markets Benchmark

For reference, we begin with the complete markets benchmark, which has an allocation that solves the following planning problem. Consider the optimal

---

1. This is not crucial, but allows for a tractable model for the stochastic process of default values. The key assumption is that the default value V_t^D varies with the punishment in effect at time t.

contracting problem between a risk-neutral principal/planner and the government. The principal chooses a consumption stream, which can be contingent on the realizations of V^D, that delivers some initial promised value to the government, v_0, subject to the limited commitment constraint that the government is always free to separate from the contract and take the current realized value of V^D as payoff.

For $v_0 < \underline{V}$, the principal finds it optimal to deliver $\underline{V}$ to avoid immediate separation. As a result, we restrict attention to initial promised values $v_0 \geq \underline{V}$.[2] It is also possible to show that it is weakly efficient to choose an allocation that avoids separation, and it is strictly optimal to do so if there is a dead-weight loss ($\rho \overline{V} < u(y)$). The reason is that there are gains from trade that are lost when the government and the lenders separate. To keep the planner's value bounded, we also assume $v_0 \leq V_{max}$ for some $V_{max} > \overline{V}$. We assume that V_{max} can be delivered with finite resources; that is, there exists some maximal level of assets $a_{max} < \infty$ such that if the government consumes $y + \rho a_{max}$ forever, it generates a value V_{max}. As we shall see, such an upper bound on the government's value does not materially affect the chosen allocation. Let $\mathbb{V} \equiv [\underline{V}, V_{max}]$ denote the domain of interest.

The complete-market's planning problem can be written in the following way. The planner chooses a deterministic consumption stream $c = \{c(t)\}_{t \geq 0}$ that is implemented until the first arrival of $\overline{V}$, at which point it can re-optimize to avoid separation. We can restrict attention to deterministic sequences prior to the first arrival of $\overline{V}$, as there is no benefit from randomizing consumption absent a change in V^D. Denote by C the space of such sequences (specifically, the space of measurable functions of time) with $c(t) \geq 0$.

What the planner does upon the first arrival of $\overline{V}$ must be consistent with its initial contract c. Specifically, let $v(t)$ denote the government's value at time t under the allocation c (see equation 4.1 below).[3] Let T denote the (random) time of the first arrival of $\overline{V}$, where T has an exponential distribution with parameter λ. Upon the realization of $\overline{V}$, the planner resets the government's value to $\max\{v(T), \overline{V}\}$. That is, if $v(T) < \overline{V}$, the planner raises the promised

---

2. We do not model the entry into the contract at promised value v_0. In particular, a patient government has no incentive to have borrowed in previous periods such that $v_0 < u(y)/\rho$. We include the full domain for completeness. Moreover, if $\rho > r^*$, a government may find it optimal to saddle future governments with a low promised value. An impatient government is discussed formally in Chapter 7.

3. Formally, we should write $v(t; c)$ to indicate that the value depends on the chosen allocation. For simplicity, we omit this extra argument.

future utility to avoid separation, as this avoids the associated deadweight losses.[4] If $v(T) \geq \overline{V}$, the planner continues with the initially promised c. Thus, c plus the stochastic process for V^D is sufficient to characterize the state-dependent evolution of consumption and the government's value.

The government's value under an allocation c is given by:

$$v(t) = \int_t^\infty e^{-(\rho+\lambda)(s-t)} u(c(s))ds + \lambda \int_t^\infty e^{-(\rho+\lambda)(s-t)} \max\{v(s), \overline{V}\}ds.$$

$$(4.1)$$

This is the expected discounted value of receiving flow utility $u(c(s))$ until the first arrival of $\overline{V}$ (which happens at time $s > t$ with probability $\lambda e^{-\lambda(s-t)}$), at which point the value jumps to the maximum of $\overline{V}$ and $v(T)$. Equation (4.1) implies that the evolution of the government's value satisfies the differential equation:

$$\dot{v} \equiv v'(t) = -u(c(t)) + (\rho + \lambda)v(t) - \lambda \max\{v(t), \overline{V}\}. \qquad (4.2)$$

Let $P^{CM} : \mathbb{V} \to \mathbb{R}$ trace out the planner's value at each $v_0 \in \mathbb{V}$. This function solves the complete-markets planning problem:

$$P^{CM}(v_0) =$$

$$\sup_{c \in C} \int_0^\infty e^{-(\rho+\lambda)t} \left[y - c(t) + \lambda \mathbb{1}_{[v(t) < \overline{V}]} P^{CM}(\overline{V}) + \lambda \mathbb{1}_{[v(t) \geq \overline{V}]} P^{CM}(v(t)) \right] dt$$

$$(4.3)$$

subject to (4.2) and $v(0) \geq v_0$ and $v(t) \in \mathbb{V}, \forall t \geq 0,$

where $\mathbb{1}_{[x]}$ is the indicator function that takes value one if x is true and zero otherwise. The complete-markets planner's value function P^{CM} is the unique bounded fixed point of this recursive equation.[5]

To solve for the optimum, we can recast the sequence problem (4.3) as a recursive differential equation. In particular, P^{CM} satisfies the following

---

4. It will not reset v to a value higher than $\overline{V}$, as there is no benefit to the planner from doing so. Moreover, a larger than necessary adjustment after the arrival of $\overline{V}$, combined with lower prior consumption to deliver present value v_0, induces excessive volatility of consumption, making it more costly to deliver a given value.

5. Note that (4.3) defines an operator on the space of bounded functions with domain $\mathbb{V}$. This operator satisfies Blackwell's sufficient condition for a contraction mapping. Hence, it admits a unique fixed point.

Hamilton-Jacobi-Bellman (HJB) equation:

$$\rho P^{CM}(v) = \max_{c \geq 0} \left\{ y - c + P^{CM\prime}(v)\dot{v} + \lambda \mathbb{1}_{[v < \overline{V}]} \left[P^{CM}(\overline{V}) - P^{CM}(v) \right] \right\},$$

$$(4.4)$$

where $\dot{v}$ is given by (4.2) evaluated at the chosen c and we suppress t as an argument of $v(t)$. Standard continuous-time dynamic programming results imply that P^{CM} is the unique bounded, continuous solution to this HJB equation.[6] The optimal complete-markets allocation takes the form of those studied in the previous chapter. To review some notation, let C denote the inverse of u. That is $u(C(x)) = x$. Let $c^{SS}(v)$ denote the "steady-state" level of consumption that ensures $\dot{v} = 0$; that is, by setting $\dot{v}$ to zero in (4.2), we have

$$c^{SS}(v) \equiv \begin{cases} C(\rho v) & \text{if } v \in [\overline{V}, V_{max}] \\ C((\rho + \lambda)v - \lambda\overline{V}) & \text{if } v \in [\underline{V}, \overline{V}). \end{cases} \qquad (4.5)$$

For $v \geq \overline{V}$, the planner simply sets consumption to the steady-state level forever:

$$P^{CM}(v) = \frac{y - c^{SS}(v)}{\rho} \text{ if } v \geq \overline{V}.$$

As $\rho = r^\star$, there is no gain in tilting consumption over time.

For $v \in [\underline{V}, \overline{V})$, the planner keeps $v(t)$ constant until the first arrival of $\overline{V}$, at which point it raises consumption to prevent separation. Thus,

$$P^{CM}(v) = \frac{y - c^{SS}(v) + \lambda P^{CM}(\overline{V})}{\rho + \lambda}.$$

Note that if there are deadweight costs associated with separation, that is, $\rho\overline{V} < u(y)$, then $c^{SS}(\overline{V}) = C(\rho\overline{V}) < y$, and $P^{CM}(\overline{V}) > 0$. This is why the planner strictly prefers to deliver $\overline{V}$ within the relationship rather than letting the government and lenders separate, as this separation yields a payoff of zero to the principal. If there are no deadweight costs, then $C(\rho\overline{V}) = y$ and the planner is indifferent between separation or continuation with the original contract. Hence, $P^{CM}(\overline{V}) = (y - C(\rho\overline{V}))/\rho$ is the deadweight cost to default in terms of goods.

---

6. See Fleming and Soner (2006) for a textbook treatment of continuous-time dynamic programming. For results specific to the environments studied in this book, see Aguiar, Amador, Farhi, and Gopinath (2012) and the online appendix to Aguiar and Amador (2020).

This completes the characterization of the complete-markets allocation. The lack of commitment involves backloading consumption, but consumption is stationary until the government is tempted to deviate by the arrival of $\overline{V}$. From the promise-keeping constraint, this implies initial consumption may be lower than the unconstrained first-best, and is not constant over time. However, eventually, on the first arrival of the high outside option, the allocation jumps to a constant level.

4.4   Incomplete Markets: A Planning Problem

We now consider allocations that are consistent with incomplete markets. Specifically, we are ultimately interested in competitive equilibria in which the government is restricted to borrowing in non-contingent bonds. This restriction on asset markets imposes restrictions on the consumption allocations that can be generated in equilibrium.

As we show in section 4.5, for the environment considered in this chapter, incomplete markets restricts the consumption allocation (conditional on no government default) to be just a function of time, but not of the realization of V^D.[7] This means that if the equilibrium consumption allocation is currently delivering a value $v < \overline{V}$ to the government, then the realization of $V^D = \overline{V}$ will necessarily lead to a government separation, which we refer to as default. The ability to generate this on-equilibrium-path default, even in the presence of deadweight losses, is a fundamental feature of the incomplete-markets assumption (and one that has important implications for quantitative work).

We proceed now to study the optimal contracting problem between the government and a lender (principal) that respects this incomplete-market restriction: that the consumption allocation is deterministic conditional on no default. As we will see in section 4.5, the solution to this contracting problem also corresponds to the decentralized equilibrium outcome, highlighting a more general result of the efficiency of financing with short-term debt.

Recall that c denotes a deterministic consumption sequence. In the complete-markets program, we allowed for adjustment upon the arrival of $\overline{V}$. Now, consumption follows a deterministic sequence until the government defaults. Hence, given an allocation c, upon the arrival of $\overline{V}$, either

7. Chapter 5 describes how this incomplete market's restriction can be imposed for more general shock processes, including shocks to the endowment.

the government defaults and receives $V^D = \overline{V}$, or continues with the initial deterministic allocation c.

For a given sequence c, the government's value is still defined by (4.1). The implicit difference is that if $v(t) < \overline{V}$, then $\overline{V}$ is delivered through default and not through adjusting the allocation. Let $P^{\star} : \mathbb{V} \to \mathbb{R}$ denote the optimal value to the lender/principal conditional on an initial promised value to the government of $v_0 \in \mathbb{V}$. This value solves the following constraint-efficient planning problem:

$$P^{\star}(v_0) = \sup_{c \in \mathcal{C}} \int_0^{\infty} e^{-(\rho + \lambda)t} \left[y - c(t) + \lambda \mathbb{1}_{[v(t) \geq \overline{V}]} P^{\star}(v(t)) \right] dt \qquad (4.6)$$

subject to $v(0) \geq v_0$ and $v(t) \in \mathbb{V}, \forall t$,

where $v(t)$ is given by (4.1) under the chosen c. Note that $P^{\star}$ is decreasing, as a lower v_0 relaxes the constraint set.

The associated HJB is:

$$\left(\rho + \mathbb{1}_{[v < \overline{V}]} \lambda \right) P^{\star}(v) = \sup_{c \geq 0} \left\{ y - c + P^{\star\prime}(v) \dot{v} \right\}, \qquad (4.7)$$

where $\dot{v}$ follows (4.2) given c. Under some technical conditions outlined in Aguiar et al. (2012), the solution to the differential equation (4.7) also solves the original sequence problem. As we shall see, there are points at which $P^{\star}$ is not differentiable, in contrast to P^{CM}; hence, we seek a generalized notion of solution to the differential equation, namely a *viscosity* solution.[8]

There is a crucial difference between (4.7) and the complete market's counterpart (4.4). In particular, when $v < \overline{V}$, they differ in what happens to the planner's value when $\overline{V}$ is realized. In the complete-market case, the value falls to $P^{CM}(\overline{V}) \geq 0$. In the incomplete-market case, the value falls to zero. Thus $P^{\star}(v) \leq P^{CM}(v)$. If there are deadweight costs of default, $P^{CM}(\overline{V}) > 0$. This implies that the principal's value will be strictly lower than under complete markets if default occurs with positive probability. In addition, the presence of default cost changes the optimal allocation conditional on no default.

In what follows, we assume that the utility function u is strictly concave and that the Inada conditions hold, so that we can restrict attention

---

8. See Aguiar et al. (2012) and the online appendix to Aguiar and Amador (2020) for the formal discussion of viscosity solutions for continuous-time dynamic programming problems in this environment.

to interior consumption allocations. Given this, the first-order condition for consumption is

$$-P^{\star\prime}(v) = 1/u'(c).\qquad(4.8)$$

The right-hand side is the cost to the planner in terms of consumption of increasing the government's flow utility today at the margin. From (4.2), the return from doing this is lowering the promises to the government going forward, which raises the value to the principal by $-P^{\star\prime}(v) > 0$. The first-order condition thus equates marginal cost to marginal benefit.

We begin by describing the straightforward case of starting from $v \geq \overline{V}$. Let $C^{\star}(v)$ denote the constrained efficient consumption given promised value v. Recall that the complete-markets allocation calls for constant consumption forever independent of the default value realization. This allocation is also achievable under incomplete markets by setting $C^{\star}(v) = c^{SS}(v)$ for $v \geq \overline{V}$. Given that the complete market's value function is an upper bound on $P^{\star}$, it follows that for $v \geq \overline{V}$:

$$P^{\star}(v) = P^{CM}(v) \text{ for } v \geq \overline{V}.\qquad(4.9)$$

For $v < \overline{V}$, recall that under complete markets, it was optimal to maintain a stationary level of consumption as long as $\overline{V}$ did not arrive. We first discuss why such a stationary level of consumption is no longer optimal under incomplete markets.

Let $P^{SS}(v)$ denote the value to the planner of setting $c = c^{SS}(v)$ for all $t \geq 0$ (until default). That is, for $v \in \mathbb{V}$, we define:

$$P^{SS}(v) \equiv \begin{cases} \frac{y - c^{SS}(v)}{\rho} & \text{if } v \geq \overline{V} \\ \frac{y - c^{SS}(v)}{\rho + \lambda} & \text{if } v \in [\underline{V}, \overline{V}). \end{cases}\qquad(4.10)$$

The first row on the right is equal to $P^{CM}(v)$. The second row is strictly less than $P^{CM}(v)$ if there are deadweight costs of default.

In Figure 4.1, panel (a), we depict three functions of v, P^{CM}, $P^{\star}$, and P^{SS}, for the case where the deadweight losses from default are strictly positive. For $v \geq \overline{V}$, all three lines coincide. For v in the neighborhood just below $\overline{V}$, the stationary value is discretely below. Hence, there is a discontinuity in P^{SS} at the boundary $\overline{V}$. This gap is the expected deadweight loss of default: $\lambda P^{CM}(\overline{V})/(\rho + \lambda) = \lambda P^{\star}(\overline{V})/(\rho + \lambda)$. If there were no deadweight costs to default, this term is zero, the complete-markets value is achievable by letting the government default, and the three lines would coincide.

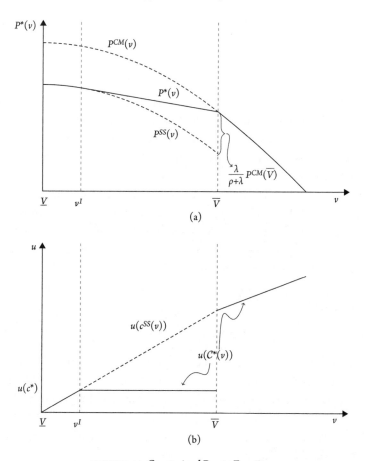

FIGURE 4.1. Constrained Pareto Frontier

Note: Panel (a) depicts the constrained efficient Pareto frontier (solid line). The vertical axis is the lenders' value and the horizontal axis is the government's value. The dashed line labeled P^{CM} is the complete-market's frontier. The dashed line labeled P^{SS} is the value from setting $c = c^{SS}(v)$. For $v \geq \overline{V}$, the three lines coincide. Panel (b) depicts the flow utility from the constrained efficient consumption policy (solid line). The dashed line depicts the utility from the stationary consumption policy, which is the complete-market's optimal policy. For $v \in [\underline{V}, \overline{V})$, the stationary policy has a slope of $(\rho + \lambda)$; for $v > \overline{V}$, the slope is ρ.

If the deadweight losses are strictly positive, then the stationary level of consumption cannot be optimal in the neighborhood below $\overline{V}$. This follows from the fact that $P^{*}(v)$ is continuous in v, and $P^{SS}(v)$ is not. The intuition for why P^{SS} is not optimal in this range can be obtained from a simple perturbation argument. Suppose, relative to c^{SS}, the planner temporarily reduces (that is, backloads) consumption slightly for v arbitrarily close (but below) $\overline{V}$. This implies $\dot{v} > 0$, and suppose as a result the government's value moves into the no-default region. Starting from the constant level of consumption, the losses to the government due to backloading of consumption are second order, and thus require a second-order increase in the present value of consumption. The reduction in the probability of default is a first-order gain to the planner if deadweight costs are positive. Thus, on net, such a perturbation strictly raises the planner's value.

This perturbation exercise leads us to conjecture that for values below but close to $\overline{V}$, it is optimal to set consumption strictly below its stationary value, so that $\dot{v} < 0$. More specifically, we conjecture that for values of v slightly below $\overline{V}$, consumption equals a constant value $c^\star < C^{SS}(\overline{V})$.[9]

Consider then equation (4.7) as we approach $\overline{V}$ from below. We have a boundary condition in $\lim_{v \uparrow \overline{V}} P^\star(v) = P^\star(\overline{V}) = P^{CM}(\overline{V})$. From (4.8), we have a mapping from $P^{\star\prime}(v)$ to consumption. In particular, $\lim_{v \uparrow \overline{V}} P^{\star\prime}(v) = -1/u'(c^\star)$. Then, using (4.7) and (4.8) and taking the limit as v approaches $\overline{V}$ from below, $c^\star$ solves:

$$(\rho + \lambda)P^\star(\overline{V}) = y - c^\star - \frac{1}{u'(c^\star)}\left(\rho\overline{V} - u(c^\star)\right). \qquad (4.11)$$

One can see that the right-hand side of equation (4.11) is non-monotonic in $c^\star$. In particular, it is strictly decreasing for $c^\star < C^{SS}(\overline{V})$ and strictly increasing for $c^\star > C^{SS}(\overline{V})$.[10] Even more, when evaluated at $c^\star = C^{SS}(\overline{V})$ the right-hand side equals $y - C^{SS}(\overline{V}) = \rho P^\star(\overline{V})$.

If there are no deadweight costs of default, then $P^\star(\overline{V}) = 0$ and $c^\star = C(\rho\overline{V}) = c^{SS}(\overline{V})$ solves (4.11).

If there are deadweight losses from default, then $P^\star(\overline{V}) > 0$, and the left-hand side of equation (4.11) will be strictly higher than the right-hand side when evaluated at $c^\star = C^{SS}(\overline{V})$. This confirms that stationary consumption is not a solution in this case, and there are potentially two values of $c^\star$ that satisfy equation (4.11). However, only $c^\star < c^{SS}(\overline{V})$ is consistent with our conjecture;

9. This conjecture that the optimal consumption is constant for a region of values above $\overline{V}$ may be a bit mysterious at this point. However, it follows from the fact that both the planner and the government discount the future at the same rate, and the fact that the probability of separation is constant for $v < \overline{V}$.

10. To see this, note that the right-hand side has a derivative with respect to $c^\star$ equal to $\frac{u''(c^\star)\dot{v}}{(u'(c^\star))^2}$, where $\dot{v} = -u(c^\star) + \rho\overline{V}$.

that is, it implies that $v(t) \to \overline{V}$. So, if there are strictly positive deadweight costs, then $c^\star < c^{SS}(\overline{V})$, and thus the value to the government increases over time as $\dot{v} > 0$ up to the point it reaches $\overline{V}$.[11]

Let us now determine the region in $[\underline{V}, \overline{V})$ where $c = c^\star$ is optimal. Note that the dynamics of v under this conjecture are given by $\dot{v} = -u(c^\star) + (\rho + \lambda)v - \lambda\overline{V}$ (see equation 4.2). For v close to $\overline{V}$, we have $\dot{v} > 0$, as discussed. However, for small enough v, it may be the case that $\dot{v} < 0$ when $c = c^\star$, which is inconsistent with our conjecture. Let v^I denote the v at which $\dot{v}$ is zero when $c = c^\star$, that is, v^I is defined implicitly by $c^\star = c^{SS}(v^I)$:

$$v^I \equiv \frac{u(c^\star) + \lambda\overline{V}}{\rho + \lambda}.$$

For $v \in [v^I, \overline{V})$, we let $c = c^\star$. The first-order condition for consumption implies that the value function must be linear in this range. The value function that solves the HJB is:

$$P^\star(v) = P^\star(\overline{V}) + \frac{1}{u'(c^\star)}\left(\overline{V} - v\right), \text{ for } v \in [v^I, \overline{V}).$$

The final step is a conjecture for the rest of the domain. For $v \in [\underline{V}, v^I)$, we conjecture that the planner no longer induces dynamics in $v(t)$, but rather switches to the stationary policy. The value v^I is the point where the planner is indifferent between moving toward the no-default region and staying put and eventually experiencing default when $V^D = \overline{V}$. For $v \leq v^I$, the cost of delaying consumption long enough to reach $\overline{V}$ outweighs the deadweight loss

---

11. The Inada conditions on utility are sufficient to guarantee the existence of $c^\star$. To see this, note that the right-hand side of (4.11) is

$$y - \frac{\rho\overline{V}}{u'(c^\star)} + \frac{u(c^\star) - u'(c^\star)c^\star}{u'(c^\star)} \geq y - \frac{\rho\overline{V}}{u'(c^\star)}$$

where the inequality follows from the concavity of u. As we take $c^\star \to 0$, $u'(c^\star) \to \infty$, and the right-hand side of (4.11) converges to a value weakly higher than y. For the left-hand side, for $v < \overline{V}$ the lender's value is bounded above by giving the government zero consumption while $v(t) < \overline{V}$ and reaching $v(T) = \overline{V}$ after $T \in (0, \infty]$ units of time. Hence, for $v < \overline{V}$, we have:

$$P^\star(\overline{V}) < P^\star(v) \leq \frac{y}{\rho + \lambda}\left(1 - e^{-(\rho+\lambda)T}\right) + e^{-(\rho+\lambda)T}P^\star(\overline{V}).$$

As $T > 0$, this implies $P^\star(\overline{V}) < y/(\rho + \lambda)$. This establishes the left-hand side of (4.11) is less than y. Thus, the right-hand side is strictly greater than the left at $c^\star = 0$ and strictly less at $c^\star = c^{SS}(\overline{V})$. This guarantees the existence of an interior $c^\star \in (0, c^{SS}(\overline{V}))$ that solves (4.11).

from default. Hence, setting $P^\star(v) = P^{SS}(v)$ on $v \in [\underline{V}, v^I)$ does not involve a discontinuity in the planner's value function. Moreover, it satisfies (4.7).[12] If $v^I < \underline{V}$, then this set is empty and $\dot{v} > 0$ for the entire domain $[\underline{V}, \overline{V})$.

Collecting results, we have now constructed a candidate $P^\star$ for the entire domain of v. We have shown that the $P^\star$ satisfies the HJB equation (4.7) at all points of differentiability, that is, for all $v \neq \overline{V}$.[13] In addition, we can show that $P^\star$ is the optimal solution and satisfies (4.7) in the viscosity sense (for this, see Aguiar et al. 2012 and the online appendix to Aguiar and Amador 2020 for details).

The associated constrained efficient consumption allocation involves stationary consumption for $v \geq \overline{V}$ and $v \in [\underline{V}, v^I]$. For $v \in (v^I, \overline{V})$, the planner sets $c = c^\star$ and $\dot{v} > 0$ when there are deadweight losses. In this region, the planner is directing $v(t)$ toward the no-default region. The government will default along the way if $\overline{V}$ arrives prior to reaching the no-default region; otherwise, the planner will successfully avoid default.

As discussed above, the reason that the planner backloads consumption is to economize on the deadweight costs of default. Equation (4.11) informs us how the optimal level of saving (or consumption) varies with $\overline{V}$. In particular, we can replace $P^\star(\overline{V})$ with $(y - C(\rho\overline{V}))/\rho$, where recall that $C(\rho\overline{V})$ is the level of consumption that delivers flow utility $\rho\overline{V}$. Implicitly differentiating condition (4.11) implies that $dc^\star/d\overline{V} > 0$ when there is a deadweight loss:

$$\frac{dc^\star}{d\overline{V}} = \frac{-\rho/u'(c^\star) + (\rho + \lambda)/u'(C(\rho\overline{V}))}{-\frac{u''(c^\star)\dot{v}}{(u'(c^\star))^2}},$$

where we use $C'(\rho\overline{V}) = 1/u'(C(\rho\overline{V}))$, as C is the inverse of u. As u is strictly increasing and concave and $\dot{v} > 0$ with deadweight costs, the denominator is positive. Moreover, as $c^\star < C(\rho\overline{V}) = c^{SS}(\overline{V})$, the numerator is also positive. Therefore, the smaller the deadweight costs of default, the larger is $c^\star$, and, from (4.2), the slower the planner moves $v(t)$ toward the no-default region.

---

12. Note that $dP^\star(v^I)/dv = dP^{SS}(v^I)/dv$, and so the function $P^\star$ is differentiable at v^I.

13. Note that $\lim_{v \downarrow \overline{V}} P^{\star\prime}(v) = \frac{-1}{u'(c^{SS}(\overline{V}))} \leq \frac{-1}{u'(c^\star)} = \lim_{v \uparrow \overline{V}} P^{\star\prime}(v)$, with strict inequality when there is a deadweight cost. Hence, $P^\star$ is not differentiable at $\overline{V}$ when deadweight losses are strictly positive.

4.5   Incomplete Markets: Decentralization

We now show that the constrained efficient allocation described above corresponds to the market equilibrium that arises when the government borrows using short-term bonds. The decentralization will allow us to connect to the approach used in the quantitative literature (such as Aguiar and Gopinath 2006 and Arellano 2008). It will also help to understand why short-term bonds implement an efficient allocation, a result that we generalize in Chapter 5 and which, as we shall see in Chapter 7, no longer holds with longer-maturity bonds. A crucial insight here is how equilibrium bond prices induce the government to internalize the deadweight costs of default despite the fact that default is strategic (that is, at the moment of default, the government strictly prefers V^D to repayment).

Let $b(t)$ denote the amount of bonds the government has outstanding at time t. We shall decentralize the efficient allocation as a Markov equilibrium (defined below) where the payoff-relevant variables are debt and V^D. We impose a No Ponzi condition on the equilibrium such that $b(t) \leq \overline{B}$ for all t. We assume $\overline{B}$ is large enough never to bind in equilibrium; sufficient for this is $\overline{B} > P^\star(\underline{V})$.

Let $V(b)$ denote the value of the government with debt b outstanding assuming repayment at this moment in time. That is, at each instant t, the government chooses $\max\{V(b(t)), V^D(t)\}$; hence, $V(b)$ denotes the value of continuing to service debt. As the arrival of $\overline{V}$ is *iid* over time, we do not need to include it as an explicit state variable in the continuation value $V(b)$. Given our interest in the efficient allocation, for ease of exposition we impose ex ante as an equilibrium condition that $V(b)$ is continuous. This raises the possibility that we are potentially ignoring interesting equilibria in which V is not continuous. The next chapter shows (in the discrete-time generalization of this model) that this is not the case.

Let $r(b)$ denote the flow equilibrium interest rate. More specifically, consider a small interval of time Δ. If the government has $b(t)$ units of bonds outstanding at time t, it must pay a flow equilibrium interest rate $r(b(t))$ until $t + \Delta$ (assuming no default). Over this interval, the government receives its endowment y. Suppose it consumes a constant $c(s) = c$ for $s \in [t, t + \Delta)$; as $\Delta \to 0$, restricting attention to a constant level of consumption over the interval is without loss. Let $b(t + \Delta)$ denote the amount of debt outstanding at the end of this interval. The flow budget constraint for the government under repayment is therefore:

$$b(t+\Delta) = b(t) + [r(b(t))b(t) + c - y]\,\Delta.$$

Subtracting $b(t)$ from both sides, dividing by Δ, and taking the limit as $\Delta \to 0$, we obtain (suppressing time arguments):[14]

$$\dot{b} = r(b)b + c - y. \tag{4.12}$$

Associated with $r(b)$ is an endogenous borrowing limit, $\bar{b}$, which is the largest debt such that $V(b) \geq \underline{V}$. For $V(b) < \underline{V}$, the government defaults immediately, and hence no lender is willing to extend a loan. That is, government debt is restricted to some range $b(t) \in [-a_{max}, \bar{b}] \equiv \mathbb{B}$, where recall that $u(y + r^{\star} a_{max})/\rho = V_{max}$. That is, $\mathbb{B}$ is an equilibrium debt domain such that $V: \mathbb{B} \to V$.

The government's problem in sequence form can be written as:

$$V(b_0) = \max_{c \in C} \int_0^\infty e^{-(\rho+\lambda)t} \left[u(c(t)) + \lambda \max\{V(b(t)), \overline{V}\} \right] dt$$

$$\text{subject to } \begin{cases} \dot{b}(t) = r(b(t))b(t) + c(t) - y \\ b(0) = b_0 \\ b(t) \in \mathbb{B} \; \forall t \geq 0. \end{cases}$$

This reflects that the government receives flow utility $u(c(t))$ until the first arrival of $\overline{V}$, at which point it chooses the maximum between continuing under repayment or default. The government's problem can be written in recursive form as the following *HJB*:

$$\rho V(b) = \max_{c \geq 0} \left\{ u(c) + V'(b)\dot{b} + \mathbb{1}_{[V(b) < \overline{V}]} \lambda \left(\overline{V} - V(b) \right) \right\}, \tag{4.13}$$

where $\dot{b}$ depends on the choice of c through (4.12). As with $P^{\star}$, V may not be everywhere differentiable, so we seek a generalized (viscosity) solution to the differential equation (4.13).[15]

To characterize the lenders' break-even condition, first note that given V, we can divide the domain of debt into two zones. For b such that $V(b) \geq \overline{V}$,

---

14. As will be clear below, $r(b)$ is such that this differential equation has a well-defined solution. At this stage of the exposition, we are implicitly assuming that an equilibrium restriction on the function r is that (4.12) has a well-defined solution given that $c(t)$ is a measurable function of time.

15. An additional restriction on the problem is that $b(t) \leq \bar{b}$, which is incorporated in the conditions that must be met by a viscosity solution to (4.13).

the arrival of the high outside option does not trigger default. Hence, we refer to the domain of debt such that $V(b) \geq \overline{V}$ as the "Safe Zone." For $V(b) \in [\underline{V}, \overline{V})$, the arrival of $\overline{V}$ triggers a default. Thus, following Cole and Kehoe (2000), we refer to this domain of debt as the "Crisis Zone." For $V(b) < \underline{V}$, the government immediately defaults, and hence this domain is not relevant in equilibrium.

The bonds are held by risk-neutral foreign lenders, who behave competitively but have enough wealth as a group that they are willing to hold any amount of bonds the government issues as long as they expect to break even relative to the (international) risk-free rate ρ. To obtain this break-even condition, again consider a short interval Δ. Take the case of $b(t)$ such that $V(b) < \overline{V}$; that is, b is in the Crisis Zone and default arrives with probability λ per unit time. As $b(t)$ is a continuous function of time, and V is continuous in b, for small enough Δ, debt will remain in the Crisis Zone over the interval. Hence, lenders face a constant hazard λ of default. In exchange, absent the arrival of $\overline{V}$, lenders receive a flow interest payment $r(b(t))$ plus the principal at the end of the interval. Lenders will be indifferent between purchasing an amount $b(t) > 0$ of government bonds versus investing in the risk-free outside asset at rate ρ as long as:

$$b(t) = \int_t^{t+\Delta} e^{-(\rho+\lambda)(s-t)} r(b(t)) b(t) ds + e^{-(\rho+\lambda)\Delta} b(t)$$

$$\Rightarrow r(b(t)) = \rho + \lambda.$$

A similar calculation implies that $r(b(t)) = \rho$ if $b(t)$ is such that $V(b) > \overline{V}$. If $V(b) = \overline{V}$, debt levels may cross into the Crisis Zone within any non-trivial interval Δ. At this boundary, we impose $r(\underline{b}) = \rho$ as our break-even condition, reflecting that the probability that the government both exits the Safe Zone and $\overline{V}$ arrives is of order Δ^2. Collecting results, the lenders' break-even condition is:

$$r(b) = \begin{cases} \rho & \text{if } V(b) \geq \overline{V} \\ \rho + \lambda & \text{if } V(b) \in [\underline{V}, \overline{V}). \end{cases} \qquad (4.14)$$

We can now define an equilibrium:

Definition 8 *A Markov competitive equilibrium (MCE) consists of a domain for debt $\mathbb{B} = [-a_{max}, \overline{b}]$, a bounded, continuous government value function $V : \mathbb{B} \to \mathbb{V}$, and an interest rate schedule $r : \mathbb{B} \to \{\rho, \rho + \lambda\}$ such that: (i) given r,* *the repayment value function V is a solution to* (4.13); *(ii) given V, the schedule r satisfies* (4.14); *and (iii)* $V(b) \geq \underline{V}$ *for* $b \in \mathbb{B}$.

It is now straightforward to show that the constrained efficient allocation can be implemented as a MCE. Let $V^\star$ denote the inverse of $P^\star$ (note that this is valid as $P^\star$ is strictly decreasing, and continuous). As b is the face value of the government's promises to lenders, efficiency requires that if $V^\star(b) = v$, then $b = P^\star(v)$.

Let $\underline{b} \equiv P^\star(\overline{V})$ and $\overline{b} \equiv P^\star(\underline{V})$. If v^I exists in the efficient allocation, let $b^I \equiv P^\star(v^I)$, otherwise replace b^I with $\overline{b}$ in the following. Inverting the expression for $P^\star$, we have:

$$V^\star(b) = \begin{cases} \frac{u(y-\rho b)}{\rho} & \text{if } b \in [-a_{max}, \underline{b}] \\ \overline{V} + u'(c^\star)\left(\underline{b} - b\right) & \text{if } b \in (\underline{b}, b^I] \\ \frac{u(y-(\rho+\lambda)b)+\lambda\overline{V}}{\rho+\lambda} & \text{if } b \in (b^I, \overline{b}], \end{cases} \tag{4.15}$$

where $c^\star$ is the same as in the constrained efficient allocation, defined by the lowest solution to equation (4.11). We depict $V^\star$ in Figure 4.2, which is the inverse image of Figure 4.1.

Panel (b) depicts the equilibrium interest rate schedule: $r(b) = \rho$ for $b \leq \underline{b}$ and $r(b) = \rho + \lambda$ for $b \in (\underline{b}, \overline{b}]$. This satisfies the break-even condition (4.14) given $V^\star$.

Note that $V^\star$ is differentiable everywhere except $\underline{b}$. At that point, it satisfies the viscosity conditions to be a solution to (4.13) detailed in Aguiar et al. (2012). Moreover, for $b \neq \underline{b}$, our candidate V satisfies (4.13) given r. Hence, V and r satisfy the conditions for a MCE. Moreover, from (4.13), $u'(c) = V'(b) = 1/P^{\star\prime}(V(b))$, and so the mapping from government values to consumption is the same as in the constrained efficient allocation. That is, the optimal consumption policy is given by

$$C^\star(b) = \begin{cases} y - \rho b \text{ if } b \in [-a_{max}, \underline{b}] \\ c^\star \text{ if } b \in (\underline{b}, b^I] \\ y - (\rho + \lambda)b \text{ if } b \in (b^I, \overline{b}]. \end{cases} \tag{4.16}$$

We do not prove that the constrained efficient allocation is the *only* MCE. However, we do so in the next chapter in the context of a more general discrete-time environment with one-period bonds.

The interesting question is why the government internalizes the dead-weight costs of default in the competitive equilibrium. Consider a level of debt

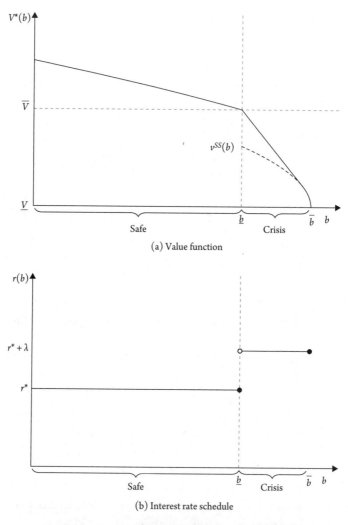

FIGURE 4.2. Equilibrium Value and Interest Rate Functions

Note: Panel (a) depicts the equilibrium value function $V^\star(b)$ (solid line). The dashed line labeled $v^{SS}(b)$ is the value from setting $c = y - r(b)b$ in the Crisis Zone until the first arrival of $\overline{V}$, and then defaulting. Panel (b) depicts the equilibrium interest rate schedule.

b_0 slightly above $\underline{b}$. At this point, $V(b_0) < \overline{V}$. The government gets a boost in value when the high outside option arrives and it defaults. Given that the expected yield on debt is the same as the government's discount rate, why doesn't the government simply await the high default value while keeping debt constant? That is, why does the government save when doing so reduces the gain upon default and tilts the path of consumption over time?

To see how saving is induced, suppose at $b_0 = \underline{b} + \epsilon$ for some arbitrarily small $\epsilon > 0$, the government sets $c = c_0 \equiv y - (\rho + \lambda)b_0 = y - (\rho + \lambda)(\underline{b} + \epsilon)$. This is the consumption that keeps debt constant at b_0. The value of this alternative policy is:

$$v^{ss}(\underline{b} + \epsilon) = \frac{u(y - (\rho + \lambda)(\underline{b} + \epsilon)) + \lambda\overline{V}}{\rho + \lambda}.$$

As u is concave, expanding u around $c = y - \rho\underline{b}$ implies

$$u(y - (\rho + \lambda)(\underline{b} + \epsilon)) \leq u(y - \rho\underline{b}) - u'(y - \rho\underline{b})(\lambda\underline{b} + (\rho + \lambda)\epsilon)$$
$$= \rho\overline{V} - u'(y - \rho\underline{b})(\lambda\underline{b} + (\rho + \lambda)\epsilon),$$

where the second line follows from the fact that $u(y - \rho\underline{b}) = \rho\overline{V}$ by definition of $\underline{b}$. Taking the limit as $\epsilon \downarrow 0$ and substituting into the previous expression, we have:

$$\lim_{\epsilon\downarrow 0} v^{ss}(\underline{b} + \epsilon) \leq \overline{V} - u'(y - \rho\underline{b})\frac{\lambda\underline{b}}{\rho + \lambda}.$$

By continuity of V, the optimal policy implies $V(\underline{b} + \epsilon) \to V(\underline{b}) = \overline{V}$. The term on the right-hand side of the above expression is strictly less than $\overline{V}$ as long as $\underline{b} = P^\star(\overline{V}) > 0$; that is, as long as there are deadweight costs. The loss incurred by the alternative policy is therefore bounded below by the loss to the planner in terms of resources times the marginal utility of consumption: $(\rho + \lambda)(\overline{V} - v^{SS}) \geq u'(y - \rho\underline{b})\lambda\underline{b} = u'(y - \rho\underline{b})\lambda P^\star(\overline{V})$. In this way, the government completely internalizes the lenders' loss in default. In Figure 4.2, $v^{ss}(b)$ depicts the value of staying put in the Crisis Zone at debt level b. We see in the neighborhood above $\underline{b}$, this value is strictly below $V^\star(b)$.

The intuition is that lenders must break even in expectation. As lenders obtain zero in default, interest rates compensate them for the full expected loss. However, default is not a zero-sum game. If there are deadweight costs, then the government does not gain as much as lenders lose. Full debt forgiveness without deadweight losses, that is $V^D = V(0) = u(y)/\rho$, would be required to make default zero sum. Thus, the government is paying the full deadweight costs. Moreover, it does so because it is rolling over its entire stock of debt every period at an interest rate that reflects the probability of default $(\rho + \lambda)$. Thus, short-term bonds fully incentivize the government to reduce the probability of default. Once b reaches $\underline{b}$, the government no longer pays the extra λ on its debt, capturing the benefits of reaching the Safe Zone.

There are two crucial ingredients to this intuition. One is that $\underline{b} > 0$. If $\underline{b} = 0$, then there is no additional cost from staying in the Crisis Zone. However, we saw that $\underline{b} = P^\star(\overline{V}) = 0$ only if deadweight costs are also zero.

The second is that the government is rolling over the entire stock of debt. That is, the additional cost is $\lambda/(\rho + \lambda)$ times the stock of debt $\underline{b}$, not just a fraction of outstanding debt. The key part of the decentralization is not short-term debt per se, but that the government fully internalizes the value of reducing the probability of default.

An equivalent decentralization uses a perpetuity (an infinite maturity bond) that pays a *variable coupon* $r(b)$ when the state is b. The market value of such a bond is always 1, as it fully compensates the holder for any change in default probability with an associated change in coupon. It provides the same stream of payments as rolling over an instantaneous bond at the equilibrium rate indefinitely. The government pays $r(b)b$ at each point in time, plus can repurchase existing bonds (or issue new bonds) at market price 1. The budget constraint is thus identical to the decentralization above, and hence so are equilibrium dynamics. With *fixed-rate* long-term bonds, the entire stock of debt is not continuously rolled over, nor are interest payments adjusted for default risk. We shall see in Chapter 7 that the constrained efficient allocation cannot in general be implemented as an equilibrium absent short-term (or variable-rate) bonds. That chapter also takes up the case when $\rho > r^\star$, and hence the government and lenders place different values on intertemporal trades.

4.6 Conclusion

The analytical model introduced in this chapter highlights the combined role that incomplete markets plus limited commitment play when default carries a deadweight loss. With short-term (or variable-rate) bonds, the government internalizes this cost. However, it is important to keep in mind that the government does not do this to avoid default per se; as emphasized above, default is optimal for the government at the time it chooses to renege on its debt. Rather, the government mitigates default risk because of how short-term bonds are priced in equilibrium. In Chapter 7, we shall see that alternative contracts, such as fixed-rate long-term bonds, do not provide the correct incentives.

In the next chapter, we explore a richer version of the model that has been used for quantitative work. The main addition will be endowment risk. We shall show that the core efficiency properties of short-term debt described above continue to hold in the model with endowment risk. Moreover, we shall show that the predictions of the quantitative models are very sensitive to the deadweight costs of default for exactly the reasons stressed in this chapter.

5

The Standard One-Period Bond Model

5.1 Introduction

The last chapter used an analytically tractable model to highlight the importance of default costs in driving debt dynamics under incomplete markets. The main takeaway was that the deadweight costs of default are a force for savings. In the competitive equilibrium, the government internalizes the full costs of default by rolling over its debt at market interest rates. This aligns the incentives of the government with the lenders to maximize the joint surplus subject to the market incompleteness.

In this chapter, we turn to the benchmark one-period bond model used in the quantitative literature. The main addition relative to the simple model of the preceding chapter is endowment risk. Under incomplete markets, endowment risk will lead to fluctuations in consumption as well as default. Despite this additional complexity, we show how to recast the competitive equilibrium in the form of a planning problem by adding an endogenous constraint that limits the amount of insurance that a planner can offer the government.

5.2 Environment

The environment is that considered in the classic paper, Eaton and Gersovitz (1981), and the subsequent quantitative literature, such as the early papers by Aguiar and Gopinath (2006), Arellano (2008), and Hamann (2002). In this chapter, we restrict attention to one-period bonds. This will be relaxed in subsequent chapters.

The basic environment is that of Chapter 2, but with incomplete markets. To quickly review, time is discrete, indexed by $t = 0, 1, \ldots,$ and there

is a single tradable good that is the numeraire. As in Chapter 2, the exogenous state $s_t \in \mathbb{S}$ follows a first-order Markov process and indexes the realized
endowment $y_t = y(s_t) \in \mathbb{Y} \subset [\underline{y}, \bar{y}]$, with $0 < \underline{y} < \bar{y} < \infty$. Let $\pi(s'|s)$ denote
the probability $s_{t+1} = s'$ given $s_t = s$. We assume $\pi(s'|s) > 0$ for all $(s, s') \in$
$\mathbb{S} \times \mathbb{S}$.

The SOE government makes all consumption, debt-issuance, and default
decisions. The government has a strictly increasing, strictly concave felicity
function u and discount factor $\beta \in (0, 1)$.

The government trades a one-period non-contingent bond with compet-
itive risk-neutral foreign lenders that discount at rate $R^{-1} = (1 + r^\star)^{-1} \in$
$(\beta, 1)$. To rule out Ponzi schemes, we assume $b \leq \bar{B}$, where $\bar{B}$ exceeds the
present value of the maximal endowment: $\bar{B} > \bar{y} R/r$.

5.2.1 Timing

The timing of a period is as follows. At the start of the period, nature draws
the state s. After observing s, the sovereign decides whether to repay outstanding debt b or to default. If it does not default, the sovereign can auction new
debt to pay off outstanding debt and consume. Note that there are two layers
of intra-period commitment involved in this timing. First, once the sovereign
decides to repay at the start of the period, it cannot default after the auction
has taken place. In Chapter 6, we relax this assumption and show that it generates additional equilibria. Second, the sovereign commits to only one auction
per period. This rules out multiple rounds of auctions, as studied, for example,
by Bizer and DeMarzo (1992) and Lorenzoni and Werning (2019). Thus, at
the time of the auction the lenders know that default will not occur this period
and how much debt will be due in the next period.

We consider equilibria in which values, policies, and prices are functions
of the state vector (s, b). Note that the notation can easily accommodate sun-
spots in the state s that coordinate beliefs and select among alternative
equilibria. It will turn out that there is no scope for coordination failures
in the current environment, but that is a result to be established, not an
assumption.

5.2.2 Equilibrium Objects

Let $V^R(s, b)$ denote the value the government obtains by repayment given
(s, b). If it defaults, the government receives value $V^D(s)$ and the lenders
receive zero. As in the previous chapter, the default payoff may depend on

the exogenous state, but does not vary with the amount of debt at the time of default. Strategic default implies the government defaults if $V^R(s, b) < V^D(s)$. We assume the government repays when indifferent.

Given the risk neutrality of lenders (and infinite collective wealth), we replace the lenders' problem and market clearing in the bond market with a break-even condition. In particular, given (s, b) and conditional on the government auctioning b' units of new debt, let $q(s, b, b')$ denote the equilibrium price of a bond that pays one next period absent default. Letting $\mathbb{1}_{[x]}$ denote the indicator function that takes the value one if x is true and zero otherwise, the lenders' break-even condition is:

$$q(s, b, b') = \begin{cases} R^{-1} \text{ if } b' \leq 0 \\ R^{-1} \sum_{s' \in \mathbb{S}} \pi(s'|s) \mathbb{1}_{[V^R(s',b') \geq V^D(s')]} \text{ otherwise.} \end{cases} \tag{BE}$$

The first row on the right-hand side says that assets carry the risk-free rate.[1] The second row reflects that debt will be repaid only if doing so is optimal for the government. The break-even condition immediately implies that q is independent of b. This follows from the timing assumption that auctions occur after the government has committed to repay b. To simplify notation, we therefore drop b as an argument of q, and redefine $q : S \times (-\infty, \overline{B}] \rightarrow [0, R^{-1}]$.

Given an exogenous state s and inherited debt b, the government's problem conditional on repayment can be written recursively as follows:

$$V^R(s, b) = \sup_{c, b' \leq \overline{B}} u(c) + \beta \sum_{s' \in \mathbb{S}} \pi(s'|s) \max\left\{V^R(s', b'), V^D(s')\right\} \tag{G}$$

subject to:

$$c \in [0, y(s) - b + q(s, b')b'],$$

for all (s, b) such that repayment is feasible (that is, the constraint set is not empty). Note that the objective assumes no default in the current period, but strategic default subsequently. This reflects the timing that the current default decision is made before issuing debt.

---

1. We have not explicitly restricted $V^D(s)$ to rule out default when the government holds assets abroad, although in most applications it would be reasonable to do this. The risk-free rate for assets can also be rationalized by assuming the counter-party of the government's assets must still fulfill the contract, perhaps to a third party, and not consume the asset in the event of default.

V^R is well-defined only if repayment is feasible. Let $\mathbb{X}_{feas}(s)$ denote the set of debt levels that are feasible to repay in state $s \in \mathbb{S}$:

Definition 9 *Given an equilibrium price schedule q, $\mathbb{X}_{feas}(s)$ is defined as:*

$$\mathbb{X}_{feas}(s) \equiv \left\{ b \mid \text{there exists } b' \leq \overline{B} \text{ such that } y(s) + q(s, b')b' - b \geq 0 \right\}. \quad (5.1)$$

Let $B^F(s)$ represent the largest amount of debt that is feasible to repay in state s:

$$B^F(s) \equiv \sup \mathbb{X}_{feas}(s). \quad (5.2)$$

Note that the feasible repayment set depends on q and hence is an equilibrium outcome. If the current amount of debt due, b, is such that $b > B^F(s)$, the government has no alternative but to default as repayment is not feasible. In that case, we let $V^R(s, b) = V_{NF}$ if $b \geq B^F(s)$, for some sufficiently low value $V_{NF}(s) < \min_{s \in \mathbb{S}} V^D(s)$.

Turning to the value of default, the canonical Eaton-Gersovitz punishment is autarky:

$$V^A(s) = \mathbb{E}_s \sum_k \beta^k u(y(s_{t+k})). \quad (5.3)$$

In Chapter 2, we discussed the alternative punishment proposed by Bulow and Rogoff (1989a), in which a government can save but not borrow after default. Let us define $V^{NA}(s, b)$ for $b \leq 0$ to be the value to the government with no access to borrowing but it can save in the international riskless bond:

$$V^{NA}(s, b) = \max_{c, b'} u(c) + \beta \sum_{s' \in \mathbb{S}} \pi(s' \mid s) V^{NA}(s', b') \quad (5.4)$$

$$\text{subject to:} \quad (5.5)$$

$$c \in [0, y(s) - b + R^{-1}b'] \quad (5.6)$$

$$b' \leq 0. \quad (5.7)$$

Clearly, $V^{NA}(s, 0) \geq V^A(s)$, as setting $b' = 0$ is a feasible choice in the above problem.

In Chapter 2, we discussed how, if the government could save (but not borrow) after a default, then absent any other punishments, there would not be any positive debt level consistent with an equilibrium. As we we will discuss later, in this incomplete-markets environment, a similar result holds. In particular, for there to be positive debt in equilibrium, it is necessary that there are some additional costs of default. That is, $V^{NA}(s, 0) \geq V^D(s)$ with strict inequality in some state. This puts a strict upper bound on default values in any equilibrium that supports borrowing.

Total financial autarky could serve as such a punishment, as $V^A(s) \leq V^{NA}(s, 0)$, and is strictly less under the typical parameter configurations assumed in the literature. Moreover, a large number of additional costs of default have been introduced in the literature that lower the value of default below V^A. For example, in Bulow and Rogoff (1989b), the same authors propose a loss of endowment in default as providing the incentive for repayment, appealing to legal ramifications and the disruption of trading arrangements.

We incorporate this by letting $y^D(s)$ denote the endowment in default, where $y^D(s)$ is related to the repayment endowment by some function ϕ : $\mathbb{Y} \times \mathbb{S} \to \mathbb{R}$, such that $y^D(s) = \phi(y(s), s)$. Note that we allow the endowment costs to depend on the state separately from the endowment in case there are stochastic punishments to default. In the computational examples, we shall discuss the function ϕ in depth.

Finally, in practice, a country's default status is not indefinite. Countries typically reach an agreement with outstanding bondholders and re-enter bond markets. Modeling that bargaining process, while interesting, will take us too far afield at this stage.[2] As a shortcut, we assume that with some constant hazard rate $\theta \in [0, 1)$, a government in default resumes its good credit standing and exits default with zero debt. Again, the latter assumption is for tractability rather than realism, as Benjamin and Wright (2008) document that governments frequently exit default with as much debt (in face value terms) as they owed at the time of default.

Hence, we can define the value of default at state s recursively by:

$$V^D(s) = u(y^D(s)) + \beta \mathbb{E}_s \left[\theta V^R(s', 0) + (1 - \theta) V^D(s') \right]. \qquad (5.8)$$

As discussed above, the government takes no actions during default, but simply waits for its good credit standing to be restored. For reference, we recursively define a lower bound on the default value by assuming $\theta = 0$:[3]

$$\underline{V}^D(s) = u(y^D(s)) + \beta \mathbb{E}_s \underline{V}^D(s'). \qquad (5.9)$$

2. See Bulow and Rogoff (1989b); Fernandez and Rosenthal (1990); Yue (2010); Benjamin and Wright (2008); Pitchford and Wright (2012) for models with post-default bargaining.

3. This is a lower bound as we establish below that $V^R(s, 0) \geq V^D(s)$ in any equilibrium.

Definition 10 *A Markov Perfect equilibrium consists of functions,* V^R :
$\mathbb{S} \times (-\infty, \overline{B}] \to \mathbb{R}$, $V^D : \mathbb{S} \to \mathbb{R}$, *and* $q : \mathbb{S} \times (-\infty, \overline{B}] \to [0, 1/R]$ *such that:*
(i) given q *and* V^D, V^R *satisfies* (G); *(ii) given* V^R, V^D *satisfies* (5.8); *and*
(iii) given V^R *and* V^D, q *satisfies* (BE).

5.3   Characterizing Equilibria

We begin characterizing equilibria by discussing the government's repayment
and default decisions. For tractability, we assume the following boundedness
conditions on utility:

Assumption 7 $u : \mathbb{R}_+ \to \mathbb{R}$ *is bounded:* $-\infty < u(0) < \overline{u} \equiv \lim_{c \to \infty} u(c) < \infty$.
Moreover, we assume there exists a $\underline{c} > 0$ *such that*

$$u(\underline{c}) + \beta V_{max} < \min_{s \in \mathbb{S}} \underline{V}^D(s), \tag{5.10}$$

where $V_{max} \equiv \overline{u}/(1 - \beta)$ *and* $\underline{V}^D(s)$ *is defined in equation* (5.9).

The assumption regarding $\underline{c}$ ensures the government always prefers to default
rather than consume zero in the current period, even if the continuation value
is at its maximal level.

The value of repayment has the following properties: (i) $V^R(s, .)$ is strictly
decreasing and continuous in b for $b \leq B^F(s)$ for all $s \in S$; (ii) for each $s \in S$,
there exists a threshold $\overline{b}(s) \in (0, B^F(s))$ such that $V^R(s, \overline{b}(s)) = V^D(s)$; and
(iii) $V^R(s, b) > V^D(s)$ for $b < \overline{b}(s)$ and $V^R(s, b) < V^D(s)$ for $b > \overline{b}(s)$. For a
formal proof of these properties, see Auclert and Rognlie (2016) or Aguiar
and Amador (2019). The properties imply that, given $s \in S$, the government is more likely to default when its debt burden is higher, with the
default decision defined by N equilibrium thresholds: $\overline{b}(s)$, $s \in S$. In particu-
lar, $\mathbb{1}_{[V^R(s,b) \geq V^D(s)]} = \mathbb{1}_{[b \leq \overline{b}(s)]}$. Plugging into (BE), this implies that $q(s, .)$ is a
weakly decreasing step function in b', with points of discontinuity confined to
$b' \in \{\overline{b}(s')\}_{s' \in S}$. Given our tie-breaking assumption, $q(s, .)$ is continuous from
the left.

The government will never default if it holds assets:

Lemma 11 *In any equilibrium with* $V^D(s) \leq V^{NA}(s, 0)$ $\forall s \in \mathbb{S}$, *for any* $b \leq 0$
we have $V^R(s, b) \geq V^D(s)$ *for all* $s \in \mathbb{S}$.

Proof. From Problem (G), we have that $V^R(s, b)$ is weakly decreasing in b in
any equilibrium for $b < B^F(s)$. This follows immediately from the fact that

b shows up only in the constraint and the constraint set is decreasing in b. Hence, it is sufficient to show that $V^R(s, 0) \geq V^D(s)$ for any $s \in S$. But the consumption allocation in $V^{NA}(s, 0)$ is feasible in the problem $V^R(s, 0)$, as the government can always choose not to borrow and rather save according to the optimal policy in V^{NA}. In this case, it also faces the risk-free price for the bonds. Hence, $V^R(s, 0) \geq V^D(s)$. □

An intuitive feature of this model is that (without the possibility of re-entry after a default) the government is tempted to default when it is forced to make a net payment to lenders. In particular, if in a given state, the government can raise enough new debt to cover the maturing debt minus the *static* loss to the endowment due to default, $y(s) - y^D(s)$, then it will not default in that state:

Lemma 12 *Suppose that $\theta = 0$. Consider an equilibrium where for some state (s, b), we have $V^D(s) \geq V^R(s, b)$. Then, for all $b' \leq \overline{B}$:*

$$q(s, b')b' \leq b - (y(s) - y^D(s)).$$

Proof. Toward a contradiction, suppose there exists b' such that $q(s, b')b' - b > y^D(s) - y(s)$. Then, the value of repayment is bounded below by choosing b':

$$V^R(s, b) \geq u(y(s) + q(s, b')b' - b) + \beta \mathbb{E}_s[\max\{V^R(s', b'), V^D(s')\}]$$

$$\geq u(y(s) + q(s, b')b' - b) + \beta \mathbb{E}_s V^D(s')$$

$$> u(y^D(s)) + \beta \mathbb{E}_s V^D(s')$$

$$= V^D(s),$$

where the second inequality follows from $\theta = 0$ and the definition of V^D and the strict inequality is the premise $y^D(s) < y(s) + q(s, b')b' - b$. This generates a contradiction. □

If $y^D(s) = \phi(y(s), s) \leq y(s)$, then according to the lemma, the government defaults only if it cannot find a b' that is sufficient to roll over the maturing bonds, that is, there is no b' such that $q(s, b')b' - b \geq 0$. The intuition for this result is as follows: rather than defaulting today, the government could issue new debt, repay maturing debt, consume more than its endowment, and default for sure tomorrow. This strategy—if available—is an improvement over default today. In other words, if the government receives a value equal to $V^D(s)$, then, if it does not default, it must be making a net payment to foreigners. This result is reminiscent of how Chapter 2's complete-markets planner delivers the autarky value.

Note that for alternative default punishments, it may be possible that the government chooses to default even if it is able to raise enough revenue to cover its current maturing debt payments. For this, it is necessary that $y^D(s) > y(s)$. One may be tempted to interpret this inequality as stating that there are no deadweight costs of default but rather there are efficiency gains. However, there are processes for the default value that feature positive deadweight costs of default but, nevertheless, when represented as (5.8) require $y^D(s) > y(s)$.[4]

The fact that default occurs, all else equal, when debt is high is a straightforward implication of the fact that $V^R(s, b)$ is decreasing in b and $V^D(s)$ is constant in b. However, how the default decision varies with the endowment is complicated by the fact that both $V^R(s, b)$ and $V^D(s)$ vary with s. One case in which we can sign this unambiguously is when s is *iid* and the default punishment is autarky. This result was first proved by Arellano (2008):

Lemma 13 (*Arellano*) *Suppose s is iid and $V^D(s) = V^A(s)$ all $s \in S$. Given b, if $V^R(s_1, b) < V^D(s_1)$ for some $s_1 \in S$, then for $s_2 \in S$ such that $y(s_2) < y(s_1)$ we have $V^R(s_2, b) < V^D(s_2)$.*

Proof. Let $y_i = y(s_i)$, $i = 1, 2$. By definition:

$$V^R(s_2, b) = \max_{b'} \left\{ u(y_2 - b + q(b')b') + \beta \mathbb{E} \max \left\{ V^R(s', b'), V^D(s') \right\} \right\}$$

$$= \max_{b'} \left\{ u(y_2 - b + q(b')b') - u(y_1 - b + q(b')b') \right.$$

$$\left. + u(y_1 - b + q(b')b') + \beta \mathbb{E} \max \left\{ V^R(s', b'), V^D(s') \right\} \right\}$$

$$\leq \max_{b'} \left\{ u(y_2 - b + q(b')b') - u(y_1 - b + q(b')b') \right\}$$

$$+ \underbrace{\max_{b'} \left\{ u(y_1 - b + q(b')b') + \beta \mathbb{E} \max \left\{ V^R(s', b'), V^D(s') \right\} \right\}}_{=V^R(s_1, b)}.$$

4. Consider for example $\theta = 0$ and two states, $s \in \{H, L\}$ with $y(s) = y$ for both s. Suppose that if default occurs in H, there is no endowment loss and $V^D(H) = V^A = u(y)/(1 - \beta)$. However, if default were to occur in state $s = L$, the country faces a strictly positive reduction

Concavity of u and $y_2 < y_1$ imply $u(y_2 - x) - u(y_1 - x)$ is decreasing in x. Thus, if $x \geq 0$, $u(y_2) - u(y_1) \geq u(y_2 - x) - u(y_1 - x)$. From Lemma 12 and the premise that $V^R(s_1, b) \leq V^A(s_1)$, we have $q(b')b' \leq b$ for all $b' \leq \bar{B}$. This implies $b - q(b')b' \geq 0$, and $\max_{b'} \{u(y_2 - b + q(b')b') - u(y_1 - b + q(b')b')\} \leq u(y_2) - u(y_1)$. Replacing in the above,

$$V^R(s_2, b) \leq u(y_2) - u(y_1) + V^R(s_1, b) < u(y_2) - u(y_1) + V^A(s_1),$$

where the second inequality is the premise of the lemma. Finally, $V^A(s_2) = V^A(s_1) - u(y_1) + u(y_2)$, giving us $V^R(s_2, b) < V^A(s_2)$.   □

The intuition for the result rests on the fact that debt is non-contingent. Suppose the government makes a net payment of $x = b - q(b')b'$ to lenders. Given the *iid* assumption, prices are independent of the current state s. From Lemma 12, x must be non-negative when $V^R(s, b) < V^D(s) = V^A(s)$. The flow utility loss relative to autarky is $u(y - x) - u(y) \leq 0$ when the endowment is y. Concavity of u implies this is weakly increasing in y when $x \geq 0$. That is, the non-contingent payment becomes a larger burden relative to autarky as the endowment falls. The lemma extends this to state that $V^R(s, b) - V^A(s)$ is weakly increasing in the endowment when $V^R(s, b) < V^A(s)$.

Recall from Chapter 2 that with complete markets, the government's participation constraint tends to bind when output is high. This reflects the insurance inherent in complete markets; namely, the government receives transfers when the endowment is low and pays when the endowment is high. As the government only has an incentive to deviate when it is supposed to make a net payment, the constraint binds when the endowment is high. As noted in Chapter 2, this property of limited commitment limits the size of net payments to the government (or debt level) in low-endowment states.

---

of its endowment forever, so that $V^D(L) = u((1 - \tau)y)/(1 - \beta) < V^A$ for $\tau > 0$. Note that this is a two-state default value process similar to that used in Chapter 4. Note as well that once the government defaults in state s, its continuation value is not stochastic. To represent this process using equation (5.8), we can define a unique $y^D(H) > y(H)$ such that $V^A = u(y^D) + \beta \mathbb{E}_H V^D(s')$. Nevertheless, there are no efficiency gains from default. In this environment, state H may be a good state to default, even if the government is able to raise enough revenue to pay the maturing debt, as next period there is the risk that the default value may revert back to $V^D(L) < V^D(H)$.

With non-contingent debt, the government must make the same pay-ment in *all* states. Due to concavity of the utility function, all else equal, this payment is more onerous when the endowment is low. The *iid* assump-tion makes the "all else equal" operative; for example, it rules out that the price schedule shifts with the endowment to make it easier to repay in a low endowment state.[5]

5.4   Two Operators

In this section, we show that the equilibrium of the Eaton-Gersovitz model with one-period bonds can be characterized as the fixed point of two alter-native operators. The first operator takes a primal approach and works from the government's Bellman equation (G). This is the standard approach for solving the model on the computer. The second operator recasts the equilib-rium as a contracting problem. This "dual" operator facilitates the comparison to the constrained efficient planning problem of the previous chapter. Under some additional assumptions, it also can be shown to have a unique fixed point.

5.4.1   The Price Operator

The "primal" operator takes the price schedule's thresholds as an argument. Specifically, recall that an equilibrium price is characterized by N thresholds, $b = \{\bar{b}_n\}_{n=1}^N$. Let T_p be an operator on $\mathbb{R}^N$. Specifically, given a candidate vector of thresholds $b \in [0, \bar{B}]^N \subset \mathbb{R}_+^N$:

1. Define a price schedule consistent with b:

$$Q(s, b'; b) \equiv \begin{cases} R^{-1} \text{ if } b' \leq 0 \\ R^{-1} \sum_{s' \in S} \pi(s'|s) \mathbb{1}_{[b' \leq \bar{b}(s')]} \text{ o.w.;} \end{cases} \tag{5.11}$$

2. Armed with this candidate price schedule, solve the government's problem (G) to obtain $v^R(s, b; b)$;
3. Compare $v^R(s, b; b)$ to $V^D(s)$ to define a new set of default thresholds b'.

Let T_p denote this mapping from b to b'; that is, $b' = T_p b$.

---

5. Such an outcome would arise, for example, if a low endowment today predicted a higher endowment in the next period. Most quantitative implementations of the model do not feature such a process, and hence in the literature default almost always coincides with low endowment states.

If there is no re-entry after default, then the operator is monotone. That is, consider two candidate threshold vectors, b_1 and b_2. If $b_1 \geq b_2$ (pointwise), then $Q(.,.; b_1) \geq Q(.,.; b_2)$. From the government's problem, we have $v^R(.,.; b_1) \geq v^R(.,.; b_2)$. Absent re-entry, $V^D(s)$ is invariant to v^R. Hence, $T_p b_1 \geq T_p b_2$.

Note that T_p maps elements of a finite-dimensional compact set, $b \in [0, \overline{B}]^N$, into itself. Monotonicity of the operator implies that, starting from $b \in [0, \overline{B}]^N$, repeatedly iterating on T_p will generate a weakly increasing sequence of thresholds that converge in the set $[0, \overline{B}]^N$. Thus, such an iterative scheme will eventually converge to an equilibrium set of thresholds, with an associated equilibrium price schedule and value function.

The monotonicity of the operator is established assuming no re-entry ($\theta = 0$ in equation (5.8)). Re-entry complicates the analysis as a greater repayment value raises the value of default (through expectations of re-entry) as well as repayment, making the impact on prices ambiguous. Nevertheless, in practice, computational approaches using the iterative scheme described above typically converge quickly for the one-period bond model. Moreover, Auclert and Rognlie (2016) and Aguiar and Amador (2019) show that many desirable properties of the no-re-entry case (such as uniqueness) extend to the case of re-entry when s is *iid*.

5.4.2 A Pseudo-Planning Problem

We now discuss a second operator that characterizes the Eaton-Gersovitz equilibrium with one-period bonds. This operator has the advantage of being a contraction and is useful for understanding the economics of the Eaton-Gersovitz model. This mapping was first established in Aguiar and Amador (2019).

Recall that $V^R(s, b)$ is strictly decreasing in b for $b \leq B^F(s)$. Let $B(s, v)$ denote the inverse of V^R. In particular, B satisfies the dual to Problem (G):

$$B(s, v) = \max_{c \geq 0, b' \leq \overline{B}} \left\{ y(s) - c + q(s, b')b' \right\}$$

subject to:

$$v = u(c) + \beta \sum_{s' \in \mathbb{S}} \pi(s'|s) \max \left\{ V^R(s', b'), V^D(s') \right\}.$$

The objective in this problem is the value to the representative lender, and the constraint ensures the government receives the associated value v. The function B is not defined for $v > V_{max}$, as delivering such a value is not feasible. Without loss, we can also restrict attention to $v \geq u(\underline{c}) + \beta V_{max}$. Recall from Assumption 7 that if $v < u(\underline{c}) + \beta V_{max}$, the government prefers to default regardless of s. Hence, define $\mathbb{V} \equiv [u(\underline{c}) + \beta V_{max}, V_{max}]$ and consider B defined on the domain $\mathbb{S} \times \mathbb{V}$.

Using the break-even constraint (BE), we can substitute for $q(s, b')$:

$$
B(s, v) = \max_{c \geq 0, b' \leq \bar{B}} \left\{ y(s) - c + b' R^{-1} \right.
$$

$$
\left. \left[\mathbb{1}_{[b' \leq 0]} + \mathbb{1}_{[b' > 0]} \sum_{s' \in \mathbb{S}} \pi(s'|s) \mathbb{1}_{[V^R(s', b') \geq V^D(s')]} \right] \right\} \quad \text{(B)}
$$

subject to:

$$
v = u(c) + \beta \sum_{s' \in \mathbb{S}} \pi(s'|s) \max \left\{ V^R(s', b'), V^D(s') \right\}.
$$

Finally, note that the choice of b' in (B) pins down the continuation value in each state next period through $V^R(s', b')$. We can make the sovereign's continuation value, $v(s')$, a choice variable subject to the restriction that $v(s') = V^R(s', b')$ for each $s' \in \mathbb{S}$ in which the government repays (that is, $v(s') \geq V^D(s')$). For s' in which the government defaults, there is no meaningful restriction on the choice of continuation value other than $v(s') < V^D(s')$. Using the fact that B is the inverse of V^R, this restriction is equivalent to $B(s', v(s')) = b'$ for $v(s') \geq V^D(s')$. That is,

$$
B(s, v) = \max_{c \geq 0, b' \leq \bar{B}, v(s') \in \mathbb{V}} \left\{ y(s) - c + b' R^{-1} \right.
$$

$$
\left. \left[\mathbb{1}_{[b' \leq 0]} + \mathbb{1}_{[b' > 0]} \sum_{s' \in \mathbb{S}} \pi(s'|s) \mathbb{1}_{[v(s') \geq V^D(s')]} \right] \right\} \quad \text{(B')}
$$

subject to:

$$
v = u(c) + \beta \sum_{s' \in \mathbb{S}} \pi(s'|s) \max \left\{ v(s'), V^D(s') \right\} \quad \text{(5.12)}
$$

$$
b' = B(s', v(s')) \text{ for all } s' \in \mathbb{S} \text{ such that } v(s') \geq V^D(s'). \quad \text{(5.13)}
$$

Problem (B') resembles the planning problem studied in the complete-markets case. However, while we have substituted out prices, the final constraint (5.13) involves an *equilibrium* object, B. By restricting how much insurance over continuation values can be provided, this constraint reflects the incompleteness of markets. In particular, it requires that in every state such that the government prefers repayment, the lenders receive the same amount.

Nevertheless, the problem clarifies that the government and lenders do not disagree on the consumption and debt issuance decisions. That is, as long as the lenders recognize the government will default if it is optimal for the government to do so, it makes no difference which party makes the consumption-savings decision. This reflects that equilibrium prices provide the government with the "correct" incentives to reduce the probability of default, a point made in the previous chapter. Similarly, the lenders have an incentive to provide a given level of utility to the government in a cost-effective way, including the possibility that the government defaults. As in Chapter 4, this efficiency property relies on short-term bonds and will not be the case for longer maturities, as discussed in Chapter 7.

The constraints in Problem (B') can be relaxed to inequalities. That is, the problem must yield *at least* v to the government, and b' is bounded above by $B(s, v(s'))$. The objective is strictly decreasing in c and weakly increasing in b' (and strictly increasing if there is at least one repayment state), and hence these constraints will bind with equality at an optimum.

Problem (B') can then form the basis of a dual operator T_d that maps the space of candidate functions $f : \mathbb{S} \times \mathbb{V} \to \mathbb{R}$ into itself:

$$(T_d f)(s, v) = \max_{c \geq 0, b' \leq \overline{B}, v(s') \in \mathbb{V}} \left\{ y(s) - c + b' R^{-1} \right.$$

$$\left. \left[\mathbb{1}_{[b' \leq 0]} + \mathbb{1}_{[b' > 0]} \sum_{s' \in \mathbb{S}} \pi(s'|s) \mathbb{1}_{[v(s') \geq V^D(s')]} \right] \right\}$$

subject to:

$$v \leq u(c) + \beta \sum_{s' \in \mathbb{S}} \pi(s'|s) \max \left\{ v(s'), V^D(s') \right\}$$

$$b' \leq f(s', v(s')) \text{ for all } s' \in \mathbb{S} \text{ such that } v(s') \geq V^D(s').$$

The equilibrium inverse function B is a fixed point of T_d.

Note that T_d is monotone. That is, if $f \geq g$, then $T_d f \geq T_d g$. To see this, note that the operated-on function only appears in the final inequality constraint. Hence, a greater function relaxes the constraint, weakly raising the maximized value.

If B is bounded, then we can restrict attention to bounded functions on $\mathbb{S} \times \mathbb{V}$. For example, if the maximal value V_{max} can be delivered with finite resources, then it is without loss to restrict attention to finite functions. In this case, T_d maps the space of bounded functions with domain $\mathbb{S} \times \mathbb{V}$ into itself. Moreover, it can be shown that $T_d(f+a) \leq T_d f + R^{-1} a$ for any $a \geq 0$. Thus, T_d discounts. This, plus monotonicity, implies that T_d satisfies Blackwell's sufficient condition for T_d to be a contraction operator, implying there exists a unique bounded fixed point of T_d.

Aguiar and Amador (2019) use the contraction property of the dual operator to establish the existence and uniqueness of an equilibrium in the one-period-bond Eaton-Gersovitz model. But there are alternatives. Auclert and Rognlie (2016) originally provided a proof of uniqueness that takes a different approach, relying on a replication argument similar to Bulow and Rogoff (1989a). In recent work, Bloise and Vailakis (2020) take an important step in generalizing the primal approach. They are able to show uniqueness even in cases in which R varies stochastically and is sometimes less than one (in which case the equilibrium operator does not satisfy discounting in the usual metric).

As a final note of this subsection, let us revisit the Bulow and Rogoff (1989a) critique in our incomplete-markets environment. Consider the case where $V^D(s) = V^{NA}(s, 0)$. That is, the only punishment available after a default is the inability to *borrow* again in the future. Let us define a generalization of V^{NA} to a domain that includes strictly positive debt in the initial period $b \leq y(s)$:

$$V^{BR}(s, b) = \max_{c, b'} u(c) + \beta \sum_{s' \in \mathbb{S}} \pi(s'|s) V^{NA}(s', b')$$

subject to:

$$c \in [0, y(s) - b + R^{-1} b']$$

$$b' \leq 0.$$

Then, one can see that $V^{BR}(s, b)$ is a fixed point of (G) when the bond price is $q(s, b') = R^{-1}$ for $b' \leq 0$ and $q(s, b') = 0$ otherwise. In addition, given

$V^D(s) = V^{NA}(s, 0)$, this value function justifies this conjectured equilibrium price: the government defaults for any strictly positive level of debt. Hence, V^{BR} and the associated q constitute a Markov equilibrium. Given the uniqueness result, it follows that for $V^D(s) = V^{NA}(s, 0)$ there is no positive debt level sustainable in equilibrium.

5.5   Quantitative Results

We now explore the quantitative properties of the one-period bond model.[6] A period is a quarter. The parameterization follows Chatterjee and Eyigungor (2012a) closely, and unless otherwise noted, the calibration numbers are from there. We set the quarterly risk-free interest rate to 1%: $R = 1.01$. This is the discount rate of the risk-neutral lenders. Our benchmark (quarterly) discount factor for the government is set to $\beta = 0.954$, which is similar to that of Arellano (2008). Given the quarterly frequency, the government is quite impatient relative to the risk-free rate. As we shall see, the model needs a fairly impatient government for default to occur in equilibrium. To provide a sense of the role of this parameter, we also discuss a radically impatient government, $\beta = 0.80$, as an alternative. Flow utility takes the standard form:

$$u(c) = \frac{c^{1-\sigma}}{1 - \sigma}.$$

We set $\sigma = 2.0$.

The government issues a one-period non-contingent bond, b. We restrict the government debt choices to a grid with 350 points spanning $b \in [0, 1.5]$. The endowment follows a first-order Markov process that approximates an AR(1) in logs. Specifically, Chatterjee and Eyigungor (2012a) use the following process based on Argentina:[7]

$$\ln y_t = \rho \ln y_{t-1} + \varepsilon_t,$$

6. The computer codes for all quantitative models can be found at https://github.com/markaguiar/TheEconomicsofSovereignDebt.

7. Chatterjee and Eyigungor (2012a) have a more complicated endowment process that involves an additional *iid* component. We include only their persistent component. The calibrated endowment process is similar to others used in the literature; the one exception is the Aguiar and Gopinath (2006) "stochastic growth" process. Aguiar, Chatterjee, Cole, and Stangebye (2016) discuss the sensitivity of the model to alternative endowment calibrations.

TABLE 5.1. Alternative Default Cost Models

Model I	$y^D = 0.9y$
Model II	$y^D = y - \max\{0, -0.188y + (0.246)y^2\}$
Model III	$y^D = \min\{y, 0.969\mathbb{E}y\}$

Note: This table details the parameterized default cost function for the three alternative models.

where $\varepsilon \sim N(0, \sigma_\varepsilon^2)$. Based on Chatterjee and Eyigungor (2012a), we set $\rho = 0.9485$ and $\sigma_\varepsilon = 0.0271$. We approximate the endowment process using Tauchen's method on a 200-point grid spanning plus and minus $3\sigma_\varepsilon^2$.

The crucial component of the calibration concerns the costs of default. The costs have two components. One is exclusion from financial markets. The other is a loss of endowment while excluded. The former proxies for the time it takes for governments to reach a settlement with their creditors. The latter is a catch-all that proxies for disruption of trade, financial markets, etc. As explained in detail in Aguiar and Gopinath (2006), exclusion is not a quantitatively significant punishment. As famously pointed out in Lucas (1987), aggregate fluctuations of consumption at business cycle frequencies do not represent a major welfare cost to a representative consumer with standard utility. That is, even if access to financial markets implied complete smoothing of business cycle risk, the welfare gain would be small. Hence, exclusion as the sole punishment results in default at counterfactually low levels of debt.

Thus, the endowment loss while in default status is the primary punishment in the calibrated model. The early paper by Aguiar and Gopinath (2006) assumed a proportional loss of endowment:

$$y_t^D = (1 - \delta)y_t,$$

with $\delta = 0.02$. In Table 5.1, this is the cost used for Model I. Chatterjee and Eyigungor (2012a) use a quadratic endowment cost:

$$y_t^D = y_t - \max\{0, \phi_0 y_t + \phi_1 y_t^2\},$$

with $\phi_0 = -0.188$ and $\phi_1 = 0.246$. The convexity of this cost implies that being in default during high-endowment states is particularly punishing. This default cost is associated with Model II below. Arellano (2008) was the first

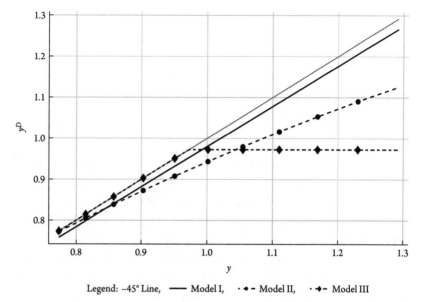

Legend: –45° Line, —— Model I, · • - Model II, · ◆ - Model III

FIGURE 5.1. Endowment in Default

Note: This figure depicts the alternative endowment costs of default. For each non-default-status endowment level on the horizontal axis, the curve depicts the corresponding level of the endowment while in default status. The default cost parameters of the three models are given in Table 5.1.

to advocate for a non-linear cost. In particular, Arellano sets:

$$y_t^D = \min\{y_t, 0.969\mathbb{E}y\}.$$

This function implies that there is no endowment loss due to default when the endowment is less than 97% of the mean. However, any endowment greater than that is lost. This is the cost used in Model III below. The alternative mappings between endowment y and default endowment y^D are depicted in Figure 5.1.[8]

Given that the endowment costs are levied during the entire period of exclusion, the rate at which a government in default is allowed to re-enter financial markets matters. Chatterjee and Eyigungor (2012a) set the re-entry hazard to 3.85% quarterly, so the expected length of exclusion is 26 quarters.

8. We refer the interested reader to Mendoza and Yue (2012) for a quantitative model where default costs are endogenous. In a recent study, Hébert and Schreger (2017) exploit the news generated by judicial rulings with regard to Argentina's default and restructuring in the 2000s to obtain a measure of the cost of default.

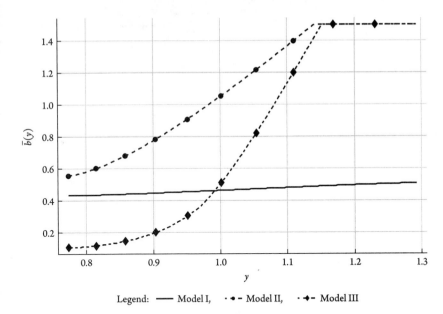

Legend: ——— Model I,   · ● - Model II,   · ◆ - Model III

FIGURE 5.2. Deadweight Costs of Default

Note: This figure depicts the debt threshold above which the government defaults given the current endowment *y* reported on the horizontal axis.

This is in line with the default durations documented by Cruces and Trebesch (2011). Aguiar and Gopinath (2006) set $\theta = 0.10$, implying a shorter average duration of 10 quarters. Arellano (2008) sets $\theta = 0.282$, which implies mean re-entry occurs after 3.5 quarters. Our benchmark sets $\theta = 0.0385$ and we explore the shorter duration $\theta = 0.282$ as an alternative.

Recall that in our analytical model, the deadweight costs of default played a prominent role. The amount lost to the lenders in default when the government is indifferent to repayment and default captures the deadweight costs in terms of the consumption good. This corresponds to the thresholds $\bar{b}(s)$ in the competitive equilibrium. The $\bar{b}$ thresholds are depicted in Figure 5.2 for the alternative models. The horizontal axis is the endowment $y(s)$.

The nearly horizontal solid black line represents the linear cost model (Model I). The flat slope represents the fact that the deadweight costs of default are similar across all endowment realizations. This stems from the proportional nature of the default cost. The upward sloping dashed line depicts the quadratic costs. The upward slope indicates a low cost of default

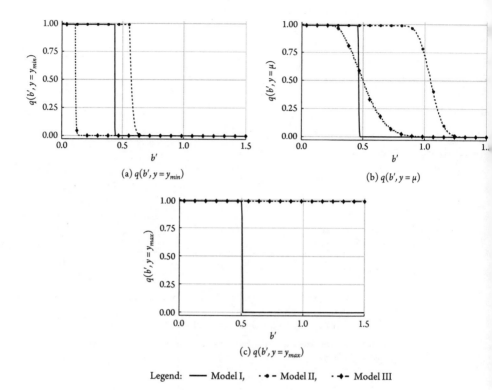

(a) $q(b', y = y_{min})$

(b) $q(b', y = \mu)$

(c) $q(b', y = y_{max})$

Legend: —— Model I,   · ◆ - Model II,   · ◆ - Model III

FIGURE 5.3. Price Schedules

Note: This figure depicts the price schedule for the three alternative models. On the horizontal axis is the amount of debt to be issued. Each panel evaluates the price schedule at a different level of endowment. Panel (a) sets the endowment to its lowest level, panel (b) sets the endowment to its long-run mean, and panel (c) sets the endowment to its highest level.

in recessions and a relatively high cost in booms. This pattern is even more exaggerated for Model III, which is the dashed-dot line. The costs of default are nearly a two-state process. For low levels of the endowment, there are essentially no deadweight costs of default. For relatively high endowment realizations, $\bar{b}$ is at the highest grid point of debt space. That is, the costs are so high that default is never optimal, even for the high levels of debt implied by the maximum debt grid point. The two-state nature of these costs is reminiscent of the analytical model. The fact that the low-endowment cost is nearly zero implies there is no incentive to reduce debt and avoid default in the competitive equilibrium.

The associated price schedules of each model are depicted in Figure 5.3. Each panel evaluates the price schedule at a different endowment point.

Panels (a), (b), and (c) represent the minimum, mean, and maximum endowment states, respectively. The horizontal axis represents the amount of debt issued at auction. The price schedules are weakly decreasing. The horizontal portions represent the risk-free price. As debt exceeds $\overline{b}(y)$ for the lowest y, default occurs with positive probability. As b' increases, the default states include more and more endowment points, until b' exceeds $\overline{b}(y_{max})$ and default occurs with probability one next period. In this case, $q = 0$.

A key feature of the price schedule is the extreme nonlinearity. This deters the government from issuing debt at the margin, as the decline in price affects the entire stock of debt issued at auction. Thus, issuance on the steeply declining portion of the price schedule is extremely expensive at the margin. As we move across panels, the price schedule shifts out or up as the endowment increases. This reflects the persistence in the endowment process and the fact that default occurs at low-endowment realizations.

Finally, the sensitivity to the current endowment differs markedly across the three alternative default costs. The linear cost model (Model I) has the same shape for each endowment realization, with simply a translation of the declining portion in response to current endowment. The non-linear-cost price schedules mimic the linear cost for low-endowment realizations, but "flatten out" at higher endowment realizations. This reflects that a high-endowment state today not only predicts high endowment tomorrow, it also predicts very high default costs tomorrow (as the costs are convex in the endowment). Hence, default is less sensitive to current debt issuance and depends more heavily on next period's endowment realization. This reduces the slope of q with respect to b'.

The associated debt-issuance policy functions are depicted in Figure 5.4. As with the previous figure, the three panels are evaluated at different endowment states. The horizontal axis is the amount of debt due in the current period. The policy functions are truncated at the level of current debt at which, given the respective endowment, the government prefers to default. As with the price schedules, the policies shift up and out with the endowment. Moreover, the debt-issuance policies are sensitive to the nature of the default costs. This reflects in part that the government faces a much different price schedule under the alternative punishment scenarios. Interestingly, a higher current endowment generates more debt issuance. This reflects the pro-cyclical price schedules depicted in Figure 5.3. The fact that the non-linear cost models displayed a greater sensitivity of price to endowment in the latter

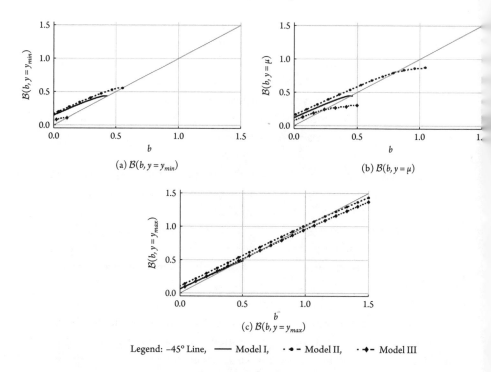

(a) $\mathcal{B}(b, y = y_{min})$

(b) $\mathcal{B}(b, y = \mu)$

(c) $\mathcal{B}(b, y = y_{max})$

Legend: −45° Line, —— Model I, · • - Model II, · ◆ - Model III

FIGURE 5.4. Policy Functions

Note: This figure depicts the debt-issuance policy functions for the three alternative models. On the horizontal axis is the amount of debt due this period. Each panel evaluates the price schedule at a different level of endowment. Panel (a) sets the endowment to its lowest level, panel (b) sets the endowment to its long-run mean, and panel (c) sets the endowment to its highest level.

figure translates into the large shifts in debt-issuance policy functions depicted across panels in Figure 5.4.

For each model, we simulate the competitive equilibrium and compute key moments of the ergodic distribution. These are reported for the benchmark calibration in Table 5.2. Following Chatterjee and Eyigungor (2012a), we condition on being in non-default status for the prior twenty quarters. This span allows the government to build up debt from zero following reentry. Thus, the moments are conditional on having been in good credit standing for at least five years. The first row is average debt issuance and the second row is the average market value of debt (or average revenue raised at auction). The third row is the average default rate, conditional on being in good credit standing coming into the period. The fourth and fifth rows are the mean and

TABLE 5.2. Benchmark Moments of the Ergodic Distribution

	Model 1 (Linear)	Model 2 (Quadratic)	Model 3 (Ceiling)
$\mathbb{E}\left[\frac{b'}{y}\right]$	0.45	0.80	0.26
$\mathbb{E}\left[\frac{q*b'}{y}\right]$	0.44	0.79	0.26
Default Rate (Annualized)	0.0003	0.002	0.007
$\mathbb{E}\left[r-r^*\right]$ (Annualized)	0.0003	0.003	0.007
StDev$(r-r^*)$ (Annualized)	0.0004	0.004	0.011
StDev$(\ln c)/$StDev$(\ln y)$	1.01	1.14	1.10
Corr$(y-c, \ln y)$	−0.22	−0.24	−0.21
Corr$(\ln y, r-r^*)$	0.02	−0.40	−0.26
Corr$(\frac{b'}{y}, r-r^*)$	−0.002	−0.21	−0.19
Corr$(r-r^*, y-c)$	−0.12	0.86	0.84

Note: This table reports key moments from the ergodic distribution of each model. All moments are conditional on being in good credit standing for the prior 20 quarters. The first row is the average level of debt issued as a fraction of the endowment. The second row is the average market value of debt issuance, again normalized by the level endowment. The third row is the annualized frequency of default. The fourth and fifth rows are the mean and standard deviation of implied spreads, respectively. Spreads are computed in annualized form as $(1/q)^4 - R^4$. The sixth row is the standard deviation of log consumption relative to the standard deviation of log income. The seventh and eighth rows are the correlation of log income with the trade balance and spread, respectively. The final two rows are the correlation of the spread with debt issuance and the trade balance, respectively.

standard deviation of the implied spread between the bonds and the risk-free rate.[9] The remaining rows depict business cycle moments.

Looking across columns, we see that the level of debt and the frequency of default are very sensitive to the functional form of default costs. The linear cost model has nearly zero default. While the non-linear cost models have default rates ten to twenty times that of the linear model, the rate is still only one default every 150 years (with Arellano 2008 cost function) or 500 years (with the Chatterjee and Eyigungor 2012a quadratic cost function). The mean and standard deviation of spreads is correspondingly low.

9. The spread is the yield implied by the price $q(b)$ minus the risk-free price: spread= $1/q(b) - 1 - r^*$.

TABLE 5.3. Alternative I: Impatient Government

	Model 1 (Linear)	Model 2 (Quadratic)	Model 3 (Ceiling)
$\mathbb{E}\left[\frac{b'}{y}\right]$	0.55	0.56	0.21
$\mathbb{E}\left[\frac{q*b'}{y}\right]$	0.54	0.55	0.20
Default Rate (Annualized)	0.0008	0.021	0.136
$\mathbb{E}\left[r - r^\star\right]$ (Annualized)	0.0009	0.023	0.171
StDev($r - r^\star$) (Annualized)	0.001	0.011	0.124
StDev(c)/StDev(y)	1.01	1.18	1.23
Corr($y - c, y$)	−0.24	−0.15	−0.08
Corr($y, r - r^\star$)	0.27	−0.11	−0.29
Corr($\frac{b'}{y}, r - r^\star$)	−0.25	−0.10	−0.42
Corr($r - r^\star, y - c$)	−0.31	0.78	0.62

Note: This table replicates the moments of Table 5.2, but recomputing each model with a governmental discount factor $\beta = 0.80$.

The procyclicality of the price schedule generates a counter-cyclical trade balance and consumption that is more volatile than the endowment. That is, governments tend to borrow in booms. The correlation of several macroeconomic aggregates with spreads are reported in the final three rows. The correlations of spreads for Model I are essentially meaningless, as the standard deviation of spreads is close to zero. For the non-linear cost models, the spreads are counter-cyclical, with debt issuances coinciding with low spreads.

Table 5.3 replicates the moments from Table 5.2, but recomputing the model with a discount factor of 0.80. At a quarterly frequency, a discount factor of 0.80 represents extreme myopia on the part of the government. The moments from Model I are remarkably stable to this alternative. This reflects that the government simply borrows out to the sharp bend in the price schedule. Thus, the model behaves similar to one with risk-free bonds but an exogenous debt limit (that varies with the state). For the non-linear models, the increased impatience generates lower debt levels in equilibrium and more default. In particular, the frequency of default increases by a factor of ten for the quadratic model and a factor of twenty for Model III. The associated spreads (both mean and volatility) are correspondingly higher.

Finally, Table 5.4 replicates the moments from Table 5.2, but recomputing the model with a re-entry hazard of 0.282, which is the value used in

TABLE 5.4. Alternative II: Short Default Duration

	Model 1 (Linear)	Model 2 (Quadratic)	Model 3 (Ceiling)
$\mathbb{E}\left[\frac{b'}{y}\right]$	0.07	0.13	0.04
$\mathbb{E}\left[\frac{q*b'}{y}\right]$	0.07	0.13	0.04
Default Rate (Annualized)	0.0009	0.009	0.033
$\mathbb{E}\left[r - r^\star\right]$ (Annualized)	0.0009	0.009	0.036
StDev$(r - r^\star)$ (Annualized)	0.002	0.010	0.050
StDev(c)/StDev(y)	1.00	1.05	1.03
Corr$(y - c, y)$	−0.11	−0.19	−0.14
Corr$(y, r - r^\star)$	−0.10	−0.67	−0.13
Corr$(\frac{b'}{y}, r - r^\star)$	0.45	−0.61	−0.24
Corr$(r - r^\star, y - c)$	−0.28	0.63	0.51

Note: This table replicates the moments of Table 5.2, but recomputing each model with a re-entry probability hazard of $\theta = 0.282$.

Arellano (2008). This high re-entry rate implies default status is a very transitory state. This sharply reduces the level of debt for Models II and III. Recall that default occurs when the endowment is low. With a short period of exclusion, it is unlikely that the endowment will be high prior to re-entry. This is important for non-linear cost models, as default costs increase steeply with the endowment. Thus, a short duration implies low costs of default. This generates less debt sustained in equilibrium, and more frequent default.

Low Discount Factor and Welfare. The need for a relatively low discount factor for the government to be able to quantitatively match empirical moments has been interpreted as the outcome of political economy frictions that push the government toward unnecessary debt accumulation. The role of political economy frictions in debt accumulation is a topic discussed in Chapter 3 in the context of a growth model. But political economy considerations also have implications for business cycles, as exemplified by the role of the government discount factor in these calibrations.[10] The fact that the

---

10. See, for example, Cuadra and Sapriza (2008) and Hatchondo, Martinez, and Sapriza (2009), which are early papers that explicitly incorporated political economy frictions into quantitative models. For more recent work, see Scholl (2017) and Chatterjee and Eyigungor (2019).

government's discount factor may not match the preferences of the under-lying domestic households also introduces the possibility that fiscal rules that constrain government spending and borrowing may be beneficial for the citizenship.[11]

Aguiar, Amador, and Fourakis (2020) propose an analytical framework to decompose the potential welfare losses from an impatient government hav-ing access to external sovereign credit. With such a decomposition, they show that, in the context of the model in this section, there are potential welfare gains from banning external borrowing. However, the gains are quantitatively not large. This is driven by the fact that total borrowing in the current envi-ronment is not large, and the procyclicality in spending generated by having access to credit is not significant enough. However, these results change once long-term bonds are introduced into this quantitative framework. This is a topic that we discuss later in Chapter 7.

5.6   Conclusion

In this chapter we verified that the insights of the analytical model carry over to the richer one-period bond environment that initiated the quantitative work in the literature. In particular, the deadweight costs of default are the key driving force behind debt dynamics and default. The mapping between a planning problem and the equilibrium also carries over, with one impor-tant caveat. With endowment shocks, the planning problem must include an "implementability" condition that captures the limitations on financial risk sharing imposed on the competitive equilibrium. A true social planner's problem is independent of market structure, and hence this is an important modification that reflects the ad hoc restriction on contracting imposed on the model. Nevertheless, the augmented planning problem is a useful ana-lytical device and highlights that the equilibrium debt dynamics maximize the joint surplus of the government and lender, subject to the contracting and limited commitment frictions. In the process, this result establishes the

11. Alfaro and Kanczuk (2017) explore the implications of fiscal rules in the sovereign debt model and found them to be beneficial. There is also a literature that explores the ben-efits of such rules in closed economies in the presence of political distortions. See, for example, Azzimonti, Battaglini, and Coate (2016) for a recent contribution.

uniqueness of the equilibrium. In the next chapter, we discuss indeterminacy (self-fulfilling crises) in a closely related model that does not have these uniqueness and efficiency properties. In Chapter 7, we show that the efficiency and uniqueness properties do not hold when the government issues fixed-rate long-term bonds in the Eaton-Gersovitz environment. In particular, "debt dilution" joins limited commitment and deadweight costs of default as an additional friction.

6

Self-Fulfilling Debt Crises

6.1 Introduction

In this chapter, we explore the "static" multiplicity of the canonical Cole and Kehoe (2000) model, as well as its extension by Aguiar, Chatterjee, Cole, and Stangebye (2019b). We refer to the multiplicity as static, as we can hold beliefs about future equilibrium behavior constant, yet still obtain alternative equilibrium prices in the current period. In the next chapter, we introduce a "dynamic" multiplicity that operates through self-fulfilling beliefs about *future* fiscal policy.[1]

6.2 Environment

To highlight the static nature of the multiplicity as well as for expositional ease, we use a simple two-period model. The basic building blocks are adapted from Chapter 4. Once the mechanism is established, the conceptual extension to many periods will be straightforward given the results of Chapter 4.

Let $t = 1, 2$ denote time. The government's preferences are given by:

$$U(c_1, c_2) = u(c_1) + \beta u(c_2),$$

1. Chapter 5 of Sachs (1984) and Alesina, Prati, and Tabellini (1990) are related antecedents to Cole and Kehoe (2000). See also Detragiache (1996), Galli (2019) and Pekarski and Sokolova (2020) for versions of multiplicity in the presence of investment. Calvo (1988) presents an alternative view of self-fulfilling crises in which there may be more than one interest rate that equilibrates the bond market. See Ayres, Navarro, Nicolini, and Teles (2018) for a full discussion of the Calvo multiplicity in versions of the one-period-bond Eaton-Gersovitz model, and Lorenzoni and Werning (2019) for Calvo multiplicity with long-term bonds. See also the recent work by Conesa and Kehoe (2017) that extends the Cole-Kehoe model to a case with output uncertainty.

where c_t is consumption in period $t = 1, 2$. The government trades a non-contingent bond with competitive risk-neutral lenders with discount factor $R^{-1} = (1 + r^*)^{-1}$.

Working backwards through time, the government enters period 2 with an amount of debt due b_2. At the start of period 2, the government receives an endowment y_2, which it uses to repay debt (absent default) and consume. As $t = 2$ is the last period, there is no issuance of new debt. For simplicity, we assume y_2 is known with certainty. Thus, consumption in period 2 conditional on repayment is:

$$c_2^R = y_2 - b_2,$$

and the value of repayment is $V_2^R(b_2) \equiv u\left(y_2 - b_2\right)$.

The government has the option to default. As in the model of Chapter 4, we model the value of default as a random variable drawn at the start of period 2. While Chapter 4 uses a two-point distribution, for the current context we assume that the value of default v^D is drawn from a continuous distribution with support on $[\underline{V}, \overline{V}]$ and cdf F_2. We assume $f_2(v^D) \equiv F_2'(v^D) > 0$ on $[\underline{V}, \overline{V}]$. As in Chapter 4, the random value of default may be interpreted as reflecting income lost due to default as well as utility costs. We assume $u(y_2) \geq \overline{V}$, so the government will never default absent a strictly positive level of debt due.

The government's decision in period 2 is thus to repay if and only if:

$$u\left(y_2 - b_2\right) \geq v^D. \tag{6.1}$$

Conditional on b_2, the ex ante probability of repayment is $F_2(u(y_2 - b_2))$. At the start of period 2, the government's expected value is:

$$V_2(b_2) = F_2\left(u(y_2 - b_2)\right) u(y_2 - b_2) + \int_{u(y_2 - b_2)}^{\overline{V}} v^D \, dF_2(v^D). \tag{6.2}$$

The first term is the probability of repayment $F(u(y_2 - b_2))$ times the utility conditional on repayment $u(y_2 - b_2)$. The second term is the expected value of default, which is the integral of possible default values v^D between the value of repayment $u(y_2 - b_2)$ and $\overline{V}$, where realizations are weighted by the probability density $dF_2(v^D) = f_2(v^D) dv^D$.

In period 1, the government begins with debt due b_1 and receives an endowment y_1 (which again is known with certainty). The government's key decisions in period 1 are whether to repay b_1 and how much debt to issue

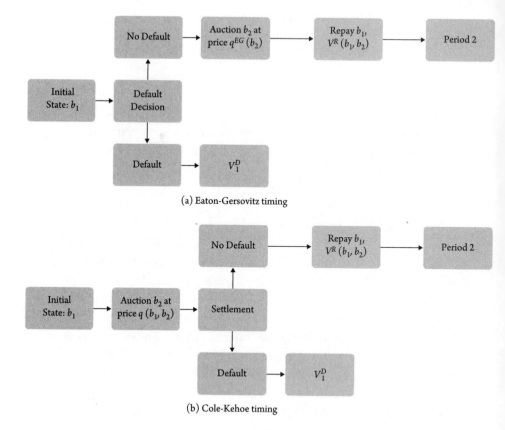

(a) Eaton-Gersovitz timing

(b) Cole-Kehoe timing

FIGURE 6.1. Period-1 Timing

for repayment in period 2, b_2.[2] If it defaults, it enjoys payoff V_1^D, which for simplicity we assume is known with certainty. We relax this last assumption below.

6.2.1   Eaton-Gersovitz Timing

We consider two alternative timing conventions for period 1, depicted in Figure 6.1. The first (panel a) is the Eaton-Gersovitz timing used in earlier chapters. Namely, the government *first* decides whether to repay b_1 or default, and then, conditional on repayment, the government proceeds to auction b_2.

2. Note that debt is one period; however, we could extend the model to include an initial amount of long-term debt existing in period 1 that is due in period 2. This would involve simply adjusting y_2 by this amount in c_2^R while leaving the distribution of the value of default unchanged.

Recall that this involves an intra-period commitment to not default after the auction, regardless of its outcome.

To set the Eaton-Gersovitz benchmark, let $q^{EG}(b)$ denote the equilibrium price under the Eaton-Gersovitz timing convention when the government issues $b_2 = b$ in $t = 1$. The lenders' break-even constraint is:

$$q^{EG}(b) = R^{-1}F_2(u(y_2 - b)). \tag{6.3}$$

Facing this price schedule, the government's value conditional on a level of b_2 is

$$V^R(b_1, b_2) = u(y_1 - b_1 + q^{EG}(b_2)b_2) + \beta V_2(b_2),$$

and the government's problem under repayment is:

$$V^{EG}(b_1) = \max_{b_2} V^R(b_1, b_2). \tag{6.4}$$

Finally, the government repays b_1 if and only if $V^{EG}(b_1) \geq V_1^D$.

Definition 14 *An equilibrium under the* Eaton-Gersovitz *timing (EG-equilibrium) is a price schedule $q^{EG} : \mathbb{R} \to [0, R^{-1}]$ and a period-1 value function under repayment V^{EG} such that (i) q^{EG} satisfies (6.3) given V^{EG} and (ii) V^{EG} is defined by (6.4).*

Note that the Eaton-Gersovitz price schedule q^{EG} is uniquely determined by primitives. This then uniquely determines the government's value in period 1. We saw in Chapter 5 that in the infinite horizon context, there was a unique equilibrium for the Eaton-Gersovitz model with one-period bonds. The same holds, as expected, in this two-period environment.

6.2.2   Cole-Kehoe Timing

We now consider an alternative timing convention, which follows Cole and Kehoe (2000), and is depicted in panel (b) of Figure 6.1. Cole-Kehoe propose the following timing: the government first auctions b_2 and *then* decides whether to repay b_1 *after* the auction is completed. Thus, the government does not commit to repay prior to the auction.

More explicitly, let $q(b_1, b_2)$ denote the equilibrium price schedule in period 1 under the Cole-Kehoe timing. As will be clear, the price schedule depends on the debt due within the period, b_1, as well as new issuances, b_2. Working backward through period 1, at the end of the period, the government decides whether to repay the debt or default (we call this stage "settlement"). If it repays, it consumes

$$c_1^R = y_1 - b_1 + q(b_1, b_2)b_2.$$

The value of repayment conditional on b_2 is:

$$V^R(b_1, b_2) = u\left(y_1 - b_1 + q(b_1, b_2)b_2\right) + \beta V_2(b_2). \tag{6.5}$$

The government repays b_1 at settlement if and only if $V_1^R(b_1, b_2) \geq V_1^{D}.$[3] The value at the start of period 1 is:

$$V(b_1) = \max\left\{\max_{b_2} V^R(b_1, b_2), V_1^D\right\}.$$

The lenders' break-even condition for $b_2 \geq 0$ is:

$$q(b_1, b_2) = R^{-1}\mathbb{1}_{[V^R(b_1,b_2) \geq V_1^D]}F_2(u(y_2 - b_2)) \tag{6.6}$$

$$= \mathbb{1}_{[V^R(b_1,b_2) \geq V_1^D]}q^{EG}(b_2),$$

where the second line uses (6.3) and recall that $\mathbb{1}_{[x]}$ is the indicator function that takes value 1 if x is true and zero otherwise. The key distinction between (6.6) and (6.3) is $\mathbb{1}_{[V^R(b_1,b_2) \geq V_1^D]}$, which can take a value of one or zero. Thus the price under the Cole-Kehoe timing is bounded above by q^{EG}. This indicator function depends on b_1 as well as b_2, and hence so does the equilibrium price schedule.

Definition 15 *An equilibrium (CK-equilibrium) under the* Cole-Kehoe *timing is a price schedule* $q: \mathbb{R} \times \mathbb{R} \to [0, R^{-1}]$ *and a period-1 value function under repayment* V^R *such that (i)* q *satisfies (6.6) given* V^R *for* $b_2 \geq 0$ *and* $q(b_1, b_2) = R^{-1}$ *for* $b_2 < 0$; *and (ii)* V^R *is defined by (6.5) given* q.

6.3   Self-Fulfilling Rollover Crises

We first discuss an equilibrium that tracks the EG-equilibrium as closely as possible under the CK timing convention. Let $\overline{V}^R(b_1, b_2)$ denote the value of repayment assuming the government faces $q^{EG}(b_2)$:

$$\overline{V}^R(b_1, b_2) = u\left(y_1 - b_1 + q^{EG}(b_2)b_2\right) + \beta V_2(b_2). \tag{6.7}$$

---

3. The original Cole-Kehoe model assumes the government consumes the auction revenue $q(b_1, b_2)b_2$ in default. For simplicity, we abstract from that possibility, and instead assume that any auction revenue is lost (to both government and lenders) in default.

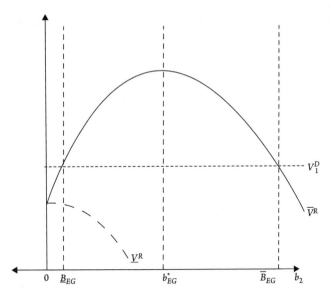

FIGURE 6.2. Value of Repayment: High Initial Debt

Note: The "humped" solid line depicts $\overline{V}^R$, the value of repayment under best-case (q^{EG}) prices. The dashed line $\underline{V}^R$ depicts the value of repayment under worst-case (zero) prices. The horizontal dotted line is the value of default.

As the CK-equilibrium q is bounded above by q^{EG}, $\overline{V}^R$ is an upper bound on the CK-equilibrium repayment value.

To guide our discussion of CK-equilibria, we use Figure 6.2. The solid line represents $\overline{V}^R(b_1, \cdot)$ as a function of b_2 for a fixed b_1. The figure is depicted assuming u and F are such that $\overline{V}^R$ is quasi-concave. The optimal choice of debt issuance when facing q^{EG} is denoted b_{EG}^*. This is the government's best response to q^{EG}. The horizontal dashed line is the value of default. As $\overline{V}^R(b_1, b_{EG}^*) > V_1^D$ in the figure's scenario, the government prefers to issue b_{EG}^* and repay at settlement rather than default.

Note that there are (off equilibrium) debt choices for which the government would rather default at settlement than repay b_1: for $b_2 < \underline{B}_{EG}$ and $b_2 > \overline{B}_{EG}$, the value of repayment is below the value of default. For the former interval, the government has issued very litttle debt (or purchased foreign assets) and finds it difficult to repay b_1. For the latter interval, the large amount of debt issued lowers the continuation payoff in period 2 to the point that default is very likely next period. In this case, $q^{EG}(b_2)$ is low enough that repayment of b_1 again becomes onerous. Thus, q^{EG} can be supported in a CK-equilibrium only for $b_2 \in [\underline{B}_{EG}, \overline{B}_{EG}]$, as outside this interval repayment at settlement is not ex post optimal.

The "best-case" CK-equilibrium price schedule $\overline{q}$ is:

$$
\overline{q}(b_1, b_2) \equiv \begin{cases} R^{-1} \text{ if } b_2 < 0 \\ q^{EG}(b_2) \text{ if } \overline{V}^R(b_1, b_2) \geq V_1^D \text{ and } b_2 \geq 0 \\ 0 \text{ otherwise.} \end{cases} \tag{6.8}
$$

The pair $\{\overline{V}^R, \overline{q}\}$ satisfies the equilibrium conditions. The price schedule satisfies the within-period perfection requirement required by the CK tim-ing: the government must be willing to repay at settlement conditional on issuing b_2 at price $q^{EG}(b_2)$; otherwise, the only valid equilibrium price is zero.

However, this is not the only valid CK-equilibrium. Suppose the govern-ment faces a price of zero for *all* $b_2 > 0$. This is a "failed" auction in which creditors are unwilling to purchase any amount of government debt. Let $\underline{q}$ denote this "crisis" price schedule:

$$
\underline{q}(b_1, b_2) \equiv \begin{cases} R^{-1} \text{ for } b_2 \leq 0 \\ 0 \text{ otherwise.} \end{cases} \tag{6.9}
$$

In this case, the value of repayment at settlement is:

$$
\underline{V}^R(b_1, b_2) = u(y_1 - b_1) + \beta V_2(b_2) \text{ for } b_2 \geq 0. \tag{6.10}
$$

Importantly, repayment always leads to period-1 consumption of $y_1 - b_1$; that is, all debt repayments must be financed out of current income. This may be painful, or even infeasible. The declining dashed line in Figure 6.2 depicts $\underline{V}^R$. As additional issuance yields zero additional auction revenue but raises the amount due in period 2, $\underline{V}^R$ is weakly decreasing in b_2, and strictly decreasing as long as repayment in period 2 is a possibility for some realizations of v^D.[4] As long as $\underline{V}^R(b_1, 0) < V_1^D$, the crisis price schedule is a valid equilibrium: faced with a failed auction, the government defaults at

---

4. Once default is certain in period 2, $\underline{V}^R = u(y_1 - b_1) + \beta \mathbb{E} v^D$.

settlement, validating the zero price.[5] From an atomistic lender's perspective, any individual purchase of debt will not shift the government's resources at settlement, implying that a zero bid is consistent with the lenders' break-even condition.

Whether multiple price schedules can be supported in equilibrium depends on the initial b_1 (as well as the other parameters). For low levels of initial debt b_1, the government prefers to repay even if it cannot issue new debt in period 1's auction. That is, $\underline{V}^R(b_1, 0) \geq V_1^D$. Cole and Kehoe refer to this domain as the "Safe Zone." Let $\underline{b}$ denote the threshold at which $\underline{V}^R(\underline{b}, 0) = V_1^D$. For $b_1 < \underline{b}$, $\underline{q}$ is no longer a valid CK-equilibrium price schedule. There may be other price schedules for this region, but we hold off that discussion until the next subsection.

For intermediate levels of b_1, the government will default in period 1 if it faces $\underline{q}$, but issue a positive amount of debt b_2^* if facing $\overline{q}$. This is the Cole-Kehoe "Crisis Zone." Whether the government defaults depends on whether creditors coordinate on the good outcome at settlement or the crisis outcome. The Crisis Zone is $(\underline{b}, \overline{b}]$, where $\overline{b}$ is defined by $\max_{b_2} \overline{V}^R(\overline{b}, b_2) = V_1^D$. At $\overline{b}$, the government is indifferent to repayment and default when facing the best-case price schedule.

At very high levels of $b_1 > \overline{b}$, the debt burden is so high that the government will default even if it were to face q^{EG}. This latter outcome coincides with the defaults in the benchmark Eaton-Gersovitz model.

The nature of the multiplicity is similar to a bank run. In the Crisis Zone, the government is solvent and will service debt if lenders are willing to "roll over" debt by purchasing new debt at auction. However, if creditors refuse to buy new debt, the government will find it optimal to default, confirming the crisis beliefs. Default is purely a coordination failure among creditors in the Crisis Zone.

6.4   Debt Issuance

With the conceptual mechanism in place, we can now extend the model to discuss debt issuance prior to period one. The threat of a rollover crisis affects the government's incentive to reduce debt over time in much the same way as the

---

5. More precisely, the crisis price schedule is a valid equilibrium if $\underline{V}^R(b_1, 0) < V_1^D$. However, the "default at settlement" statement requires as well that saving is dominated by default: $\underline{V}^R(b_1, b_2) < V_1^D$ for all $b_2 \leq 0$.

threat of default did in the model of Chapter 4. The parallel can be shown in a transparent way by introducing a period prior to $t = 1$ in the above model, call it $t = 0$. In this initial period, we consider the price schedule the government faces in its choice of b_1. For now, we restrict attention to one-period bonds, and discuss long-term bonds in Section 6.5.

First, we need to put some structure on which equilibrium price schedule is operative in period 1. This is necessary to pin down the period-0 prices. Following Cole and Kehoe (2000), suppose a sunspot is realized at the start of period 1. Depending on the realization of the sunspot, creditors coordinate on $\bar{q}$ or $\underline{q}$. Suppose creditors coordinate on the crisis price schedule with probability λ, and the best-case price schedule with probability $1 - \lambda$.

The default decision in period one is thus as follows. If b_1 is in the Safe Zone $(-\infty, \underline{b}]$, the government repays with probability one. If b_1 is in the Crisis Zone $(\underline{b}, \bar{b}]$, the government repays only if creditors coordinate on the best-case scenario, which occurs with probability $1 - \lambda$. Finally, if $b_1 > \bar{b}$, the government defaults with probability one.

Now consider the period 0 bond-market equilibrium. For simplicity, assume zero debt at the start of the period, so we can abstract from default in period 0, and let $q_0(b_1)$ denote the period-zero price schedule. The lenders' break-even condition implies:

$$
q_0(b) = \begin{cases} R^{-1} \text{ if } b \leq \underline{b} \\ (1 - \lambda)R^{-1} \text{ if } b \in (\underline{b}, \bar{b}] \\ 0 \text{ otherwise.} \end{cases}
$$

The nature of q_0 is identical to the price schedule studied in Chapter 4. Specifically, there is a threshold above which the government must compensate lenders for default risk. The only distinction is that default in the current setup is driven by a coordination failure among creditors, rather than a high default value realization. Hence, as in the earlier analysis, the government has an incentive to reduce the probability of default by saving toward the Safe Zone. In fact, the incentive is stronger, as the government defaults when it would strictly prefer to repay under the best-case prices, implying greater deadweight losses.

Cole and Kehoe (2000) as well as Aguiar, Amador, Farhi, and Gopinath (2012) consider infinite horizon versions of the above rollover-crisis model and establish that in the neighborhood just above the Safe Zone, the government chooses to reduce debt over time. If βR is close enough to one, the Safe Zone becomes an absorbing state. We omit the details as the analysis of debt dynamics in the infinite horizon model are essentially the same as that of Chapter 4.

6.5 The Security of Long-Term Bonds

The fact that the level of b_1 determines the government's vulnerability to a rollover crisis speaks to the value of longer maturity bonds as a shield against self-fulfilling crises. To see this, consider the equilibirum path of debt $\{b_1, b_2^*\}$ under the best-case price schedule q^{EG}. The net payment in period 1 is $\rho \equiv b_1 - \bar{q}(b_1, b_2^*)b_2^*$.

An alternative way to support the same path of net payments (in period "zero") is to issue a two-period bond that promises a coupon ρ in period 1 and the principal b_2^* in period 2. In this case, the government never needs to auction bonds in period 1, and there is therefore no scope for the crisis equilibrium. Hence, longer maturity bonds are one way to reduce the vulnerability to self-fulfilling crises of the type studied by Cole and Kehoe.

6.6 Extensions: Sudden Stops and Over-Borrowing

The Cole-Kehoe rollover crisis model highlights the vulnerability to a self-fulfilling failed auction. At a point in time, a country may be able to easily roll over its debt or be forced to default, depending on creditors' (self-fulfilling) beliefs about imminent default. Aguiar et al. (2019b)—henceforth ACCS—show that the same framework can generate a rich set of alternative scenarios beyond these two extremes. The simple two-period model introduced above can be used to highlight two additional self-fulfilling outcomes.

6.6.1 Sudden Stops

The first is a "sudden stop" or "forced austerity," in which the government does not default, but finds itself able to issue only a limited amount of debt at auction. To explore this possible outcome, consider Figure 6.3. This figure is similar to Figure 6.2, but with a lower initial debt, b_1. This shifts up the repayment schedules at each choice of b_2. In particular, assume b_1 is low enough that $\underline{V}^R(b_1, 0) > V_1^D$.

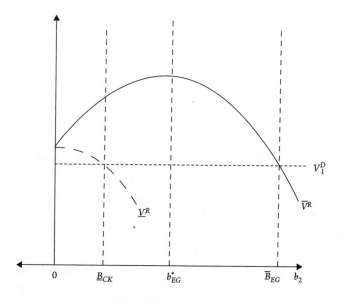

FIGURE 6.3. Value of Repayment: Low Initial Debt

Note: This figure reproduces the objects of Figure 6.2 but evaluated at a lower initial debt b_1.

The fact that $\underline{V}^R(b_1, 0) > V_1^D$ implies that we are in the Cole-Kehoe Safe Zone. That is, a price of zero is not sustainable for *all* choices of debt issuances. In Figure 6.3, $\underline{B}_{CK} \in (0, b_{EG}^*)$ denotes the lowest level of b_2 at which a price of zero can be supported in equilibrium. This is the threshold such that $\underline{V}^R(b_1, \underline{B}_{CK}) = V_1^D$. For choices $b_2 < \underline{B}_{CK}$, $\bar{q}$ is the only equilibrium price schedule.

Now consider the following two alternative outcomes. One is the best-case scenario: the government faces $\bar{q}$ for the entire domain $b_2 > 0$, issues b_{EG}^*, and does not default.

The alternative is that the government faces $\bar{q}$ only on the *restricted* domain $b_2 \leq \underline{B}_{CK}$. For $b_2 > \underline{B}_{CK}$, the government faces $q(b_1, b_2) = 0$. The optimal choice is $b_2 = \underline{B}_{CK} < b_2^*$.[6] At this choice (and associated price), the government's repayment value is $\overline{V}^R(b_1, \underline{B}_{CK}) > V_1^D$. Hence, it does not default at settlement. However, as long as $\underline{B}_{CK} < b_{EG}^*$, its value is below that under the alternative equilibrium price schedule.

6. Note that we have assigned the best-case scenario price at the boundary $\underline{B}_{CK}$ to ensure a well-defined optimal choice of b_2.

This scenario is a self-fulfilling "sudden stop." Lenders are willing to purchase bonds, but only in limited quantities. Creditors worry that additional issuances will lower the continuation value to the point the government defaults on b_1 at settlement. These expectations are self-fulfilling—if instead creditors coordinate on the best-case scenario, the government auctions a larger quantity of debt yet does not default.

6.6.2   Over-Borrowing and Prolonged Crises

Another scenario considered by Aguiar et al. (2019b) has the opposite outcome to a sudden stop; namely, the government issues $b_2 > b_{EG}^*$. The launching point for this scenario is to enrich the key distinction between the CK and EG timings; that is, the gap between auction of new debt and repayment of maturing debt within the period. In the canonical model, there is perfect foresight between these two events. ACCS introduce some intra-period uncertainty, motivated by the fact that high-frequency risk is a common feature observed in financial markets. We shall show that the "over-borrowing" (relative to the best-case equilibrium) reassures creditors that the government has ample resources to repay debt regardless of the uncertainty.

Suppose that the default value in period 1 is $V_1^D + \sigma\epsilon$, where σ is a parameter that scales the extent of risk and ϵ is a random variable with compact support and cdf $F_1(\epsilon)$. We assume $f_1(\epsilon) \equiv F_1'(\epsilon)$ is strictly positive on the support. The limits of the support are arbitrary given the presence of σ (and V_1^D), and hence we normalize to $\epsilon \in [-1, 0]$. The government draws ϵ *after* period-1's auction, but before settlement. Hence, ϵ represents intra-period risk to the creditors. This risk represents high-frequency news regarding the costs (or benefits) of default, whether financial or political.[7]

As above, let $V^R(b_1, b_2)$ denote the equilibrium value of repayment in period 1 conditional on initial debt b_1 and issuances of b_2. At settlement, the government repays if and only if $V_1^D + \sigma\epsilon \le V^R(b_1, b_2)$. That is, if

$$\epsilon \le \underbrace{\frac{1}{\sigma}\left(V^R(b_1, b_2) - V_1^D\right)}_{\equiv \Delta}. \qquad (6.11)$$

---

7. ACCS also provide an alternative formulation in which the government seeks a third-party bailout at settlement, the size of which is unknown at auction. This makes the value of repayment rather than default a random variable, but the economics work in a similar manner as having uncertainty over the value of default.

Let Δ denote the difference in parentheses on the right-hand side, where the notation omits explicit reference to the fact that this difference depends on the equilibrium value $V^R(b_1, b_2)$. Thus, at the time of auction, the probability of repayment at settlement is $F_1(\Delta/\sigma)$.

In this environment, the lenders' period-1 break-even condition is:

$$q(b_1, b_2) = F_1(\Delta/\sigma)q^{EG}(b_2). \tag{6.12}$$

The difference between this expression and equation (6.6) is that the zero-one indicator variable in the latter equation has been replaced with a $F_1(\Delta/\sigma) \in [0, 1]$.

The novel equilibrium arises when creditors coordinate on *intra-period risk*. Suppose there is a threshold, $\tilde{\epsilon}$, such that the government repays if $\epsilon \leq \tilde{\epsilon}$, and defaults otherwise. Associated with this threshold is a price, $\tilde{q}(b_1, b_2) = F_1(\tilde{\epsilon})q^{EG}(b_2)$. For a given (b_1, b_2), let $\tilde{\Delta}$ be Δ evaluated at this price. An equilibrium is a fixed point of (6.12) such that $\tilde{q} = F_1(\tilde{\Delta}/\sigma)q^{EG}$. If $\tilde{\epsilon} \in (-1, 0)$ and $\tilde{q} \in (0, q^{EG})$, there is intra-period uncertainty at the time of auction. The uncertainty of whether the government defaults or not remains unresolved until ϵ is realized. This was not the case with the failed auction or the best-case scenario, which feature perfect foresight within the period.

ACCS show that if zero and q^{EG} are valid equilibria, there is a third equilibrium price in which the government may or may not default at settlement, introducing an additional level of risk. This equilibrium price schedule exists even as $\sigma \to 0$. That is, no matter how small the intra-period uncertainty, there exists a set of states and beliefs such that the government may face a price strictly between zero and q^{EG}.

The "interior" price schedule poses an interesting dilemma for the government. It is able to issue bonds at positive prices, but must compensate lenders for this additional source of risk. ACCS show that under fairly general conditions, this provides an incentive for the government to issue *more* debt than it would under the best-case q^{EG} beliefs. By issuing additional debt, the government can raise sufficient revenue to credibly assure auction participants that it will repay maturing debt at settlement. However, the additional debt raises the probability of default in the second period. ACCS show that this may be the optimal response to such creditor beliefs. Thus, the government achieves intra-period certainty at the cost of higher default risk in the future. Despite the static nature of multiplicity, creditor beliefs today can generate a prolonged crisis through the evolution of the endogenous state variable.

6.7 Domestic Currency Bonds and Rollover Risk

A conventional wisdom holds that bonds denominated in local currency are not vulnerable to rollover risk. According to the logic, the issuing government can always print money to pay off maturing bonds in the event of a failed auction. Aguiar et al. (2012) (henceforth AAFG) and Aguiar, Amador, Farhi, and Gopinath (2015) explore this premise formally in a small open economy and in a monetary union, respectively.[8]

The starting point of their analysis is that feasibility is only one criterion entering a government's decision to repay debt. Governments default in situations in which it is feasible to repay, but the costs of repayment outweigh the costs of default. The same calculus applies to domestic currency bonds; namely, the government trades off the costs of default against any distortion that arises from expanding the money supply. AAFG model the latter through a weakly convex cost of inflation, and consider alternative environments that differ in the severity of this cost. They show that the ability to monetize debt insures against failed auctions only for intermediate costs of inflation.

Specifically, for very low costs, the government will resort to inflating away debt regardless of whether creditors coordinate on a high or low price. Low-cost inflation dominates reducing consumption (or distortionary taxation) as the primary response to maturing bonds. In equilibrium, creditors anticipate this inflation and are unwilling to lend in domestic currency (or do so only at arbitrarily high rates as the costs of inflation become negligible). Thus, for countries with weak monetary policy credibility, borrowing in foreign currency may be the optimal or even only viable option.

For very high costs of inflation, repayment through monetization is dominated by outright default. As the country rarely, if ever, resorts to inflation, local currency and foreign currency debt are near perfect substitutes. The government can borrow in local currency, but is vulnerable to rollover risk as if it had borrowed in foreign currency.

At an intermediate cost of inflation, the government resorts to monetization only in extenuating circumstances. When facing high prices, the country

8. There is significant work exploring the interactions between inflation, nominal bonds, devaluations, and default. See for example, Araujo, Leon, and Santos (2013), Nuño and Thomas (2015), Corsetti and Dedola (2016), Du and Schreger (2016b), Engel and Park (2018), Bianchi and Mondragon (2018), Na, Schmitt-Grohé, Uribe, and Yue (2018), Hur, Kondo, and Perri (2018), Bassetto and Galli (2019), Ottonello and Perez (2019), Galli (2020), Sunder-Plassmann (2020), and Du, Pflueger, and Schreger (2020).

prefers to service debt via real resources, as maturing principal can be rolled over at favorable prices. However, in the event of a failed auction, it will resort to inflating maturing bonds rather than default, eliminating the zero price as an equilibrium outcome. The intermediate commitment to low infla- tion provides the government with a credible state-contingent approach to monetizing debt, with low inflation when facing equilibrium prices but a credible off-equilibrium promise of monetization that provides protection against runs.

Aguiar et al. (2012) take the costs of inflation as a primitive of the environment. Aguiar et al. (2015) show how the composition of a monetary union generates an endogenous commitment to low inflation. The intermediate cost of inflation described above can be generated by a monetary union comprised of a mix of high-debt and low-debt economies. An objective function that values both of the two heterogeneous membership classes can generate low inflation along the equilibrium path, but credibly promise to step in and inflate away maturing debt in the event of a failed auction.[9]

While domestic currency may rule out Cole-Kehoe style rollover crises in this manner, it does open the door to a different type of multiplicity first studied by Calvo (1988). In particular, suppose the government uses a combination of real (tax) resources and inflation to pay off debt, and the level of ex post inflation is increasing in the amount of debt issued. The second element Calvo introduces is that the government has to raise a certain amount of revenue from auctioning debt; that is, it has relatively tight constraints on the size of the deficit to be financed. In such an environment, if creditors anticipate high inflation next period, bonds will be sold at a deep discount at auction, and the government will be forced to issue a large amount of face value to cover its deficit. The large debt generates the anticipated inflation in the next period when repayment is due, fulfilling creditor expectations. Conversely, optimistic inflation expectations lead to a high price at auction, and the government issues a small amount of face value, supporting low inflation next period. This type of multiplicity is explored further in models of foreign currency debt in Lorenzoni and Werning (2019) and Ayres, Navarro, Nicolini, and Teles (2015), and is discussed in the context of nominal bonds by Aguiar et al. (2012) and Bacchetta, Perazzi, and van Wincoop (2018).

---

9. Corsetti, Kuester, Meier, and Müller (2014) explore belief-driven deflationary crises in the euro area using a model with nominal rigidities.

6.8   Policy Responses and Debt Design

Rollover crises closely parallel bank runs. In a bank run, a "lender of last resort" can step in and guarantee liquidity, using bank assets as collateral. In the canonical model of Diamond and Dybvig (1983), the mere presence of such a backstop can eliminate the run equilibrium, without extending any emergency lending along the equilibrium path. A third-party facility (such as the International Monetary Fund) could accomplish the same function in the Cole-Kehoe environment by guaranteeing a floor on bond prices. As long as prices are such that the government is willing to repay maturing bonds, the zero-price equilibrium is eliminated.[10]

However, the analysis so far raises two important concerns about a lender of last resort. The first relates to the analysis of Section 6.6.2. If creditors are uncertain about whether and to what extent the lender of last resort is willing to lend at settlement, then this opens the door to self-fulfilling risk that may be priced into bond markets.

The second concern is taken up in Chapter 7, Section 7.8, in which we identify a different, dynamic source of multiplicity. In that environment, a debt floor can inefficiently select an equilibrium with excessive borrowing.

The threat of rollover risk also suggests the value of long maturities. However, this must be balanced against the dilution risk discussed in Chapter 7. One middle approach suggested by the models presented in this book is long-term debt with floating-rate coupon payments. As pointed out at the end of Chapter 4, Section 4.5, a perpetuity with a floating coupon tied to the price of an instantaneous bond implements the efficient allocation in the analytical model. The absence of principal payments provides some protection against rollover risk. The floating coupon payments provide incentives to mitigate default risk.[11]

10. At the height of the European debt crisis in July 2012, European Central Bank (ECB) president Mario Draghi pledged to do "whatever it takes to preserve the euro." This statement was quickly followed by the announcement of an institutional structure for Outright Monetary Transactions (OMTs) to formalize the process of backstopping sovereign debt markets. This sequence of events coincided with a sharp drop in spreads for distressed euro-area sovereign bonds. A common (but not exclusive) interpretation of this sequence is the ECB promising to serve the role of lender of last resort, thereby eliminating the run equilibrium. See Bocola and Dovis (2019) for a quantitative analysis of this episode. See Abrahám et al. (2018) for a normative analysis of an optimal stabilization fund.

11. Hatchondo, Martinez, and Sosa-Padilla (2016) quantitatively explore a closely related debt covenant and compute the welfare gains.

A few qualifications are in order regarding floating-rate debt. One is it requires the benchmark rate for the coupon. For example, a short-term bond that is regularly auctioned would serve this purpose. The market needs to be large enough that liquidity of the bonds is not an issue, but not too large to raise the danger of a rollover crisis.[12] See Alesina et al. (1990) for the problems encountered when Italy issued floating-rate bonds.

Second, a floating rate alters the hedging properties of long-term bonds. The government is exposed to fluctuations in world interest rates and risk premia. It is a quantitative question of whether such hedging properties are of the same magnitude as dilution risk.[13]

6.9   Conclusion

The risk of a rollover crisis looms large in sovereign debt markets. Its presence motivates governments to extend maturities in restructurings, despite the fact that such bonds may exacerbate fundamental risk, as we discuss next in Chapter 7. Even in tranquil periods, governments frequently auction longer-term bonds in order to repurchase bonds that are not yet due but that mature in the near future. Such maturity swaps are used in part to avoid the risk of a failed auction at the time the maturing bonds come due (see Aguiar and Amador 2021 for an analysis of such swaps). As noted above, longer maturities combined with floating-rate coupons represent one approach to balancing rollover and fundamental risks, as is third-party assistance in the event of a failed auction. Nevertheless, it is not clear that there exists a single instrument or policy that can completely remove both the rollover risk of short-term bonds and the dilution risk of longer maturities. The preceding chapters outlined both the efficient properties and vulnerabilities of short-term debt. The topic of the next chapter is long-maturity bonds, which introduce a number of novel implications for debt dynamics and default.

12. A cap on the floating interest rate can be used to avoid a self-fulfilling spike in the short-term rate, as in the model of Calvo (1988).

13. Chatterjee and Eyigungor (2012a) find that dilution costs dominate the benefits of hedging in their long-term bond model. A similar argument is made in Hatchondo et al. (2016).

7

Long-Term Bonds

7.1 Introduction

In this chapter we extend the models of Chapters 4 and 5 to include fixed-rate long-term bonds. Longer maturity debt is the primary source of government financing around the world. Moreover, as we shall see, the quantitative properties of sovereign debt models with longer maturity bonds bring the model predictions closer to the data. Conceptually, longer maturity debt introduces a novel friction relative to the preceding chapters. Specifically, long-term bonds open the door to "debt dilution." By debt dilution, we mean that bondholders are vulnerable to future fiscal decisions by the government. For example, by issuing additional debt in the future, the original bondholders will see the value of their claims fall due to the increased probability of default. A goal of this chapter is to understand how this channel affects both equilibrium prices and the government's equilibrium fiscal policy. We not only show that long-term bonds can lead to excessive borrowing, we also highlight that the extent of this dilution may be "self-fulfilling." That is, a low-debt and high-debt equilibrium may both be supportable, and which equilibrium is realized depends only on self-fulfilling creditor beliefs about future fiscal policy.

As with the one-period bond model, our approach is to first isolate the key economics using the simple analytical model of Chapter 4. Within this analytical framework, we assume that the government borrows only using a long-term bond whose maturity is taken as a primitive parameter. We discuss the properties of equilibrium and highlight the inefficiency generated by long-term financing.[1]

---

[1]. The inefficiency is a property of Markov equilibria. In the concluding section of this chapter, we discuss an alternative equilibrium concept studied by Dovis (2019) in which long-term debt plays an important role in implementing a constrained efficient allocation.

We then introduce an additional instrument into the framework and allow the government to issue new debt using a short-term bond. We study the maturity choice problem and show that in equilibrium, the government manages its debt portfolio by using only the short-term bond. It does not issue or buy back the long-term bond. We discuss that if the government were to become active in the long-term bond margin, bond prices would adversely move against its trades, generating losses. We also discuss the Pareto gains from restructuring an inherited debt portfolio, the role that holdouts play in a restructuring, and the result that the yield curve is not informative about maturity choice.

We also establish that the primary inefficiency introduced by long-term debt—debt dilution—also generates indeterminacy. In particular, creditor beliefs about future fiscal policy can be self-fulfilling. This contrasts with the uniqueness of the Eaton-Gersovitz equilibrium involving short-term debt. The multiplicity of equilibria highlights not only that do long-term bond prices reflect creditor beliefs about fiscal policy, but that the government's incentive to dilute depends in turn on the equilibrium price schedule it faces. We show that in the standard long-term bond model, this interaction may have multiple equilibrium fixed points.

Finally, we turn to a richer quantitative model to show how the introduction of debt dilution affects the model's quantitative properties. In the concluding section, we discuss why a government would choose to issue long-term bonds.

7.2   Environment

Let us consider again the continuous-time environment described in Chapter 4. As before, let y denote a constant endowment stream, ρ the government's discount rate, and $u(c)$ the government's utility function given consumption flow c.

The only source of risk is the value of default, $V^D \in \{\underline{V}, \overline{V}\}$. Recall that $\underline{V}$ is the normal default value, but with Poisson probability λ, the government has the option to default at the higher value $\overline{V} > \underline{V}$. If the government defaults, its continuation value is $\overline{V}$, while if it forgoes the option to default, it continues to service debt and the default value returns to $\underline{V}$ until the next (random) arrival of $\overline{V}$.

Given a deterministic consumption stream c, government preferences are given by (4.1), which we repeat here:

$$v(t) = \int_t^\infty e^{-(\rho+\lambda)(s-t)} u(c(s)) ds + \lambda \int_t^\infty e^{-(\rho+\lambda)(s-t)} \max\{v(s), \overline{V}\} ds.$$

The government can borrow from an international financial market populated by risk-neutral lenders. As before, we assume that the risk-neutral lenders' discount rate is $r^\star$. For the benchmark analysis we assume $r^\star = \rho$; later, we allow for asymmetry in time preference and generalize to $r^\star \leq \rho$.

The key modification to the environment is the structure of the financial markets. Rather than restricting attention to an instantaneous bond we studied in the decentralization in Chapter 4, we now let the government borrow using an exponential bond. To incorporate maturity in a tractable manner, we follow Leland (1994), Hatchondo and Martinez (2009), and Chatterjee and Eyigungor (2012a) and consider random maturity bonds.[2] Each bond matures with a constant Poisson hazard rate δ, at which point a principal payment of 1 is due. We assume that bonds mature independently such that a deterministic fraction δ of any portfolio of bonds matures each instant.

We normalize the fixed coupon of a bond to be the risk-free rate $r^\star$ so that a risk-free bond has price one.[3] This serves as the upper bound on the price of the sovereign's bond in equilibrium.

The expected maturity of a bond is $1/\delta$. Thus, δ parametrizes the inverse maturity. This formulation implies that each bond that has not yet matured is identical going forward, regardless of when it was issued.[4] Note that $\delta = 0$ corresponds to a perpetuity with a constant coupon and thus has an infinite maturity. The limit as δ approaches ∞ corresponds to the instantaneous bond (i.e., an average maturity of 0 periods).

---

2. Hatchondo and Martinez (2009) introduce a bond with an exponentially decaying coupon. That approach is isomorphic to the random maturity bond.

3. To see this, a bond pays $r^\star$ every period through maturity, at which point it also pays one. The survival probability through t periods is $e^{-\delta t}$, and the probability a bond matures in period t is $\delta e^{-\delta t}$. Discounting at $r^\star$, we have $\int_0^\infty e^{-r^\star t}(r^\star + \delta)e^{-\delta t} dt = 1$.

4. Note as well that δ also parametrizes the Macaulay duration of the bond absent default. A unit measure portfolio of bonds pays $(r^\star + \delta)e^{-\delta t}$ in period t. Discounting at $r^\star$, we have:

$$\int_0^\infty e^{-r^\star t}\left[t(r^\star + \delta)e^{-\delta t} \right] dt = \frac{1}{r^\star + \delta}.$$

7.2.1   The Government's Problem

We continue to focus on Markov equilibria, in which equilibrium objects are functions only of payoff-relevant state variables. In particular, let $b(t)$ denote the face value of outstanding debt at time t, $q(b)$ an equilibrium price schedule that maps the stock of debt into market value, $q(b)b$, and $V(b)$ denote the government's value given b conditional on repayment this period. Let $\mathbb{B} \equiv [-a_{max}, \overline{b}]$ denote the relevant domain of debt, where $\overline{b}$ is the endogenous equilibrium borrowing limit. Specifically, $V(b) \in [\underline{V}, V_{max}] = \mathbb{V}$ for all $b \in \mathbb{B}$, and $V(b) < \underline{V}$ and $q(b) = 0$ for all $b > \overline{b}$. Henceforth, we restrict attention to the relevant equilibrium domain $\mathbb{B}$.

In case of no default, the government finances consumption and coupon payments using its endowment y and new debt issuances. Let $\dot{b} \equiv b'(t)$ denote the change in the face value of debt at time t. A decline of $-\delta b$ is due to a fraction δ of bonds maturing. The additional change, $(\dot{b} + \delta b)$, if any, represents the auction of new debt (or repurchases of debt if negative). Thus, the amount raised at auction from new debt issuances is:

$$q(b) \left(\dot{b} + \delta b \right).$$

The government's budget constraint conditional on no default can then be expressed:

$$c(t) + (r^\star + \delta)b(t) = y + q(b(t)) \left(\dot{b}(t) + \delta b(t) \right),$$

or, suppressing the time argument:

$$\dot{b} = \frac{c + (r^\star + \delta)b - y}{q(b)} - \delta b. \tag{7.1}$$

The government's problem in recursive form can then be stated using the following Hamilton-Jacobi-Bellman equation:

$$\rho V(b) = \max_{c \geq 0} \left\{ u(c) + V'(b)\dot{b} + \mathbb{1}_{[V(b) < \overline{V}]} \lambda \left(\overline{V} - V(b) \right) \right\}, \tag{7.2}$$

where $\dot{b}$ depends on c through (7.1). Note that this is the same problem as (4.13); the lone difference is the presence of long-term bonds in the budget constraint. Assuming c is interior, the first-order condition for consumption is:

$$u'(c) = -V'(b)/q(b). \qquad (7.3)$$

Given V and q, this pins down the equilibrium consumption function $C(b)$.

As in the short-term bond model of Chapter 4, given that $V(b)$ will be decreasing in b, we can define thresholds $\{\underline{b}, \overline{b}\}$ such that $V(\underline{b}) = \overline{V}$ and $V(\overline{b}) = \underline{V}$. Thus, the state space can be divided into a Safe Zone ($b \leq \underline{b}$) and a Crisis Zone $b \in (\underline{b}, \overline{b}]$. In the Safe Zone, the government does not default on the arrival of $\overline{V}$, while in the Crisis Zone the government defaults with probability λ. For $b > \overline{b}$, the government defaults regardless of the default value. This latter case will not be relevant in equilibrium, as $\overline{b}$ is the endogenous debt limit.

7.2.2 Lenders' Break-Even Condition

With long-term bonds, the lender is concerned about more than the probability of default in the next "instant." In particular, it needs to forecast the probability that future coupon and principal payments will be made. Given an equilibrium price schedule q, the government's problem defines a debt path $b(t)$ conditional on repayment through time t. Moreover, the lenders anticipate the government will default on the arrival of $\overline{V}$ if $b \in (\underline{b}, \overline{b}]$. Let

$$\Lambda(b) = \begin{cases} 0 \text{ if } b \leq \underline{b} \\ \lambda \text{ if } b \in (\underline{b}, \overline{b}]. \end{cases} \qquad (7.4)$$

The price is such that lenders are indifferent between holding the bond or selling it:

$$q(b(t)) = \int_t^\infty e^{-(r^\star + \delta)(s-t) - \int_t^s \Lambda(b(v))dv} (r^\star + \delta)ds. \qquad (7.5)$$

The integral reflects that the bond promises a coupon $r^\star$ through maturity. With probability $e^{-\delta(s-t)}$, the bond has not matured by time s, and first matures at time s with probability δ times the survival probability. The payments are also discounted by $\Lambda(b)$, as the bonds become worthless with that hazard rate.

Differentiating with respect to t, we have:

$$q'(b)\dot{b} = [r^\star + \delta + \Lambda(b)]q(b) - (r^\star + \delta). \qquad (7.6)$$

Or, rearranging,

$$r^\star q(b) = r^\star + q'(b)\dot{b} + \delta(1 - q(b)) - \Lambda(b)q(b).$$

The left-hand side is the opportunity cost of holding the bond. The right-hand side is the benefit of holding the bond, which is composed of four terms: the coupon payment, $r^\star$, the instantaneous capital gain in case of no default, $q'(b)\dot{b}$, the net gain from the fraction δ of maturing bonds, $\delta(1 - q(b))$, and the expected capital loss that arises because of default risk, $-\Lambda(b)q(b)$.

An important feature of the above price equation is the capital gain term $q'(b)\dot{b}$. This term is not relevant for short-term debt, as those bonds either paid their full promised value or zero. With long-term bonds, the bond-holders recognize that even if default is not realized, the government may continue to alter the amount of debt outstanding prior to the initial bonds maturing, affecting their price. The capital gain term is why long-term bond-holders may be subject to "debt dilution" by the future fiscal policy of the government.

7.2.3   Equilibrium with Long-Term Bonds

We first define a competitive equilibrium in the current long-term bond environment:

Definition 16 *A Markov competitive equilibrium (MCE) consists of a domain for debt* $\mathbb{B} = [-a_{max}, \bar{b}]$, *a bounded, continuous government value function* V : $\mathbb{B} \to \mathbb{V}$ *and a price schedule* $q : \mathbb{B} \to [0, 1]$ *such that: (i) given q, the repayment value function V is a solution to* (7.2); *(ii) given V, the schedule q satisfies* (7.6); *and (iii)* $V(b) \geq \underline{V}$ *for* $b \in \mathbb{B}$.

7.3   Characterizing Competitive Equilibria

7.3.1   The Safe Zone

We begin our analysis of competitive equilibria by noting that the planning problem in the current environment is the same as the planning problem in Chapter 4. The role of incomplete markets in that planning problem is reflected in the fact that consumption is not contingent on the realization of V^D. It places no other restrictions on the planning problem.[5] The maturity

---

5. This is not the case with income fluctuations. In the pseudo-planning problem (B') of Chapter 5, incomplete markets also restricted continuation values absent default through the

of the bonds does not introduce new constraints, as the ability of the planner to deliver payments to lenders conditional on no default is not affected by it. As before, we will use the constrained efficient allocation as a reference when characterizing the equilibrium.

In the efficient allocation, the Safe Zone is absorbing and consumption is constant. Hence, we conjecture and verify that the same policy holds in equilibrium, and the equilibrium price is one (the risk-free price). Specifically, for $b \leq \underline{b}$, we have:

$$V(b) = \frac{u(y - r^\star b)}{\rho}$$

$$q(b) = 1.$$

The edge of the Safe Zone is determined by $V(\underline{b}) = \overline{V}$, and thus:

$$\underline{b} = \frac{y - u^{-1}(\rho \overline{V})}{r^\star}. \tag{7.7}$$

7.3.2 The Crisis Zone

In the Crisis Zone, recall that in the efficient allocation, the planner chooses a consumption sequence such that the government saves toward the Safe Zone. We now explore a similar conjecture for the equilibrium behavior with long-term bonds. In the Crisis Zone, we can rewrite the government's HJB (7.2) as:

$$(\rho + \lambda)V(b) = H(V'(b), q(b), b),$$

where, for general slope p, price m, and debt b, we define

$$H(p, m, b) \equiv \max_{c \geq 0} \left\{ u(c) + p \left(\frac{c + (r^\star + \delta)b - y}{m} - \delta b \right) + \lambda \overline{V} \right\}. \tag{7.8}$$

The right-hand side is continuous and strictly concave in c, and hence has a unique maximizer. Let $\hat{C}(p, m, b)$ denote the maximizer of (7.8).

An equilibrium in the Crisis Zone solves the following system of two differential equations:

---

implementability condition. This constraint, in general, will be affected by the maturity of the bonds, as the maturity of the bonds changes the spanning of the underlying asset, and hence the set of continuation values that are feasible with a given amount of debt.

$$(\rho + \lambda)V(b) = H(V'(b), q(b), b) \tag{7.9}$$

$$r^\star q(b) = r^\star + q'(b)\dot{b} + \delta(1 - q(b)) - \lambda q(b), \tag{7.10}$$

with

$$\dot{b} = \frac{\hat{C}(V'(b), q(b), b) + (r^\star + \delta)b - y}{q(b)} - \delta b. \tag{7.11}$$

The boundary conditions for the system of ODEs are given by the Safe Zone values:

$$V(\underline{b}) = \overline{V} \tag{7.12}$$

$$q(\underline{b}) = 1. \tag{7.13}$$

Equation (7.9) is an implicit differential equation. The function H is convex in $V'(b)$ (a standard result for HJBs), and hence there are at most two values for $V'(b)$ that solve (7.9) given $V(b)$ and $q(b)$. Only one solution is associated with saving, and hence is consistent with the conjectured equilibrium behavior. This is the same point made in Chapter 4 in connection with equation (4.11) and the determination of the efficient consumption in the Crisis Zone. To mirror that discussion, we can use the first-order condition for consumption, $u'(c) = -V'(b)/q(b)$, to note that the optimal consumption satisfies:

$$(\rho + \lambda)V(b) - \lambda\overline{V} = u(c) - u'(c)\left(c + [r^\star + \delta(1 - q(b))]b - y\right). \tag{7.14}$$

For fixed $(b, q(b))$, the right-hand side of (7.14) is plotted as a function of c in Figure 7.1. The function is convex with slope $-u''(c)q(b)\dot{b}$. The minimum is $c^{ss}(b) = y - [r^\star + \delta(1 - q(b))]b$, the level of consumption that sets $\dot{b} = 0$. For $c < c^{ss}$, we have $\dot{b} < 0$ and the function is decreasing, and vice versa for $c > c^{ss}$. In general, there are two roots to (7.14), one with $\dot{b} < 0$ and one with $\dot{b} > 0$. The latter implies borrowing and is therefore inconsistent with the conjectured equilibrium dynamics of saving toward the Safe Zone. The "saving" root below c^{ss}, denoted $C(b)$, is a valid solution and determines the equilibrium level of consumption at b. We can then set $V'(b) = -q(b)u'(C(b))$.

At some b far enough from the Safe Zone, it may no longer be optimal to save. Specifically, given $\rho = r^\star$, there may exist a b^I such that $C(b^I)$ equals the stationary level of consumption. For $b > b^I$, the optimal consumption is $C(b) = c^{ss}(b) = y - [r^\star + \delta(1 - q(b))]b$, and the associated value is $V(b) = \frac{u(C(b)) + \lambda\overline{V}}{\rho + \lambda}$. As $\dot{b} = 0$ on this region of the Crisis Zone, the associated price is

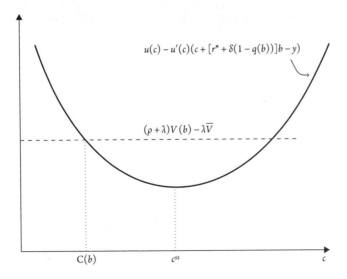

$$u(c) - u'(c)(c + [r^* + \delta(1 - q(b))]b - y)$$

$$(\rho + \lambda)V(b) - \lambda \overline{V}$$

$C(b)$ $\qquad$ c^{ss} $\qquad$ c

FIGURE 7.1. Consumption Choice

Note: The "U"-shaped solid line depicts the right-hand side of equation (7.14) as a function of c. The horizontal dashed line is the left-hand side of (7.14). The intersection labeled $C(b)$ denotes the optimal consumption choice. c^{ss} denotes the consumption associated with $\dot{b} = 0$.

$q(b) = \underline{q} = (r^* + \delta)/(r^* + \delta + \lambda)$. Continuity of V requires the government to be indifferent to a policy of saving toward the Safe Zone versus setting $\dot{b} = 0$ at b^I.

Collecting results, the equilibrium in the Safe Zone is characterized by the government rolling over its debt at risk-free prices. In the Crisis Zone, the government saves near the boundary $\underline{b}$, with values and prices given by the ODE system (7.9) and (7.10). Finally, there may be a level of debt in the Crisis Zone above which the government no longer saves, but rolls over its debt at a constant price $\underline{q} < 1$. The endogenous borrowing limit is pinned down by $V(\bar{b}) = \underline{V}$. We shall solve for equilibria in example economies below. Before doing that, we discuss how the equilibria with long-term bonds differ from the efficient allocation.

7.4 Inefficiency and Long-Term Bonds

As a first step in understanding the inefficiency of long-term bonds, we consider behavior in the Crisis Zone near the boundary $\underline{b}$. Consider a given debt level $b \in (\underline{b}, \bar{b}]$. Let us denote by $T(b) \in \mathbb{R}_{++} \cup \{\infty\}$ the equilibrium time that it takes for the government to reduce the debt down to $\underline{b}$ starting from $b > \underline{b}$; that is, the amount of time to exit the Crisis Zone. With this, it is possible to obtain the price of the bonds. From (7.5), we have

$$q(b) = \int_0^{T(b)} e^{-(r^\star+\delta+\lambda)t}(r^\star + \delta)dt + e^{-(r^\star+\delta+\lambda)T(b)}q(\underline{b}), \qquad (7.15)$$

where the first term in the right-hand side is the present discounted value of payments over the first $T(b)$ periods, where the discounting reflects the hazard rate of default λ in the Crisis Zone; and the second term is the present discounted value of the coupons after period $T(b)$, where, conditionally on reaching that time, there is no longer default risk and the bond is worth $q(\underline{b}) = 1$.

With this, we obtain that

$$q(b) = \frac{r^\star + \delta + e^{-(r^\star+\delta+\lambda)T(b)}\lambda}{r^\star + \delta + \lambda}. \qquad (7.16)$$

This formula is helpful, as it highlights how the price is affected by the equilibrium exit time. The faster the government exits the Crisis Zone, that is, the lower $T(b)$, the higher the price. Note that as $T(b) \to 0$, the price converges to 1, the risk-free price. Similarly, as $T(b) \to \infty$ (so that the government never exits the Crisis Zone), the price converges to $\underline{q} \equiv \frac{r^\star+\delta}{r^\star+\delta+\lambda}$, the lowest possible price in the Crisis Zone.

Now we contrast saving behavior with long-term bonds relative to the efficient allocation. We first do this heuristically and then proceed more formally below. As the Safe Zone is absorbing when $\rho = r^\star$, $\underline{b}$ is independent of maturity, and hence consider a b in the neighborhood of $\underline{b}$ for arbitrary δ. Associated with b and δ is an exit time $T(b)$ and price given by (7.16). Substituting for $q(b)$ in equation (7.14), the equilibrium consumption satisfies:

$$(\rho + \lambda)V(b) - \lambda\overline{V} = u(c) - u'(c)\left(c + (r^\star + \tilde{\lambda}(b))b - y\right), \qquad (7.17)$$

where

$$\tilde{\lambda}(b) = \lambda\delta\left(\frac{1 - e^{-(r^\star+\delta+\lambda)T(b)}}{r^\star + \delta + \lambda}\right). \qquad (7.18)$$

To compare this to the efficient allocation, recall from Chapter 4 that the efficient allocation can be decentralized with short-term (instantaneous) bonds that pay a coupon $r(b) = r^\star + \lambda$ in the Crisis Zone. Moreover, in the neighborhood just above $\underline{b}$, efficient consumption $c^\star$ is constant and satisfies:

$$\rho \overline{V} = u(c^\star) - u'(c^\star) \left(c^\star + (r^\star + \lambda)\underline{b} - y \right). \tag{7.19}$$

Comparing the right-hand side of (7.17) to (7.19), we see that the implicit cost of debt differs by the gap between $\tilde{\lambda}(b)$ versus λ. As $b \downarrow \underline{b}$, $T(b) \to 0$ and we have $\tilde{\lambda}$ discretely less than λ. The left-hand sides of (7.17) and (7.19) both approach $\rho \overline{V}$ as b approaches $\underline{b}$. Thus, the right-hand side of (7.17) is strictly above the right-hand side of (7.19), while the left-hand sides converge to the same value. In terms of Figure 7.1, the convex curve is shifted down in the efficient allocation relative to the equilibrium with long-term bonds, and hence the efficient consumption is lower: $c^\star < C(b)$ for b in the neighborhood above $\underline{b}$. The saving behavior with long-term bonds is "as if" the government faces a lower default premium as it rolls over bonds. This reflects that it is only rolling over a fraction of the face value. The default premium provides the incentive to reduce the risk of default in the decentralization of the efficient allocation, and we see with long-maturity bonds this incentive becomes under-powered.

We now show more formally that the planning solution cannot be decentralized as an equilibrium for *any* non-instantaneous maturity:

Proposition 17 *If the efficient allocation features saving (that is $y > \rho \overline{V}$), then the equilibrium with long-maturity bonds is not constrained efficient.*

Proof. To obtain a contradiction, suppose an equilibrium $\{V, q\}$ with maturity parameter δ decentralizes the efficient allocation. For a given b in the Crisis Zone, let $v = V(b) \in [\underline{V}, \overline{V})$. Efficiency requires $P^\star(v) = q(b)b$, where recall $P^\star$ is the maximum expected present value of payments to lenders as a function of the government's value. Let $c^\star$ denote the efficient consumption level at v, which by premise is the equilibrium consumption level at b. The equilibrium requires that (7.17) is satisfied:

$$(\rho + \lambda)v - \lambda\overline{V} = u(c^\star) - u'(c^\star) \left(c^\star + [r^\star + \delta(1 - q(b))]b - y \right).$$

The HJB from the planning problem (4.7) implies:

$$(\rho + \lambda)v - \lambda\overline{V} = u(c^\star) - u'(c^\star) \left(c^\star + [r^\star + \lambda]P^\star(v) - y \right),$$

where we use the first-order condition $u'(c^\star) = -1/P^{\star\prime}(v)$. Subtracting the two conditions and using the premise $P^\star(v) = q(b)b$, we have

$$0 = u'(c^*) \left[(r^* + \delta + \lambda) - \frac{r^* + \delta}{q(b)} \right] P^*(v). \qquad (7.20)$$

As $P^*(v) > 0$ for $v < \overline{V}$, the term in brackets must be zero for the premise to be valid. This is only the case if $q(b) = \underline{q} = (r^* + \delta)/(r^* + \delta + \lambda)$. Recall that $\underline{q}$ is the break-even price if the government remains in the Crisis Zone indefinitely. However, as long as $y > \rho\overline{V}$, the government saves near the Safe Zone, and on this domain we have $q(b) > \underline{q}$. As b was an arbitrary point in the Crisis Zone, we have a contradiction. Thus, an equilibrium with long-term bonds *cannot be efficient.* □

The fact that the efficient allocation is not an equilibrium in the Crisis Zone is informative about the equilibrium fiscal policy. In particular, consider again a $b > \underline{b}$, with an associated equilibrium value $V(b) = v$ to the government. The inefficiency result guarantees that $P^*(v) > q(b)b$, where q is the equilibrium price function. That is, the expected payments to lenders is reduced in the equilibrium relative to the efficient outcome. For a given government value v, this implies that the probability of default is inefficiently high. As the arrival probability λ is constant, we have that the government spends an inefficiently long period of time in the Crisis Zone. In short, *the government reduces its debt at a slower rate than what is efficient.*

In Chapter 4, we decentralized the efficient allocation with instantaneous bonds. This cannot be done with fixed-rate longer maturity bonds. Intuitively, with instantaneous bonds, the government fully captures the efficiency gains from reducing the debt in the Crisis Zone. This is because it rolls over its entire stock of debt at every instant, and thus pays the full cost of remaining in the Crisis Zone and yields the full benefit of entering the Safe Zone. With longer maturity bonds, a $\delta > 0$ provides some incentive to exit the Crisis Zone, as the fraction maturing will be rolled over at a higher price in the Safe Zone. However, for $\delta < \infty$, the government does not capture the full gain, as some of the gain accrues to the bondholders of non-maturing debt, and thus the incentive to reduce debt is inefficiently weak.

7.5   Maturity Choice, Debt Buybacks, and Restructuring

The inefficiency of long-term bonds raises the question of whether a government could engineer an improvement by buying back outstanding bonds and switching to instantaneous bonds. That is, suppose the government has some legacy long-term bonds issued in previous periods and now considers rebalancing its portfolio to the efficient portfolio of only instantaneous bonds. In this section, we show that the answer is no if we restrict attention to arms-length market transactions, but an improvement could be implemented with a coordinated restructuring. We also establish how this result affects maturity management.[6]

7.5.1   A Modified Planning Problem

Suppose a government has b_ℓ long-term bonds outstanding. For simplicity, we assume these are perpetuities ($\delta = 0$) that promise a coupon $r^\star$ forever. The same result holds for arbitrary $\delta < \infty$, but the notation is messier.

Now suppose the government writes a constrained-efficient contract with a new representative lender. That is, consider a modified planning problem in which the planner maximizes expected payments to the new lenders subject to the government obtaining some value v_0 and subject to a constraint imposed by the presence of legacy lenders. The latter constraint states that absent default, the government must pay promises on b_ℓ.

Specifically, consider the problem:

$$\tilde{P}(v_0; b_\ell) = \sup_{c \in C}\left\{\int_0^\infty e^{-(r^\star+\lambda)t}\left[y - r^\star b_\ell - c(t) + \lambda \mathbb{1}_{[v(t)\geq \overline{V}]}\tilde{P}(v(t); b_\ell)\right]dt\right\}$$

(7.21)

subject to: $v(0) \geq v_0$ and $v(t) \in \mathbb{V}, \forall t$.

Comparing this to the original planning problem of Chapter 4, equation (4.6), the lone difference is that the objective is reduced by payments to legacy bondholders. It is "as if" the endowment is reduced by an amount $r^\star b_\ell$ every period, but with one crucial difference. If the government defaults, the presence of legacy lenders is irrelevant. As the new lender/planner and government both see $r^\star b_\ell$ as a pure loss stemming from repayment, this provides an incentive to deviate from the fully efficient allocation $c^\star(v_0)$ to make default more likely.[7]

---

6. This section draws from Aguiar, Amador, Hopenhayn, and Werning (2019a).

7. See Hatchondo, Roch, and Martinez (2019) for an extension of the planning problem to a model with endowment risk. In particular, they extend the "dual" planning problem introduced in Chapter 5, equation (B') in the context of one-period bonds to an environment with long-term bonds.

In particular, let $Q(b_\ell, v_0, c)$ denote the expected value to legacy lenders given an allocation c:

$$Q(b_\ell, v_0, c) = \int_0^\infty e^{-(r^*+\lambda)t} \left[r^* b_\ell + \lambda \mathbb{1}_{[v(t)\geq \overline{V}]} Q(b_\ell, v(t), c) \right] dt,$$

where $v(t)$ is the government's value along the repayment path given consumption c. Q is the market value of the legacy perpetuities given a path of consumption c. We can rewrite the objective of problem (7.21) as

$$\tilde{P}(v_0; b_\ell) = \sup_{c\in C} \left\{ \int_0^\infty e^{-(r^*+\lambda)t} \left[y - c(t) + \lambda \mathbb{1}_{[v(t)\geq \overline{V}]} \left(\tilde{P}(v(t); b_\ell) \right. \right. \right.$$

$$\left. \left. \left. + Q(b_\ell, v(t), c)) \right] dt - Q(b_\ell, v_0, c) \right\}.$$

Thus, the objective of problem (7.21) is the $P^\star$ planning problem objective minus the market value of legacy bonds. Intuitively, the legacy bondholders will receive their contractual payments as long as the government does not default, and thus their expected present value of payments (which is Q) represents a loss in the new planning problem (7.21). Note that if Q did not depend on the chosen path c, the problem is isomorphic to (4.6) with $P^* = \tilde{P} + Q$; however, as written the optimal allocation in this problem will not in general coincide with (4.6).

Let $c^\star$ denote the constrained efficient allocation given promise v_0 studied in Chapter 4. As the efficient allocation delivers promised value v_0, it is feasible for problem (7.21). Hence,

$$\tilde{P}(v_0; b_\ell) \geq P^\star(v_0) - Q(b_\ell, v_0, c^\star),$$

where $P^\star$ is the constrained efficient value discussed in Chapter 4. The inequality reflects that new lenders can deliver v_0 in a privately optimal manner by lowering the expected payments to legacy lenders Q; that is, by increasing the probability the government defaults.

To characterize the solution to (7.21), let $\tilde{y} \equiv y - r^* b_\ell$. Substituting that into (7.21), we have a problem that is isomorphic to the planning problem (4.6) of Chapter 4, but with a different endowment level. The key distortion in the model of Chapter 4 is the deadweight cost of default: $u(y) - \rho \overline{V}$. In the modified planning problem, the implicit cost is $u(\tilde{y}) - \rho \overline{V} < u(y) - \rho \overline{V}$. Thus, the modified planning problem is like the "true" planning problem under a smaller deadweight cost of default.

With this re-interpretation, the analysis of Chapter 4 yields two insights about the solution to the modified planning problem. One is that the rate at which the government saves is lower, reflecting the smaller deadweight costs of default. This is the result established in Chapter 4, Section 4.4. The second one is about maturity choice, to which we now turn.

7.5.2   Maturity Choice

We now show that the modified planning problem's solution can be decentralized by adding instantaneous bonds to the long-term bond model. In addition, the prediction of the model is that the government will not actively manage its portfolio of long-term debt.

The environment is as follows: the government starts with a portfolio (b_S, b_ℓ), where b_S represents the amount of instantaneous bonds and b_ℓ represents the amount of long-term bonds outstanding. Starting from this portfolio, the government sequentially manages its debt portfolio, choosing the amount of instantaneous bonds to issue, as well as whether to issue or repurchase additional perpetuities, and whether to default or not. In case of a default, all holders of bonds receive a payoff of zero.[8]

The re-interpretation of the planning problem above guides us to the following result. Suppose that the government never issues new long-term bonds or buys back outstanding ones. Under this assumption, we can then decentralize the solution in the modified planning problem in (7.21) with short-term bonds in the same way as we did in Chapter 4, but with the modified income process $\tilde{y} = y - r^* b_\ell$.

But what if the government decides to issue new long-term bonds or to buy back some of the inherited ones? To answer this question, we need to describe the price at which the government buys and sells long-term bonds in equilibrium. For any (b_S, b_ℓ), let $v_0(b_S, b_\ell)$ be such that $b_S = \tilde{P}(v_0(b_S, b_\ell); b_\ell)$. We then solve the modified planning problem in (7.21) and let $c^{MP}(v_0(b_S, b_\ell), b_\ell)$ represent a corresponding solution path for consumption. Let us define the price of the long-term bond to be $q(b_\ell, b_S) = Q(b_\ell, v_0(b_S, b_\ell), c^{MP}(b_S, b_\ell))/b_\ell$. This price represents what a foreign investor is willing to pay to hold a unit of the long-term bond, if the equilibrium

---

8. In the data, the haircuts received by bondholders in a default episode are different depending on the maturity of the bonds they hold. For evidence on this, see Asonuma, Niepelt, and Ranciere (2017).

consumption path corresponds to $c^{MP}(v_0(b_S, b_\ell), b_\ell)$. Note that in this way, we can construct a long-term bond price for different portfolio positions. Because different portfolio positions generate different consumption paths, this long-term bond price is a "schedule" that depends on the current portfolio of outstanding bonds.

It turns out that when facing such prices for its long-term bonds, it is optimal for the government to refrain from trading in the long-term bond market. That is, *it is an equilibrium for the government to manage its total debt without ever issuing or repurchasing long-term bonds*. If the solution calls for savings, then the government pays down its instantaneous position, b_S, until it reaches the Safe Zone, at which point the government's value equals $\overline{V}$.[9] As noted above, the speed at which it approaches the Safe Zone is less than in the constrained efficient allocation, reflecting the presence of legacy long-term bondholders. The legacy long-term bonds are paid their coupon conditional on no default, but are not repurchased and no additional long-term debt is issued.[10] The reason this is the case is the subject of the next section.

7.5.3   *Buybacks vs. Restructuring: The Role of Holdouts*

We can use the diagram in Figure 7.2 to study buybacks, restructuring, and maturity management. The solid line traces out $\tilde{P}(v, b_\ell)$ as a function of long-term debt b_ℓ, holding v constant. As b_ℓ increases, more resources are promised to legacy bondholders, and the expected payments to the new lender are reduced. Hence, the negative slope for a given v.

For a given v, $\tilde{P}$ is convex in b_ℓ. To see this, the promise-keeping constraint implies the planner always has the option of keeping the same consumption allocation in response to an increase in b_ℓ. This lowers the objective linearly in b_ℓ, providing a lower bound on the shape of $\tilde{P}$. However, it may be possible to

---

9. Let $\tilde{V}(b_S, b_\ell)$ be the government's value function in the decentralized equilibrium. If the government reaches zero instantaneous bonds before reaching the Safe Zone, that is, $\tilde{V}(0, b_\ell) < \overline{V}$, then the government simply stays put at this portfolio until the first arrival of $\overline{V}$, at which point it defaults. With zero short-term bonds, the government is not rolling over any debt, and has no incentive to reduce debt further. See Aguiar et al. (2019a) for details.

10. This result also holds if the long-term bonds are not a perpetuity (in which case, the government also pays, in addition to the coupon, the maturing principal when $\delta > 0$). It is actually more general, and independent of the maturity structure of the long-term bonds. See Aguiar et al. (2019a).

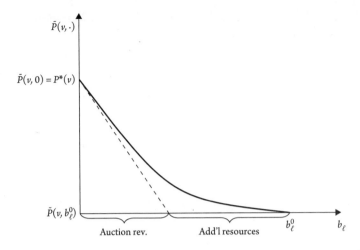

FIGURE 7.2. Debt Buybacks

Note: This figure depicts the discussion of the buyback operation of Section 7.5.3. The downward sloping solid line is $\tilde{P}$ as a function of b_ℓ for a fixed government value v. It traces out the locus of one-period debt (vertical axis) and long-term debt (horizontal axis), holding constant the promised government value v. The dashed line is tangent to the vertical intercept of $\tilde{P}$, and has a slope equal to minus the price of long-term bonds at the vertical intercept.

improve on this outcome by choosing a different allocation, making $\tilde{P}$ decline less than linearly in b_ℓ. This convexity will be useful to understand why buying back legacy bonds is sub-optimal.

The envelope condition applied to problem (7.21) implies $\frac{\partial \tilde{P}}{\partial b_\ell} = -q(b_\ell)$, where q is the market price of an individual perpetuity under the chosen allocation. In the decentralization discussed above, at each b_ℓ, the value $\tilde{P}(v, b_\ell)$ represents the face value of instantaneous debt that delivers v to the government in equilibrium. As we increase b_ℓ and decrease the amount of short-term debt, the price of b_ℓ—or the absolute value of the slope of $\tilde{P}$—decreases. This reflects that the government reduces debt at a slower rate when the portfolio of outstanding debt shifts toward long-term bonds.

Now consider the following thought experiment. Suppose the government starts with only long-term debt of face value b_ℓ^0, which is indicated along the horizontal axis at coordinates $(0, b_\ell^0)$. Suppose, in an effort to achieve an efficient outcome, the government considers issuing short-term debt and buying back all outstanding long-term debt. After such a purchase, the government has only short-term debt and we know from Chapter 4, Section 4.5

that the equilibrium will track the constrained efficient allocation. Does this transaction make sense for the government?

To answer this, note that the vertical intercept, $\tilde{P}(v, 0) = P^\star(v)$, represents the amount of instantaneous debt that delivers the same value, v, as the initial portfolio. If the government issues $P^\star(v)$ in short-term bonds, how much of its long-term bonds can it repurchase? The price of long-term bonds *at the new allocation* is the slope of $\tilde{P}$ at the vertical intercept. Given the convexity of $\tilde{P}$, this is larger (in magnitude) then the slope (price) at the initial allocation $\tilde{b}_\ell^0$. Lenders recognize that a more efficient allocation going forward reduces the probability of default and raises the value of long-term bonds, and therefore demand a higher price to take part in the exchange. At this price, the government can only retire the amount labeled "Auction Rev." The remaining long-term bonds require additional resources. Or, to put it another way, to repurchase existing long-term bonds would require issuing an additional amount of short-term bonds beyond $P^\star(v)$, *lowering* the government's value below v.

Thus, repurchasing long-term bonds is not optimal for the government in equilibrium. This is because it does not capture enough of the benefits of moving to the efficient allocation. The optimal strategy for the government is to be active in managing its stock of instantaneous bonds, but not trade in long-term bonds.

An alternative thought experiment is a coordinated restructuring, in which the lenders *as a group* agree to swap their long-term bonds for short-term bonds at some intermediate price. The exact price depends on how the surplus is split between the government and lenders, but is strictly below the market price of a long-term bond after the exchange.[11] This achieves the efficient outcome, but cannot be done through arms-length market trades. The reason is that an individual long-term bondholder would prefer to hold out and enjoy a larger capital gain, rather than agree to the exchange. Thus, the efficient exchange requires bargaining rather than market buybacks. We show in Section 7.7 that a Pareto improvement can be attained even in the absence

---

11. In particular, an offer of $\tilde{P}(v, 0) = P^\star(v)$ to lenders keeps the government indifferent and gives the lenders all the additional surplus. At the other extreme, if we take a line tangent to $\tilde{P}$ at $(0, b_\ell^0)$ and extend it to the vertical axis, the intercept keeps the lenders' market value constant and gives all the surplus to the government. This uses the fact that market prices at $(0, b_\ell^0)$ are the slope of the tangent line. Anything in between these values is also a valid split of the Pareto improvement.

of short-term bonds, but again must be implemented through a non-market mechanism.

The analysis above implies that efficient restructuring shortens maturity. We highlight two key elements missing in the environment in this section that may alter this result. First, lengthening of maturities is justified empirically because they provided "breathing room" from an ongoing confidence crisis in the government's ability to repay its debts. As we discuss in footnote 34 in the conclusion to this chapter, such extensions can be justified in the presence of rollover risk. Second, restructurings of sovereign debt usually involve official lenders, such as the International Monetary Fund. These renegotiations are usually accompanied by conditions on subsequent fiscal policy and budget deficits (e.g., IMF "conditionality"), which, if credible, reduce the negative incentive effects of long-term borrowing highlighted previously.[12]

The sub-optimality of buybacks is reminiscent of the point made by Bulow and Rogoff (1991). In the Bulow-Rogoff model, there is a non-zero recovery value of defaulting bonds, and repurchases must compensate lenders for this payment as well as the value in repayment. This raises the cost of buybacks for the government. The argument presented above involves dynamic incentives, rather than a recovery value. To see the difference, in the Bulow-Rogoff environment, the government would benefit by issuing *more* debt, diluting the existing creditors' recovery claims. In the current model, issuing more long-term debt is welfare *reducing*, as the price of newly issued long-term bonds will be low in anticipation of the higher probability of default going forward.[13]

This result begs the question of why the government issues long-term bonds in the first place. We discuss this in the concluding section of the chapter.

---

12. For a recent contribution within a quantitative model on the role of maturity in a sovereign debt restructuring, see Dvorkin, Yurdagul, Sapriza, and Sanchez (forthcoming). Also related is Mihalache (2020). For studies of the role of the IMF, see Díaz-Cassou, Erce, and Vázquez-Zamora (2008) and Stefanidis (2020).

13. This can be seen in the diagram by starting at zero long-term debt, point $(0, P^{\star}(v))$, and considering issuing b_ℓ to pay off its short-term debt (moving to point $(b_\ell, 0)$). The price/slope at $(b_\ell, 0)$ is small in magnitude, indicating that the auction revenue would be less than the amount of short-term debt due (trace the tangent at $(b_\ell, 0)$ to the vertical axis to see the gap). Thus, issuing long-term bonds would make achieving v more expensive as well. The optimal strategy is to neither issue nor repurchase long-term bonds.

7.5.4   *The Yield Curve and the Elasticity of the Bond Price*

Section 7.5.2 discussed the incentives for the government to rely on short-term bonds to adjust debt at the margin. It is instructive to relate this conclusion to the equilibrium yield curve (which we define and derive below). In particular, does the slope of the yield curve provide an informative signal about optimal maturity issuance?

Consider a situation in which the government starts with some initial stock of instantaneous bonds, denoted b_S, and of perpetuities, denoted b_ℓ. Again, let v_0 denote the government value such that $b_S = \tilde{P}(v_0; b_\ell)$. Suppose that this portfolio is such that $v_0 < \overline{V}$, and, in the modified planning problem (7.21), it is optimal to increase the government's value until $\overline{V}$. That is, the decentralized equilibrium debt dynamics point toward the Safe Zone such that the government reduces its stock of instantaneous bonds up to the point where $\bar{b}_S = \tilde{P}(\overline{V}, b_\ell)$. Along the way, the instantaneous default probability is initially equal to λ, dropping to zero once the government reaches the Safe Zone.

We can now describe the corresponding equilibrium "yield curve." The yield curve is a commonly used summary of bond prices, describing the theoretical yield of a zero-coupon bond at different maturities. In any equilibrium, we can compute the yield of a hypothetical government bond of arbitrary maturity by asking how much are the international investors willing to pay to hold an infinitesimal unit of such bond. The assumption of an infinitesimal unit implies that the presence of this new bond does not alter the equilibrium behavior of the government—that is, the equilibrium path of government consumption and default remains unaltered. In particular, we consider a hypothetical zero coupon bond that pays 1 at some arbitrary date τ periods in the future.

To price such a bond, let $T(b_S, b_\ell)$ denote the equilibrium time to reach the Safe Zone. The price of the zero coupon bond of maturity τ, denoted q^τ, is then:

$$q^\tau = e^{-r^*\tau} e^{-\lambda \min\{\tau, T(b_S, b_\ell)\}}$$

where the first term is the discount factor of foreign lenders and the second term represents the probability that the government reaches period τ without defaulting. This is the equivalent of equation (7.15) but for a zero coupon bond.

The implied yield i^τ of this bond is given by:

$$e^{-i^\tau} = q^\tau,$$

which is the internal rate of return for an asset that costs q^τ and pays 1 in τ periods. Substituting in for q^τ and solving, we obtain:

$$i^\tau = r^\star + \lambda \frac{\min\{\tau, T(b_S, b_\ell)\}}{\tau}.$$

As we vary the maturity τ, the associated change in i^τ traces out the equilibrium yield curve. Note that the yield of the zero coupon bond equals the risk-free rate, $r^\star$, plus the hazard rate of default *averaged* over the bond's horizon. At the short end of maturities, the yield of the instantaneous bond is $i^0 = r^\star + \lambda$. This exactly corresponds to the instantaneous interest rate demanded by foreign lenders to compensate them for the hazard rate of default λ to which they are exposed. Note that for all maturities in $[0, T(b_S, b_\ell)]$, the yield remains equal to $r^\star + \lambda$. This reflects that the foreign lenders face a constant hazard rate of default of λ for the entire life-span of any bond that matures before the government enters the Safe Zone.

For values of $\tau > T(b_S, b_\ell)$, the yield is $i^\tau = r^\star + \lambda T(b_s, b_\ell)/\tau$. Note that this yield is *decreasing* in τ. For these bonds, the yield reflects the average of time spent in the Crisis Zone and time spent in the Safe Zone until maturity. The longer the maturity, the more weight is on the latter, for which the hazard of default is zero. In the limit as τ approaches infinity, the yield of the zero coupon bond converges to the risk-free rate $r^\star$.[14]

A common and perhaps natural view is that the relative attractiveness of long-term borrowing can be deduced from the slope of the yield curve. If implied yields are lower at longer maturities, such a view goes, then borrowing long term is "cheaper." However, we have just described an equilibrium in which the yield curve slopes down, yet the government finds it sub-optimal to issue longer maturity bonds. In our environment, the yield curve reflects the expected evolution of default probabilities. Because the default probability is decreasing over time (the government eventually reaches the Safe

14. It is worth pointing out that the perpetuity ($\delta = 0$) does not correspond to $\tau = \infty$. The perpetuity has an infinite maturity but features a constant stream of coupon payments (so it is not the limit of a zero coupon bond).

Zone), the yield curve, in our example, is downward sloping. The long bond yield is lower than the short. But this does not impact the result that the government, in equilibrium, does not issue long-term bonds. Thus, *the shape of the yield curve is not an indicator of the benefits or costs of borrowing long-versus short-term.*

The reason is that the yield curve represents the *average* compensation a lender requires to hold a bond of a given maturity. But it does not reflect the *marginal* cost of financing for the government. That is, were the government to issue or buy back long-term bonds, it would also find it optimal to change the time it takes to reach the Safe Zone. This changes default probabilities and, as a result, the equilibrium bond prices. Thus, government fiscal policy changes the equilibrium yield curve, and this change must be factored into the portfolio decision. It is this elasticity of the bond price with respect to the government's policy that deters the government from trading in the long-maturity market: the long-term bond price increases when the government buys back bonds and decreases when it issues new ones.

Sovereign debt crises are typically periods in which the yield curve is downward sloping, yet governments reduce their reliance on longer-maturity issuances.[15] The model rationalizes why this occurs. The yield for long-term bonds does not reflect the *marginal* cost of borrowing long term: if the government were to issue additional long-term bonds, the long-term bond price would fall. It is that elasticity that deters the government from going long and instead points it toward the "short route."

7.6   Example Equilibria

In this section, we show example equilibria with long-term bonds.

---

15. Broner, Lorenzoni, and Schmukler (2013) showed that during times of sovereign crisis in emerging markets (that is, when the spreads of their government bond yields relative to developed countries are high), emerging market governments reduce significantly their issuances of long-term maturity bonds. Arellano and Ramanarayanan (2012) also confirmed this result for four emerging market economies. Perez (2017) extended the sample to incorporate a larger group of emerging markets and found a similar pattern. In the case of the recent sovereign debt crisis in Europe, the yield curve for several of the stressed countries flattened and sometimes inverted (that is, became downward sloping) while at the same time, the corresponding governments significantly reduced or completely eliminated the issuances of long-term bonds at the height of the crisis. See Bocola and Dovis (2019) for a discussion of the Italian case. A similar pattern also holds for Spain and Portugal.

7.6.1   A Closed-Form Solution: The Case of Perpetuities

While $\delta \rightarrow \infty$ replicates the efficient outcome, at the other extreme of $\delta = 0$ (i.e., perpetuities) the government *never* saves out of the Crisis Zone. For this case, we can provide a closed-form solution to the equilibrium. We guess and verify that the equilibrium consumption level $C(b) = y - r^{\star}b$ for all b. From the budget constraint in (7.1), it follows that $\dot{b} = 0$ for all b: the government keeps the debt stationary at all times (including the Crisis Zone). With perpetuities, the government's consumption policy is completely insulated from prices—it simply pays its coupon and never issues or repurchases bonds. This is the opposite extreme from the decentralization from Chapter 4 in which the government rolled over its entire stock of debt at market prices every period.

The government's value function is then:

$$V(b) = \begin{cases} \frac{u(y - r^{\star}b)}{\rho} & \text{, for } b \leq \underline{b} \\ \frac{u(y - r^{\star}b) + \lambda \overline{V}}{\rho + \lambda} & \text{, for } b \in [\underline{b}, \overline{b}] \end{cases}$$

where $\underline{b}$ is as in (7.7). Note that $V(b)$ is continuous. The equilibrium price is then

$$q(b) = \begin{cases} 1 & \text{for } b \leq \underline{b} \\ \frac{r^{\star}}{r^{\star} + \lambda} & \text{for } b \in (\underline{b}, \overline{b}]. \end{cases}$$

This coincides with the stationary allocation associated with equation (4.10) from Chapter 4.

To verify that this is indeed an equilibrium, we need to check that the candidate functions and associated consumption policy satisfy the equilibrium conditions. This is immediate for the Safe Zone. For the Crisis Zone, the price schedule ensures the lenders break even given the conjectured policy of $\dot{b} = 0$. For the government, in the Crisis Zone, we have that $V'(b) = -r^{\star}u'(y - r^{\star}b)/(r^{\star} + \lambda) = -u'(c)q(b)$, satisfying the first-order condition (7.3), and thus, the candidate V satisfies the HJB equation, (7.2). With perpetuities, debt is never rolled over, and the government has no incentives to save out of the Crisis Zone.

Recall that in the discussion of the efficient allocation of Chapter 4 we considered and discarded the stationary policy of (4.10) due to the discontinuity in the planner's value function. A small perturbation of the stationary policy around this discontinuity led to a discrete gain. Why does a similar perturbation not apply for the equilibrium with perpetuities?

To see why, suppose at some point in time (which we normalize to zero), debt is in the Crisis Zone: $b > \underline{b}$. The equilibrium calls for keeping $b(t) = b$ for all $t \geq 0$. However, consider a deviation such that consumption is constant and debt is reduced to $\underline{b}$ over an interval of time $t \in [0, \Delta]$. After Δ, the government is in the Safe Zone and rolls over debt by setting $c = y - r^\star \underline{b}$. Let $\hat{c}$ denote the constant deviation consumption while the government saves.

In the Crisis Zone, the equilibrium price of a perpetuity is $q(b) = \underline{q} = r^\star/(r^\star + \lambda)$ and $\dot{b}(t) = (c + r^\star b(t) - y)/\underline{q}$. Integrating with respect to t over the interval $[0, \Delta]$, we have

$$\hat{c} = y - r^\star b - \frac{r^\star(b - \underline{b})}{e^{(r^\star + \lambda)\Delta} - 1} < y - r^\star b = c^{ss},$$

where $c^{ss} = y - r^\star b$ is the equilibrium (stationary) consumption level at b and associated value $V(b)$. The deviation thus involves reducing consumption below the stationary consumption level for a period of length Δ and then increasing consumption to $y - r^\star \underline{b} > c^{ss}$ thereafter. Letting $\alpha \equiv 1 - e^{-(r^\star + \lambda)\Delta} \in (0, 1)$, we have $c^{ss} = \alpha\hat{c} + (1 - \alpha)(y - r^\star \underline{b})$.

Let $\hat{V}$ denote the value under the deviation. We then have (using $\rho = r^\star$):

$$(r^\star + \lambda)(\hat{V} - V(b)) \equiv (r^\star + \lambda)$$

$$\left[\int_0^\Delta e^{-(r^\star + \lambda)s} \left[u\left(\hat{c}\right) + \lambda\overline{V} \right] ds + e^{-(r^\star + \lambda)\Delta}\overline{V} - V(b) \right]$$

$$= \alpha u(\hat{c}) + (1 - \alpha)u(y - r^\star \underline{b}) - u(\bar{c}),$$

where the second line uses $r^\star \overline{V} = u(y - r^\star \underline{b})$ and $(r^\star + \lambda)V(b) = u(\bar{c}) + \lambda\overline{V}$ as well as the definition of α. As long as u is strictly concave, we have $\hat{V} < V(b)$. Hence this strategy of saving to the edge of the Safe Zone is dominated by the equilibrium strategy of staying put.[16] In this case of perpetuities, the gains

---

16. It is interesting to note that $\hat{V} = V(b)$ if u were linear. In that case, the government would be indifferent between the equilibrium strategy and the proposed alternative strategy. Note, however, that the proposed alternative strategy is not an equilibrium in this case. If it were, then prices during the Δ period would not be constant, and instead, they would be strictly increasing toward one as the amount of debt is reduced and the exit time comes closer. But this means that the alternative strategy of saving to the Safe Zone is *more expensive* for the government (as it is buying back debt) than in the calculation in the text. As the government was indifferent

from saving and the associated decline in default risk are completely captured by legacy bondholders as a capital gain. Thus, there is no incentive in equilibrium for the government to save.

7.6.2   An Example with Intermediate Maturity

For intermediate values of δ (that is, $\infty > \delta > 0$) we do not have a closed-form solution.[17] However, we can explore the properties of the equilibrium using numerical solutions to the ordinary differential equation system (7.9)–(7.10) with boundary conditions (7.12)–(7.13).[18] For the following numerical exercises, we set $r^* = 0.05$, $\lambda = 0.20$, $u = log$, $y = 1$, and $\underline{V} = u((1 - \underline{\tau})y)/r^*$, $\overline{V} = u((1 - \underline{\tau})y)/r^*$ where $\underline{\tau} = 0.05$ and $\overline{\tau} = 0.3$. These examples are illustrative; we turn to a richer and more realistic quantitative version of the model in Section 7.9.

We consider the equilibrium when $\delta = 0.2$, or an expected maturity equal to five units of time. The results are plotted in Figure 7.3. Panels (a) and (b) show the equilibrium of the model for consumption and prices. The three vertical lines correspond to the values of $\underline{b}$, b^I, and $\overline{b}$ in increasing order. The value of b^I is the point where saving out of the Crisis Zone is no longer an equilibrium outcome, and instead, the government remains put in the Crisis Zone. The dynamics can be observed in the consumption policy plot in panel (a). The dashed line in this plot is the stationary consumption level, that is, the level that given current prices would keep $\dot{b} = 0$. For values in the Safe Zone ($b < \underline{b}$) and for values in the Crisis Zone such that $b \in (b^I, \overline{b}]$, equilibrium consumption equals the stationary consumption level. Hence, debt remains constant in these areas, conditional on no default. Note that the slopes of the stationary consumption levels are different in these two regions, reflecting the fact that the interest rate payments are higher (the bond price is lower) in the Crisis Zone than in the Safe Zone because of the default risk. In the savings region of the Crisis Zone ($\underline{b}$, b^I), consumption is below the stationary consumption level, and thus debt is falling over time. Panel (b) shows that indeed the bond price approaches 1 as debt is reduced in this region, reflecting

---

when prices did not adversely move against it, staying put in the Crisis Zone would always be preferable.

17. A closed-form solution is possible when utility is linear. See Section 7.8.

18. The computer codes that solve this model can be found at https://github.com/markaguiar/TheEconomicsofSovereignDebt.

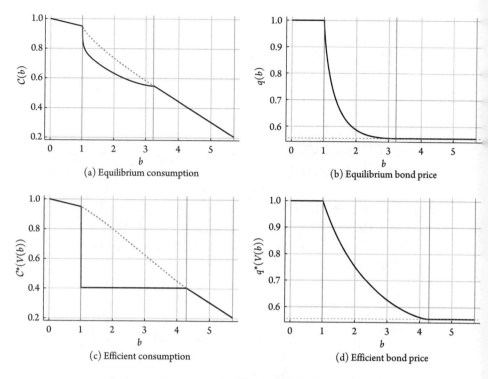

FIGURE 7.3. Equilibrium with $\delta = 0.2$

Note: Equilibrium and efficient allocations for $\delta = 0.2$. The three vertical lines represent $\underline{b}$, b^I, and $\overline{b}$ in increasing order. The value b^I represents the point where the government decides to stop saving and remain instead in the Crisis Zone. In panels (a) and (c), the dashed line represents the stationary consumption level.

the default risk over the lifetime of the bond is going to zero as the exit time from the Crisis Zone goes to zero.

To compare to the equilibrium and constrained efficient allocations, recall that $C^\star(v)$ is the solution to the planner's problem. Panel (c) plots $C^\star(V(b))$ as a function of b. That is, if the planner initiated a consumption sequence designed to maximize the market value of debt while delivering $v = V(b)$ to the government, it would select $C^\star(V(b))$ as its initial consumption.

In the efficient allocation, consumption is constant while exiting in the Crisis Zone. Compare this with the equilibrium behavior: as the exit time approaches, consumption rises (an implication of the fact that the equilibrium incentives to exit are reduced as the current bond price approaches 1).

Associated with an efficient consumption sequence is an exit time $T^\star(V(b))$. That is, starting from $v = V(b)$, $T^\star$ is the duration under the constrained efficient allocation until $v(t) = \overline{V}$. Substituting $T^\star$ into (7.16), we obtain the value of a bond, $q^\star(V(b))$, *if* the constrained efficient allocation were chosen starting from $v = V(b)$. This price is depicted in panel (d), which shows the effect of the efficient consumption policy on the value of the long-term bond. The price is higher in the efficient allocation with respect to the equilibrium, as the exit time from the Crisis Zone is correspondingly lower.

7.7   The Pareto Frontier and the Debt Laffer Curve

In Section 7.5, we showed that coordinated restructuring to shorter maturities can generate a Pareto improvement. In this section, we show that even without using alternative maturities, a Pareto improvement can be achieved through debt *forgiveness*.

The point can be made explicitly using the closed-form solution of the perpetuities equilibrium presented in Section 7.6.1. The fact that equilibrium consumption is the stationary level with perpetuities implies there is a discontinuity in the price of debt at $\underline{b}$. For $b \leq \underline{b}$, the price is one. For $b > \underline{b}$, the price is $r^\star/(r^\star + \lambda) < 1$. This implies a discontinuity in the market value of debt at $\underline{b}$ as long as $\underline{b} > 0$, which is the same discontinuity discussed in Chapter 4 when comparing $P^\star$ to P^{ss} in the neighborhood of $\overline{V}$. Hence, a small reduction in debt around the default threshold increases the value of the government at the same time it generates a discontinuous increase in the value to the lenders. If all the lenders and the government could coordinate, they could renegotiate the debt down, and the value to all would increase. Indeed, near the Safe Zone threshold, a partial debt forgiveness generates a discrete jump in the market value of debt. In equilibrium, however, this debt reduction does not occur as the government has no incentives to reduce (or, in this case with perpetuities, buy back) any portion of the outstanding debt.

Another way of stating this property is that the debt "Laffer curve" may be downward sloping. The debt Laffer curve plots market value of bonds against face value. In the perpetuities case, the discontinuity in price at $\underline{b}$ implies the Laffer curve also has a downward discontinuity at $\underline{b}$. This is a property of long-term debt models with general maturity.

Figure 7.4 plots the debt Laffer curve for the $\delta = 0.2$ case solved numerically in Section 7.6.2. While for most of the debt domain, market value

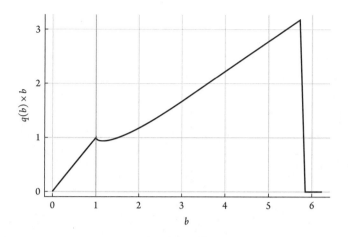

FIGURE 7.4. Equilibrium Debt Laffer Curve

Note: Debt Laffer curve for $\delta = 0.2$. The vertical line represents $\underline{b}$, the edge of the Safe Zone.

increases with face value, this is not the case near the boundary of the Safe Zone. The slow dynamics combined with the hazard of default lowers the expected payments to bondholders below what they would achieve if debt were lower.[19]

This relationship shows that, around the Safe Zone threshold, there are pairs of distinct debt levels that deliver *the same market value* to the lenders. Consider, for example, the pair $\underline{b}$ and $b_0 > \underline{b}$, where $\underline{b}$ is the boundary of the Safe Zone. For b_0 close enough to $\underline{b}$, we have $q(b_0)b_0 < q(\underline{b})\underline{b} = \underline{b}$. It would be a Pareto improvement for the government and all the lenders to swap the current amount of bonds b_0 for a new amount equal to $\underline{b}$. This delivers a higher market value and a higher value to the government. *This swap cannot happen in equilibrium*: to reduce the debt from b_0 to $\underline{b}$, in equilibrium, the government must buy bonds back. Given that those bonds have a positive price, the government must spend resources—making this strategy suboptimal.[20]

19. Note that the market value decreases again at $b \geq \bar{b}$. This is because the price is zero on this domain as default would be immediate. Differently from the area around the Safe Zone, these high values of debt are never chosen in equilibrium as they exceed the endogenous borrowing limit.

20. Hatchondo, Martinez, and Padilla (2014) show evidence that there are debt restructurings in the data that reduce the face value of debt but generate an increase in the ex post market value of outstanding claims. They construct a quantitative model in which lenders and

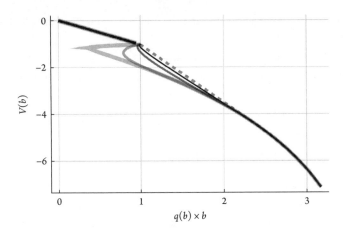

FIGURE 7.5. Pareto Frontier and Equilibrium Values

Note: Each solid line traces out pairs of equilibrium values, $v = V(b)$ and $q(b)b$, for the government and lenders as we vary b. Each solid line represents an equilibrium with maturity parameter $\delta \in (0.02, 0.1, 0.3, 0.7)$ where thicker lines represent lower values of δ. The dashed line represents the constrained efficient frontier. The equilibrium at the threshold of the Safe Zone is always on the frontier at $q(b)b = 1$.

To assess the efficiency of the equilibrium, we plot the Pareto frontier between the government and lenders. Figure 7.5 plots $v = V(b)$ against the market value of debt, $q(b)b$. The latter is the value to lenders, and hence this diagram traces out the respective values the equilibrium delivers to the government and lenders. The figure does this for several maturities: $\delta \in \{0.02, 0.1, 0.3, 0.7\}$. The thicker the solid lines, the lower is δ and the longer is expected maturity. For reference, the Safe Zone boundary is associated with a market value of one, regardless of maturity.

The constrained Pareto frontier is given by the dashed line. This corresponds to the planning problem solved in Chapter 4; specifically, it depicts the same points as Figure 4.1 panel (a) of Chapter 4, but with the axes switched.

As discussed above, the equilibrium values lie below the frontier when the efficient allocation calls for saving. More strikingly, *close to the edge of the Safe Zone, the equilibrium payoff frontier is upward sloping!* As noted above, it would

---

the government are allowed to restructure existing bonds with some constant hazard probability. From the above logic, this is an ex post Pareto improvement. Interestingly, Hatchondo et al.'s (2014) quantitative model suggests that allowing for this possibility may *reduce* ex ante welfare. This reflects that debt restructurings weaken the incentive to reduce debt along the equilibrium path.

be better to forgive some of the debt in this area, which raises the payoff to both lenders and the government.

As δ increases (maturity shortens and the lines become thinner), the inefficiency is reduced, and the equilibrium payoff frontier converges toward the efficient one. As we have established in Chapter 4, full efficiency is achieved in the limit as $\delta \to \infty$.

7.8   Self-Fulfilling Debt Dilution

In Chapter 6, we explored self-fulfilling runs and failed auctions. These crises feature a "static" multiplicity. By that, we mean the multiplicity does not involve different beliefs about *future* equilibrium behavior, but does involve a coordination problem in the current-period auction.

Dilution introduces a "dynamic" multiplicity, in which expectations about future equilibrium behavior take center stage.[21] The indeterminacy involves the extent to which the government will dilute existing long-term bondholders going forward. Depending on self-fulfilling beliefs, the government either pursues a conservative fiscal policy that reduces debt or pursues a profligate policy of high debt and eventual default. Which outcome is observed in equilibrium is not pinned down by fundamentals, but instead depends on self-fulfilling beliefs among market participants (creditors and government) about future behavior.

We shall see that long-term debt is crucial for this "self-fulfilling dilution." For this reason, it provides a stark contrast to the rollover crises in the Cole-Kehoe paradigm of Chapter 6. In the latter, longer maturities (for a given face value) provide safety against failed auctions, as the government rolls over only a fraction (if any) of debt in a period. As we shall see, the dynamic multiplicity study here arises *precisely because the government does not roll over the debt frequently enough.*

7.8.1   *Environment*

We continue with our continuous-time analytical model. We make two changes, one substantive and one for transparency. The substantive change is that we allow the government to be more impatient than lenders: $\rho \geq r^{\star}$,

21. This section draws on Aguiar and Amador (2020). See Stangebye (2020) for a related discussion of multiplicity with long-term bonds.

where ρ is the discount factor of the government and r^* is the risk-free interest rate. As we shall establish, multiplicity in this framework rests on a relatively impatient government. For transparency, we assume the government has linear felicity: $u(c) = c$. This allows for convenient closed-form expressions, but does not otherwise play a role in generating multiplicity. With linear utility, consumption may not be interior. We assume consumption is chosen from a compact set, $[\underline{C}, \overline{C}]$, and then take limits as $\underline{C} \to -\infty$ and $\overline{C} \to \infty$. In the online appendix to Aguiar and Amador (2020), we present the model with finite bounds.

7.8.2 Efficient Allocations with Relative Impatience

In Chapter 4 we solved for a constrained efficient allocation. Recall that the planning problem solves the following HJB equation:

$$(r^* + \mathbb{1}_{[v < \overline{V}]}\lambda)P^*(v) = \max_{c \in [\underline{C}, \overline{C}]} \left\{ y - c + P^{*\prime}(v)\dot{v} \right\},$$

where, with linear utility, $\dot{v} = -c + \rho v - \mathbb{1}_{[v < \overline{V}]}\lambda\left[\overline{V} - v\right]$.

For the case $\rho = r^*$, as we saw before, if $v \geq \overline{V}$, the optimal allocation is to set $\dot{v} = 0$ (and $c = \rho v$) and never default. If $\rho > r^*$, the government may be sufficiently impatient that avoiding no default is no longer efficient. That is, it may be efficient to give the government higher initial consumption at the cost of future default. We therefore characterize two candidate allocations and then establish under which parametrizations either is optimal.

Borrowing Allocation. Relative impatience suggests a novel allocation as a candidate for efficiency. Specifically, a "borrowing" allocation in which the planner frontloads consumption until the value promised to the government reaches its lowest value, $v = \underline{V}$. Letting a subscript B denote the efficient *borrowing* allocation, we have $C_B^*(v) = \overline{C}$ for $v > \underline{V}$, and $C_B^*(\underline{V}) = c^{ss}(\underline{V})$, where we recall from Chapter 4 that c^{ss} is the consumption that sets $\dot{v} = 0$. With linear utility, $c^{ss}(\underline{V}) = \rho\underline{V} - \lambda(\overline{V} - \underline{V})$.

For $v > \underline{V}$ as $\overline{C} \to \infty$, the transition from v to $\underline{V}$ occurs immediately, and the allocation approaches a lump-sum payment to the government of $v - \underline{V}$, after which the government receives $c^{ss}(\underline{V})$ until the first arrival of $\overline{V}$, at which point it defaults.

The corresponding value to the planner/lenders when $\overline{C} \to \infty$ is:

$$P_B^\star(v) = -(v - \underline{V}) + P_B^\star(\underline{V})$$

$$= -(v - \underline{V}) + \frac{y - c^{ss}(\underline{V})}{r^\star + \lambda}, \qquad (7.22)$$

for $v \in \mathbb{V} = [\underline{V}, V_{max}]$. This is the value to planner/lenders of giving the government a lump-sum payment of $v - \underline{V}$ and then receiving $y - c^{ss}(\underline{V})$ until the government defaults.

Saving Allocation. The alternative allocation features saving toward the safe region, as was the case in Chapter 4. We call this an efficient "saving" allocation. The key feature that distinguishes this allocation from the borrowing allocation is that the Safe Zone is absorbing: that is, at $v = \overline{V}$, we have $\dot{v} = 0$ and $c = \rho \overline{V}$. This may be optimal even if $\rho > r^\star$, as indulging the government's relative impatience exposes the allocation to deadweight losses due to default risk.

Letting a subscript S indicate the efficient "savings" allocation, we have $C_S^\star(\overline{V}) = c^{ss}(\overline{V}) = \rho \overline{V}$, and $P_S^\star(\overline{V}) = (y - \rho \overline{V})/r^\star$.

For $v > \overline{V}$, as utility is linear and $\rho \geq r^\star$, it is without loss (and strictly optimal if $\rho > r^\star$) to frontload the government's consumption until $v = \overline{V}$. That is, $C_S^\star(v) = \overline{C}$ for $v > \overline{V}$. For $v < \overline{V}$, the savings allocation conjectures that the planner sets $\dot{v} > 0$ until $v = \overline{V}$. Given the linearity, we conjecture that while saving, $C_S^\star(v) = \underline{C}$, which is the fastest trajectory to the Safe Zone.

The corresponding value to the planner/lenders when $\overline{C} \to \infty$ and $\underline{C} \to -\infty$ is:

$$P_S^\star(v) = -(v - \overline{V}) + P_S^\star(\overline{V})$$

$$= -(v - \overline{V}) + \frac{y - \rho \overline{V}}{r^\star}, \qquad (7.23)$$

for $v \in \mathbb{V} = [\underline{V}, V_{max}]$.

This is the value to planner/lenders of giving the government (or receiving, if negative) a lump-sum payment $v - \overline{V}$ and then receiving $y - \rho \overline{V} \geq 0$ thereafter.

Efficiency. We can now turn to the question of whether and when saving is efficient relative to borrowing. We restrict attention to the limit case where $\overline{C} \to \infty$ and $\underline{C} \to -\infty$. $P_S^\star$ and $P_B^\star$ are linear functions that have the same slope but potentially different intercepts. Hence, it is sufficient to compare the two possible allocations at a single point. The crucial point of comparison for finite $\{\underline{C}, \overline{C}\}$ is $\overline{V}$.[22] With a little algebra, we have for all v

$$P_S^\star(v) \geq P_B^\star(v) \Longleftrightarrow P_S^\star(\overline{V}) \geq P_B^\star(\overline{V}) \Longleftrightarrow \frac{\lambda\left(y - \rho\overline{V}\right)}{r^\star} \geq (\rho - r^\star)\left(\overline{V} - \underline{V}\right).$$

The left-hand side of the last inequality is a measure of how costly is default. Recall that $y - \rho\overline{V}$ is a measure of the deadweight costs of default. The larger this quantity (times the probability λ of default), the greater the incentive to pursue the saving allocation. The right-hand side involves $\rho - r^\star$, which measures the relative impatience of the government. The larger this value, the greater the incentive to have the government consume earlier rather than later. Whether the efficient allocation features borrowing or saving thus turns only on this tradeoff.

7.8.3 Competitive Equilibria Revisited

We construct competitive equilibria following the same procedure as the efficient allocations. That is, we conjecture either a "borrowing" or "saving" equilibrium, and then verify when either satisfies the conditions for equilibrium set out in Definition 16. In particular, a candidate $\{V, q\}$ must satisfy the government's HJB (7.2) and the break-even condition (7.5).

Borrowing Equilibrium Conjecture. To construct a "borrowing equilibrium" conjecture, we assume that the government always borrows to its borrowing limit, $\overline{b}_B$, where again we use the subscript "B" to denote a borrowing allocation. Specifically, the government sets $C_B(b) = \overline{C}$ for $b < \overline{b}_B$, and then sets $\dot{b} = 0$ at $\overline{b}_B$. This allocation coincides with the efficient borrowing allocation described in the previous subsection. To simplify the calculations, in what follows we again take the limit as $\overline{C} \to \infty$.

The associated bond price is

$$q_B(b) = \underline{q} \equiv \frac{r^\star + \delta}{r^\star + \delta + \lambda}$$

for all $b \in (0, \overline{b}_B]$.

---

22. See Aguiar and Amador (2020) for the formal statement.

To understand the above price, note that the Crisis Zone is absorbing, and thus in this zone, the bond price is the value of receiving the coupon $r^\star$ and principal δ until the first arrival of $\overline{V}$, which happens with constant hazard λ and at which point the bonds become worthless. Now, because $\overline{C} \to \infty$, the government reaches the borrowing limit arbitrarily fast starting from any v outside of the Crisis Zone. Thus the bond price converges to $q_B(b) = \underline{q}$ for all $b \in (0, \overline{b}_B]$.

Let $V_B(b)$ denote the government's value function in the conjectured borrowing equilibrium. As the policy is the same as in the efficient borrowing allocation, the associated values to the government and lenders must also be the same. In particular, if $V_B(b) = v$, then $q_B(b)b = P_B^\star(v)$. Using this and inverting (7.22), we have:

$$V_B(b) = \underline{V} + \underline{q}(\overline{b}_B - b). \tag{7.24}$$

Intuitively, the government issues $\overline{b}_B - b$ in debt, consumes it in lump-sum fashion, and then has value $\underline{V}$ thereafter. To obtain the thresholds $\{\underline{b}_B, \overline{b}_B\}$, where $\underline{b}_B$ is the Safe Zone threshold in the borrowing equilibrium, we use the indifference conditions $V_B(\underline{b}_B) = \overline{V}$ and $V_B(\overline{b}_B) = \underline{V}$, which in this case imply $\underline{b}_B = P_B^\star(\overline{V})/\underline{q}$ and $\overline{b}_B = P_B^\star(\underline{V})/\underline{q}$.

To verify if $\{q_B, V_B\}$ is a valid equilibrium, note that $\underline{q}$ satisfies the break-even condition under the conjectured consumption policy. The other requirement is that V_B satisfy the government's HJB (7.2). The first-order condition for consumption is satisfied given the conjectured V_B and q_B. However, it also must be the case that $V_B(b)$ for any $b \leq \underline{b}_B$ dominates staying put in the Safe Zone.

The necessary and sufficient condition for borrowing to be a valid equilibrium is:[23]

$$V_B(b) \geq \frac{y - [r + \delta(1 - \underline{q})]b}{\rho} \text{ for all } b \in [0, \underline{b}_B]. \tag{7.25}$$

The right-hand side is the value to the government of keeping debt constant (rolling over the debt) in the Safe Zone forever at price $q_B(b) = \underline{q}$. This price incorporates the equilibrium conjecture that the government borrows into

23. This follows from Proposition 3 in Aguiar and Amador (2020).

the Crisis Zone. Differently from the planning problem, a government contemplating setting $\dot{b}=0$ in the Safe Zone necessarily takes into account at what equilibrium price it rolls over debt.

The planning problem effectively evaluates staying in the Safe Zone at risk-free prices. In particular, as discussed before, borrowing is efficient if $P_B^\star(\overline{V}) \geq P_S^\star(\overline{V})$, or equivalently, if

$$P_B^\star(\overline{V}) \geq \frac{y - \rho\overline{V}}{r^\star} \iff \overline{V} \geq \frac{1}{\rho}\left(y - r^\star(\underline{q} \times \underline{b}_B)\right). \qquad (7.26)$$

To interpret the difference between (7.25) and (7.26), evaluate the former at $\underline{b}_B$ (using $V(\underline{b}_B) = \overline{V}$:

$$\overline{V} \geq \frac{1}{\rho}\left[y - \left(\frac{r^\star + \delta(1 - \underline{q})}{\underline{q}}\right)(\underline{q} \times \underline{b}_B)\right].$$

Comparing this with (7.26), we see that efficiency evaluates the alternative strategy of staying put in the Safe Zone using the risk-free interest rate paid on a given lender's value $\underline{q}\underline{b}_B$. The government, in equilibrium, however, evaluates the alternative to borrowing at market prices, which require a strictly greater implicit rate of return for the given market value. This reflects that creditors anticipate the government to borrow and default, and price bonds accordingly. These beliefs (and prices) are held fixed by the government when considering alternative fiscal policies.

This gap between efficiency and equilibrium arises because the government cannot credibly commit to remain in the Safe Zone, and therefore considers the alternative to borrowing to be rolling over debt at low equilibrium prices. This reduces the temptation to remain in the Safe Zone, even when doing so is efficient. Thus, borrowing can be an equilibrium outcome even if the borrowing allocation is inefficient.

Note that $q_B(b)$ is increasing in δ (or decreasing in expected maturity). Thus, if borrowing is an equilibrium for a given δ_0, it is also an equilibrium for any $\delta < \delta_0$. Conversely, as $\delta \to \infty$, the equilibrium coincides with the planning problem, as in Chapter 4.[24]

Saving Equilibrium Conjecture. The saving equilibrium tracks the case of $\rho = r^\star$ described in Section 7.2.3. That is, we conjecture that the Safe Zone is

---

24. The limit of $\delta \to \infty$ is taken before letting $\overline{C} \to \infty$, so bonds are maturing arbitrarily fast relative to debt dynamics. See Aguiar and Amador (2020) for details.

absorbing and that for an interval of debt next to the Safe Zone threshold, the government chooses to reduce its debt until it reaches the Safe Zone. However, differently than the efficient saving allocation, the government does not save as quickly as feasible, despite the linear utility. In fact, Aguiar and Amador (2020) show that in an equilibrium $\dot{b} \geq -\delta b$; that is, the government never saves faster than the rate at which debt matures, echoing the "no buyback" logic of Section 7.5.

Given this conjecture, prices are risk-free in the Safe Zone. The boundary of the Safe Zone, $\underline{b}_S$, is therefore pinned down by $\overline{V} = (y - r^\star \underline{b}_S)/\rho$, which is the value of keeping debt constant at $\underline{b}_S$, rolling it over at risk-free prices forever. Note that this threshold coincides with the efficient saving allocation threshold.

To check that saving is a valid equilibrium, we need to verify that saving into the Safe Zone dominates borrowing out of the Safe Zone. It turns out that it is necessary and sufficient to verify that at the boundary of the Safe Zone, the value of saving dominates the value from the borrowing equilibrium.[25] That is, the saving equilibrium conjecture is an equilibrium if and only if $V_S(\underline{b}_S) \geq V_B(\underline{b}_S)$.

Note that $V_S(\underline{b}_S) = \overline{V} = V_B(\underline{b}_B)$ by the definition of $\underline{b}_i$, $i = S, B$. Thus, the condition for a saving equilibrium is equivalent to $V_B(\underline{b}_S) \leq V_B(\underline{b}_B) = \overline{V}$, or, as V_B is strictly decreasing,

$$\underline{b}_S = \frac{y - \rho \overline{V}}{r^\star} \geq \underline{b}_B.$$

This states that in terms of *face value*, the saving equilibrium Safe Zone is larger than that of the borrowing equilibrium.

Let us compare this condition with the condition for the efficiency of the saving allocation. The latter is that the *market value* at the threshold is greater for the saving allocation than the borrowing allocation: $P_S^\star(\overline{V}) \geq P_B^\star(\overline{V})$. As $P_S^\star(\overline{V}) = \underline{b}_S$ and $P_B^\star(\overline{V}) = \underline{q}\underline{b}_B$, efficiency of saving requires

$$\underline{b}_S \geq \underline{q} \times \underline{b}_B.$$

Thus, as $\underline{q} < 1$ the condition for saving to be an equilibrium imposes a higher threshold than for saving to be efficient. That is, efficiency of the saving allocation is a necessary but not sufficient condition for the saving equilibrium:

---

25. This follows from Proposition 5 of Aguiar and Amador (2020).

it may be privately optimal for the government to borrow, but not socially optimal.

Multiplicity. Working with the conditions, one can show that there is a region of the parameter space in which a saving and borrowing equilibrium can both be supported. For this, saving must be efficient, which requires that the deadweight costs of default $(\lambda(y - \rho\overline{V}))$ dominate impatience $(\rho - r^\star)$. This ensures that for very short maturity debt, saving is the only equilibrium. However, as δ falls (maturity lengthens), the borrowing equilibrium becomes viable as well if $\rho > r^\star$. Thus, for intermediate values of δ given deadweight costs and $\rho > r^\star$, both equilbria can be supported.

The source of the multiplicity is that equilibrium prices depend on creditor beliefs about *future* fiscal policy. If they anticipate future dilution, prices in the Safe Zone are low and the government has no incentive to reduce the likelihood of default by deleveraging. If they anticipate that the government remains in the Safe Zone, deleveraging is rewarded by a high price once the Safe Zone is reached. Thus, creditor beliefs, through equilibrium prices, generate self-fulfilling debt dynamics.[26]

This source of multiplicity has novel implications for third-party policies. Recall from Chapter 6 that a price floor promised by, for example, the International Monetary Fund or European Central Bank can eliminate the crisis equilibrium without costing resources in equilibrium. A price floor in the current context has perverse consequences. The saving equilibrium is supported by the large differential in prices between the Safe Zone and the Crisis Zone. The steeply declining price schedule punishes borrowing and rewards saving. A price floor that extends into the Crisis Zone deters saving and may actually select the borrowing equilibrium. Moreover, the third party will have to expend resources to defend the floor. The appropriate policy is for the third party to guarantee a high price *conditional* on the government reducing its debt sufficiently. This mimics the incentives provided by the saving equilibrium price schedule and can eliminate the borrowing equilibrium.

---

26. The multiplicity thus arises because of the ability of the government to adjust its spending decision to market prices. Lorenzoni and Werning (2019) emphasized instead the inability of the government to react as a potential source of multiplicity. In Aguiar and Amador (2020), section VII, we discuss how introducing a lower bound on consumption in the environment of this section can generate a failed auction multiplicity, as emphasized by Cole-Kehoe. See also the work Stefanidis and Paluszynski (2020) studying the role of adjustment frictions in spending in generating a "borrow into default" pattern in a quantitative framework.

7.9   Quantitative Models

Comparing the model just presented to that of Chapter 4. The key difference is that longer maturities discourage the government from reducing the probability of default; that is, the saving motive is dampened. We now turn to full-blown quantitative versions of the model with long-term bonds.[27] The insights from the analytical model are all clearly reflected in the quantitative implications of the long-term bond model.

We revisit the environments presented in Chapter 5. Other than allowing for longer maturity bonds, the only additional modification to the environment is augmenting the endowment process. In particular, following Chatterjee and Eyigungor (2012a), let x_t denote the total endowment realization in period t, with

$$x_t = y_t + z_t.$$

The first component, y_t, follows the same process as in Chapter 5. The second component, z_t, is *iid* over time and drawn from a continuous distribution. This additional shock is introduced for computational reasons, as explained in detail in Chatterjee and Eyigungor (2012a). Let $s = (y, z)$ denote the exogenous state, and let $\mathbb{E}_s$ denote expectation over the next period's state conditional on today's state being s.

In discrete time, a bond at time t matures in $t + 1$ with probability $\delta \in [0, 1]$. If it matures, it pays off the face value of the bond, which is normalized to one. With probability $1 - \delta$, the bond pays a coupon κ. The corresponding risk-free price of a bond is $q^{RF} \equiv (\delta + (1 - \delta)\kappa)/(r^\star + \delta)$.[28]

The government's Bellman equation conditional on repayment is:

$$V^R(s, b) = \max_{c \geq 0, b' \leq \overline{B}} \left\{ u(c) + \beta \mathbb{E}_s \max \left\{ V^R(s', b'), V^D(s') \right\} \right\} \tag{G}$$

subject to:

$$c \leq y(s) + z(s) - \delta b - \kappa(1 - \delta)b + q(s, b')(b' - (1 - \delta)b).$$

27. The computer codes for all quantitative models can be found at https://github.com/markaguiar/TheEconomicsofSovereignDebt.

28. It is important to highlight that the value of κ is effectively a normalization of what is promised to a unit of face value in the model. Changing the value of κ changes the contract that corresponds to a bond of face value 1, but does not alter the solution after appropriate re-scaling face values and prices. In the previous subsections, we normalized the risk-free price

This is the same as the one-period model with the exception of the budget constraint. The term $b' - (1 - \delta)b$ represents the amount of debt issued at auction. A fraction δ of b is paid out in principal and the remaining fraction receives coupon κ. Let $\mathcal{B}(s, b)$ denote the government's debt-issuance policy function.

The break-even condition for lenders is:

$$(1 + r^\star)q(s, b) = \mathbb{E}_s \mathbb{1}_{[V(b,s') \geq V^D(s')]} \left\{ \delta + (1 - \delta)[\kappa + q(s', \mathcal{B}(s', b))] \right\}.$$

The term on the left is the opportunity cost of purchasing the bond at price q. The left-hand side is the expected value of the bond's return next period. In each state, the indicator function $\mathbb{1}_{[(.)]}$ takes the value one if the government repays and zero otherwise. Conditional on repayment, the lender receives coupon κ on non-maturing debt plus the principal on a fraction δ of the bond.[29] The final term is novel to long-term debt. Namely, the lender anticipates the government will issue $\mathcal{B}(s', b)$ in state s' given that it is bringing in debt of b, and hence the market value of the non-maturing $1 - \delta$ fraction of bonds has value $q(s', \mathcal{B}(s', b))$. The fact that the government's debt-issuance policy function (and not just its default policy) as well as the next period price schedule appears in the break-even condition makes the long-maturity model much more difficult to compute.

The calibration is the same as the quadratic cost model of Chapter 5 (Model II) and follows Chatterjee and Eyigungor (2012a). In particular, a period is a quarter. We set $R = 1.01$ and $\beta = 0.954$. The process for $\log y$ is an (approximated) AR(1) with $\rho_y = 0.9485$ and a standard deviation for the innovation equal to 0.0271. The iid income shock z_t is drawn from a truncated Normal distribution with mean zero and standard deviation $\sigma_z = 0.003$, and truncation points $\pm 2\sigma_z$. Such a small magnitude for σ_z implies that the shock z_t plays little role in the business cycle moments of the model, but is nevertheless useful for computation, as discussed in Chatterjee and Eyigungor (2012a).

---

to 1, which in this case requires setting $\kappa = r^\star/(1 - \delta)$. However, in this subsection, we follow the quantitative literature and let κ be determined by the actual profile of government bonds.

29. We can think of q as the price of a unit measure of individual bonds with idiosyncratic maturity probability of δ. Alternatively, we can think of a single unit and δ is the probability it matures. For risk-neutral lenders, the expected value is the same.

The quadratic default punishment is the same as in Chapter 5. Specifically,

$$y^D = y - \max\left\{0, -0.188y + 0.246y^2\right\}.$$

If the government defaults at time t, the z_t shock is set to its lowest value $(-2\sigma_z)$, and then for $t+1$ onward resumes being drawn from its baseline distribution.[30] The re-entry hazard rate is $\theta = 0.0385$.

We set the coupon payment $\kappa = 0.03$ and the expected maturity to five years ($\delta = 0.05$ quarterly).[31] For comparison, we shall recompute the model with $\delta = 1$ (one-period bonds) and $\delta = 0.025$ (ten-year bonds).

Figure 7.6 plots the price schedule as a function of alternative next-period face values b'. Each price is normalized by the risk-free price for the respective maturity. Panel (a) evaluates the persistent component of income at the lowest value, panel (b) at the mean, and the final panel at the maximum value. One notable feature is that even at debt levels close to zero, the price of a long-maturity bond is strictly below the risk-free price. Lenders recognize that the government will eventually borrow into a region where default is likely, reducing the value of their bonds. We saw the same phenomenon in the "borrowing" equilibrium of Section 7.8. Recall that the borrowing equilibrium arose when the government is relatively impatient and deadweight costs of default are low. This is the case in the quantitative model as well. We have $\beta R = 0.96$, and recall from Chapter 5 that the quadratic default cost function implies small deadweight losses in low endowment states (which are the states relevant for default).

In addition to depressing the level of the price, longer maturity also flattens the slope of the price schedule. Longer-maturity bond prices incorporate not only current levels of debt but also anticipated issuances in the future; hence, the sensitivity to a given current level of issuance is reduced.

As was the case in the analytical model, the reduction in the marginal impact of an additional debt issuance on auction revenues (that is, $\partial q(b, y)/\partial b$) reduces the cost of borrowing into a region in which default is likely (and

30. The ad hoc value of z_t in the first period of default status is for computational reasons. In particular, the value of default is independent of the realization of z in that period. Whether the minimum, mean, or maximum of z is chosen for the default payoff is not crucial, as the remaining parameters of default costs (d_0, d_1, θ) can always be adjusted to yield a similar tradeoff between repayment and default as we vary z.

31. Chatterjee and Eyigungor (2012a) selected these values as an approximation to the outstanding portfolio of government bonds issued by Argentina, documented by Broner et al. (2013).

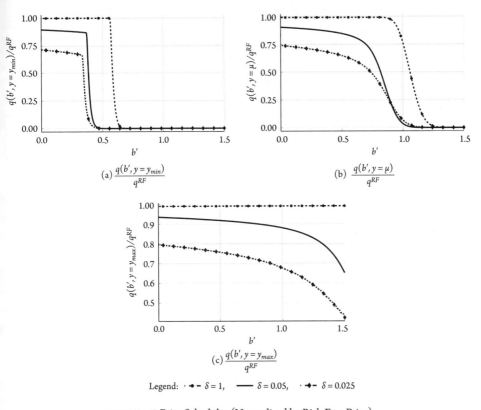

Legend: $\cdot$-$\bullet$-$\cdot$ $\delta = 1$, —— $\delta = 0.05$, $\cdot$-$\bullet$-$\cdot$ $\delta = 0.025$

FIGURE 7.6. Price Schedules (Normalized by Risk-Free Price)

Note: This figure depicts the price schedule for the three alternative maturities. Prices are normalized by the risk-free price for the respective maturity given coupon $\kappa = 0.03$: $q^{RF} = (\delta + (1 - \delta)\kappa)/(R - (1 - \delta))$. On the horizontal axis is the amount of debt to be issued. Each panel evaluates the price schedule at a different level of endowment. Panel (a) sets the endowment to its lowest level, panel (b) sets the endowment to its long-run mean, and panel (c) sets the endowment to its highest level.

reduces the benefit of saving out of such a region). This was how the borrowing equilibrium in Section 7.8 was sustained even when saving is efficient. Moreover, this flattening of the price schedule is sensitive to the output realization, as the probability of future default varies with current output due to persistence. In equilibrium, this generates more frequent default and higher volatility of spreads, as we discuss next.

The moments of the ergodic distribution of three simulations are reported in Table 7.1. The first column sets $\delta = 1$, replicating the one-period bond model of Chapter 5. The middle column is the benchmark five-year maturity model. The final column extends expected maturity to ten years. The moments are computed in the same way as in Chapter 5; namely, the sample

TABLE 7.1. Long-Term Bond Model Moments

Expected Maturity	One-Period Bonds 1 Quarter	Long-Term Bonds I 20 Quarters	Long-Term Bonds II 40 Quarters
$\mathbb{E}\left[\frac{b'}{y}\right]$	0.81	0.70	0.75
$\mathbb{E}\left[\frac{q*b'}{y}\right]$	0.80	0.70	0.61
Default Rate (Annualized)	0.002	0.068	0.111
$\mathbb{E}\left[r-r^\star\right]$ (Annualized)	0.002	0.081	0.153
StDev$(r-r^\star)$ (Annualized)	0.004	0.044	0.086
StDev(c)/StDev(y)	1.13	1.11	1.06
Corr$(y-c,y)$	−0.24	−0.43	−0.36
Corr$(y,r-r^\star)$	−0.42	−0.65	−0.62
Corr$(\frac{b'}{y},r-r^\star)$	−0.23	−0.03	0.28
Corr$(r-r^\star,y-c)$	0.88	0.77	0.72

Note: This table reports the simulated moments of alternative long-term bond models. The moment definitions are the same as in Table 5.2. The first column reports the case of one-period bonds ($\delta = 1$), the second column the benchmark maturity of 5 years ($\delta = 0.05$), and the last column the longer maturity of 10 years ($\delta = 0.025$). The coupon $\kappa = 0.03$ is held constant across columns.

is restricted to periods at which the government has been in good credit standing for at least twenty quarters.

In the first row we report the average face value of debt issuance relative to (the persistent component of) income. Note that as we vary maturity, the face value of a bond represents a different stream of promised payments, so the numbers are not easily comparable.[32] The second row reports market value, which is the economically more relevant statistic. Comparing across rows, the government sustains a larger face value of debt in equilibrium for shorter maturity bonds. This may seem surprising as longer maturities incentivize borrowing, as discussed previously. However, comparing face value to market value, we see that ten-year bonds sell at a deep discount relative to shorter maturity bonds.

Rows three through five highlight that longer maturities lead to more frequent default, higher mean spreads, and more volatile spreads. This brings the long-term bond model closer to the data discussed in Chapter 1. Viewed through the lens of the model, it is the interaction of non-linear default

32. Additionally, the one-period bond has a coupon of 3% in the current environment, and had zero coupon in Chapter 5.

costs and longer maturities that drives the volatility of spreads and recurrent defaults.

The other business cycle moments reported in Table 7.1 are relatively stable across maturities and comparable to the models of Table 5.2 in Chapter 5. In particular, consumption is more volatile than income and both net exports and spreads are counter-cyclical. The one moment that displays a difference across maturities is the correlation of debt and spreads, which reflects the relative magnitude of the shift in the price schedule versus movement along the schedule.

In this calibrated version of the long-term bond model, we are only able to compute a single equilibrium. However, as discussed in the previous subsection, the long-term bond model can potentially allow for multiple equilibria. It is indeed possible to obtain calibrations where multiple equilibria can be computed with slight modifications to the environment. Aguiar and Amador (2020) modify the income process by incorporating a "disaster state."[33] This addition, besides being empirically relevant, also allows for the computation of multiple equilibria in this environment.

Finally, we noted at the end of Chapter 5 that the low discount factor is often interpreted as being due to political economy frictions rather than the time preference of domestic citizens. In the one-period bond model, the welfare loss due to excessive borrowing by an impatient government is relatively modest, primarily because of the low levels of debt and rare instances of default in equilibrium. However, with long-term bonds, debt dilution exacerbates the efficiency consequences of borrowing and generates frequent default. Under the current calibration, Aguiar, Amador, and Fourakis (2020) find large welfare losses for households at relatively small levels of discount rate disagreement with the government. The reason for the sharp difference relative to the one-period bond case is that the simulated economy spends a significant fraction of time in the default state.

7.10 Conclusion

In this chapter, we established that long-term bonds are prone to dilution. Beyond providing an incentive to over-borrow (relative to the efficient benchmark), this additional friction has numerous interesting theoretical

---

33. See also Paluszynski (2019) and Rebelo, Wang, and Yang (2019) for sovereign debt models that incorporate disaster risk.

implications. It makes debt buybacks unattractive to the government, despite the fact that swapping maturity could lead to a Pareto improvement. Debt forgiveness may raise the market value of bonds. Finally, we showed that dilution gives rise to self-fulfilling equilibria.

These results beg the question of why a government would choose to issue long-term bonds. There are two main omissions from the model of this chapter that provide a counter-balance in favor of longer maturities. The first is rollover risk, as discussed at length in Chapter 6. With short-term bonds, the government must constantly issue a full set of new bonds to repay maturing bonds, making them vulnerable to a failed auction.[34]

The second reason to issue long-term bonds is hedging. With incomplete markets, a rich maturity structure can increase the span of assets, improving insurance.[35] Even with a single maturity, as in the above model, long-term bonds with a fixed coupon help insure against shocks to primitives. For example, if the arrival rate λ of $\overline{V}$ varied stochastically in the analytical model, the government would be exposed to time-varying prices. A long-term bond with a fixed coupon provides insurance against such an event.[36] A similar risk appears in the quantitative model, as shocks to the endowment shift the price schedule (Figure 7.6).

It is not clear in practice whether the insurance properties of long-term bonds outweigh the additional frictions due to dilution. Chatterjee and

---

34. The working paper version of Aguiar and Amador (2013) studies an example (see their section 4) where the government faces the possibility of a default as a result of a confidence crisis. Hence, maturity choices must balance the negative incentive effects of long-term bonds with the ability to insulate the economy from a self-fulfilling run. This tradeoff between incentives and protection against runs is at the heart of the quantitative analysis of Bocola and Dovis (2019). Using a quantitative model, Sánchez, Sapriza, and Yurdagul (2018) also point to the importance of "sudden stops" as driving maturity choice in favor of long-term bonds. In recent work, Aguiar and Amador (2021) study how sovereign debt swaps undertaken by the government can be used to separate confidence-crisis risk from fundamental risk, as swaps have distinct implications for the behavior of bond prices (and welfare) depending on the source of default risk.

35. The role of the maturity structure in allowing the government to hedge risk under incomplete markets is the focus of analysis in the work of Angeletos (2002) and Buera and Nicolini (2004) for closed-economy environments without default risk (see also Faraglia, Marcet, Oikonomou, and Scott 2019 and Bhandari, Evans, Golosov, and Sargent 2019). In the context of a sovereign debt model with equilibrium default, see the subsequent work of Arellano and Ramanarayanan (2012), Dovis (2019), Niepelt (2014), and Fernandez and Martin (2015).

36. See the discussion in Aguiar et al. (2019a).

Eyigungor (2012a) explore this question in their quantitative model. Absent rollover risk, they show that the government's welfare (at zero debt) is maximized when bonds are short term, indicating that in the model, the dilution costs dominate the hedging benefits.

One way to view the long-term bond model is that in tranquil times, a government issues a range of maturities for a number of reasons: to hedge, provide liquid benchmarks for private financial markets, synchronize debt payments with tax revenues, etc. However, in a crisis, default risk comes to the forefront, and the lessons of this chapter become the first-order concern. This potentially explains why, in a crisis, governments skew issuances heavily toward the short end of the yield curve.

There are several dimensions that we have not explored in this chapter. One of them is to analyze how the model's implications and its quantitative performance change once capital accumulation is introduced. We refer the reader to the recent work of Gordon and Guerron-Quintana (2018), who have recently done such analysis in the context of a long-bond model.[37] Also recently, Esquivel (2020) analyzed a multi-sector version of the model with capital accumulation in the context of economies that discover oil and shift their production toward that sector.

Related to the portfolio choice governments face, it is important to mention that governments sometimes accumulate significant levels of foreign reserves (usually in the form of safe assets issued by developed countries' governments) and in addition, maintain high stocks of external debt. An early paper by Alfaro and Kanczuk (2009) pointed out the difficult job that quantitative sovereign debt models with one-period debt face when trying to account for this behavior.[38] The reason is that the low discount factor of the government that makes the government willing to borrow also makes it reluctant to save. However, recent work by Bianchi, Hatchondo, and Martinez (2018) has shown that a model with long-term bonds extended to incorporate risk-premium shocks to the lenders is indeed capable of generating significant reserve accumulation.[39]

37. See Bai and Zhang (2012a), Park (2017), and Roldán-Peña (2012) for versions of quantitative sovereign debt models incorporating capital and investment, but with one-period bonds.

38. On this issue, see also Salomao (2013).

39. For previous work emphasizing roll-over risk for reserve accumulation see Aizenman and Lee (2007) and Hur and Kondo (2016).

Finally, our analysis of long-term bonds is restricted to Markovian equilibria, in which historical actions are relevant only through credit standing and the face value of outstanding debt. But there are other approaches. For example, Dovis (2019) considers a richer set of equilibria that allows for prices (and other equilibrium outcomes) to depend on the entire history of actions. In particular, this allows for trigger strategies as in the models of Chapters 2 and 3, where autarky is a potential punishment for any deviation from the candidate allocation. Dovis also includes a limited possibility for "excusable" defaults (partial repayment) in the spirit of Grossman and Van Huyck (1988). In an environment with productivity shocks, limited commitment, and hidden information, Dovis (2019) shows that a constrained efficient allocation with complete markets can be decentralized with a portfolio of debt, including long-term bonds. The maturity structure provides insurance, and the fact that equilibrium prices and lending depend on histories, and not just payoff-relevant states, is sufficient to solve the threat of dilution.

8

Conclusion

We began this book by identifying key frictions that govern the behavior of sovereign debt markets. The preceding chapters studied these underlying frictions in analytical as well as larger quantitative models that help illuminate real-world contexts.

The main friction we have emphasized is *limited commitment*. This is a natural assumption for the study of sovereign debt as there is no controlling legal authority that can enforce repayment or oversee a bankruptcy of a sovereign nation. Chapter 2 explored the implications for risk-sharing between a government and its external creditors under just this one friction. A general lesson in that context is that it is efficient for a "patient" government to reduce the level of indebtedness or save through reserve accumulation in the presence of this friction. In addition, we described how direct punishments or external sanctions are necessary to sustain any positive level of debt, a message that quantitatively also applies to models with incomplete markets.

While it is almost tautological that debt-market frictions can be overcome by not borrowing, the data suggest that emerging-market countries frequently accumulate large amounts of external debts, and recurrently find themselves in fiscal crises that sometimes lead to default. This begs the question of why countries are prone to such levels of indebtedness (maybe because of government impatience/political economy frictions), and why (what seem to be costly) defaults occur in equilibrium.

There is a natural supposition that some developing economies accumulate external debt because they rely on external finance and need it for investment and economic growth. However, the data from the last forty years suggest that debt induces volatility *and* is not associated with growth. Governments of emerging markets with stronger than average growth records if anything accumulate reserves and reduce public indebtedness. Those that maintain a high level of debt (or accumulate more debt) have inferior growth outcomes. Note that this is a pattern observed at the half-century frequency, and is not speaking to smoothing shocks at business cycle frequencies. Chapter 3 introduced an additional friction to help explain these patterns, namely that *political leaders may be myopic or self-serving,* and shows how, coupled with limited commitment, external borrowing distorts investment and capital accumulation. As growth is perhaps the only method for significantly alleviating poverty, the negative relationship between growth and debt should be at the forefront, even in addressing a short-run debt crisis.[1]

Chapters 4 and 5 introduced *incomplete markets* as another friction: the debt contract is one period and cannot be made contingent on shocks. This now allows for the possibility of default occurring in equilibrium. Chapter 4 showcased a stylized and tractable model without income risk that highlighted the implications for consumption and debt dynamics that emerge from this environment. Again, we showed that a patient government reduces its debt so as to avoid the deadweight losses that a future default can generate. And we also showed how short-term bonds can decentralize the constrained efficient allocation as an equilibrium outcome. Chapter 5 generalized this environment by introducing income risk. We described how the efficiency result in Chapter 4 survived in this environment and how it also guarantees a unique equilibrium. We also explored the quantitative implications of this one-period bond model and discussed the characteristics of the equilibrium, its empirical success in generating a volatile consumption as well as the cyclicality of the trade balance.

As detailed in Chapters 4 and 5, short-term bonds align the government's payoffs with the socially efficient returns. However, as is well understood, short-term debt also exposes the government to the risk of a market run or a failed auction. In Chapter 6, we discussed how a modification of the timing in the model allows for this "static" multiplicity to arise. In particular, we showed how if fundamentals are sufficiently weak (that is, if the debt is sufficiently large), a government may be at the mercy of market's beliefs about its willingness to repay. In terms of policy, we discussed how long maturity bonds can reduce this type of vulnerability to runs, how floating-rate debt can be of help, and how a lender of last resort could eliminate the bad equilibrium outcomes. The role of a lender of last resort has been exemplified by the Mexican

---

1. For an alternative perspective on the role of debt, see Ventura and Voth (2015).

debt crisis in 1994, as well as the European debt crisis of the early 2010s. In both of these, third-party interventions (in the Mexican case, the US Treasury and the IMF, while in the European case, the European Central Bank, the European Commission, and the IMF) were crucial in alleviating the crisis.

Chapter 7 extends the model to include fixed-rate long duration bonds. The introduction of long-term bonds opens the door to "debt dilution": bondholders are now affected by future borrowing decisions by the government, as those increase future default probabilities within the life-span of the bond. We showed in a tractable environment how long-term bond borrowing can lead to inefficient outcomes. With long-term bonds, only a fraction of the debt needs to be rolled over in a period, decreasing the incentives to reduce debt. As a result, the government reduces debt at a lower rate than what is efficient, and default risk can remain inefficiently high in equilibrium. We also used this environment to discuss why a market-based swap of long-term debt for short-term debt does not make sense for the government. In addition, we showed that, if given a maturity choice for new issuances, the equilibrium incentivizes a government to borrow short term and not to buy or sell long-term bonds. We also discussed that the intuition from Chapter 6 with regard to the advantage of long-term financing in alleviating self-fulfilling crises is fragile. We showed that long-term borrowing also suffers from coordination failures, but that in this case involves a "dynamic" multiplicity. In particular, at the time of auction for long-term bonds, creditors must forecast future fiscal policy. A negative forecast can be self-fulfilling, as pricing in the anticipation of future borrowing reduces the reward to the government of fiscal prudence going forward. In an incomplete market environment, long-term bonds have additional benefits, as a government may use the maturity structure to hedge against future shocks. We ended this chapter highlighting the quantitative properties in an environment that features income risk and thus the potential that long-term bonds provide a hedging benefit. We showed how introducing long-term bonds generates a significant improvement of the fit of the model.

More generally, the lack of state contingency in sovereign debt markets makes it an imperfect source of insurance. There have been cases in which GDP-indexed warrants have been included in debt contracts (as in Argentina's 2005 and Greece's 2012 restructured bonds). However, these are modest in scope. It is unclear whether they can be used at a larger scale given the moral hazard problems (for example, manipulation of government statistics).

Moreover, it is not clear how to insure against failed auctions, political crises, and risk premia shocks. The data suggest only a weak correlation between growth and debt market outcomes such as default or spreads. There is a significant correlation with measures of investor sentiment in world financial markets (such as the VIX) and US monetary policy, the so-called global financial cycle.[2] Absent private insurance such as options or other contracts based on world financial indicators, longer maturities can provide a hedge against high-frequency movements in risk premia. However, as we discussed, long-maturity bonds introduce debt dilution and are themselves vulnerable to runs.

One policy implication of the preceding chapters is that variable-rate debt represents a happy coincidence of reducing dilution as well as rollover risk. As the debt's principal is not continuously rolled over, the government is less vulnerable to runs or changes in risk premia. At the same time, the variable rate provides some discipline on the government by rewarding a government that moderates default risk over the bond's life-span. Such debt requires frequent auctions of a benchmark short-term loan that indexes coupon payments. However, such auctions do not need to be large to reflect high frequency updates on the government's fiscal policy. Alternative disciplining mechanisms have been tried, such as fiscal rules and conditionality. However, these are often difficult to enforce ex post. Returning to the market frequently provides a market-based approach to discipline fiscal policy. Combining floating rates with long maturities provides correct incentives while moderating rollover risk.

The models discussed in this book indicate that the field has matured along some dimensions. In particular, economists have successfully developed medium-scale quantitative models that replicate a number of moments observed in emerging economies. We also have tractable, analytical models that clearly identify the forces at work. However, much work remains to be done.

For example, in both the theoretical and quantitative models, the deadweight costs of default play a prominent role. Measuring these costs in the data is difficult, as it requires knowing what the counterfactual world of no default (or repayment, depending on the context) would look like. One interesting empirical attempt at measuring this is Hébert and Schreger (2017). Part of the costs reflects the length of time it takes to restructure debt. Models

2. See Miranda-Agrippino and Rey (2020).

of delays in bargaining in the context of sovereign debt have recently been proposed.[3] Additional default costs are due to the disruption of the financial system after default, particularly if the domestic banking system holds government bonds on their balance sheets.[4] We view that understanding the costs of default, and the political economy decisions of the government and private agents to nevertheless borrow and pay these costs, as exciting areas of ongoing research.

3. See Bi (2008); Benjamin and Wright (2008); Bai and Zhang (2012b); Pitchford and Wright (2012); Asonuma and Joo (2020).

4. The adverse effects of sovereign risk on the banking sector has been an area of active research, specially after the European debt crisis. Basu (2009), Brutti (2011), Bolton and Jeanne (2011), Gennaioli, Martin, and Rossi (2014), Sosa-Padilla (2018), Perez (2018), and Chari, Dovis, and Kehoe (2020) are models that incorporate this mechanism. The work of Bocola (2016) quantitatively assesses how sovereign risk passes through to the banking sector by studying the case of Italian banks during the European debt crisis. For additional empirical work on this channel, see also Gennaioli et al. (2014) and Baskaya and Kalemli-Ozcan (2016). The recent work of Arellano, Bai, and Bocola (2017) explores the heterogeneous effects of sovereign risk on firms with access to banks with different holdings of sovereign bonds. The interaction can also flow in the other direction: problems in the financial sector can generate a sovereign debt crisis. Together this forms the so-called doom loop between banks holding government bonds as assets and fiscal authorities standing as guarantors of the banking system. See, for example, Acharya, Drechsler, and Schnabl (2014), Farhi and Tirole (2018), and Cooper and Nikolov (2018). For recent evidence that default costs are generated not just through the effects on the banking sector balance sheet, see Asonuma, Chamon, Erce, and Sasahara (2020).

BIBLIOGRAPHY

Abbas, S. Ali, Pienkowski, Alex, and Rogoff, Kenneth, editors. *Sovereign Debt: A Guide for Economists and Practitioners*. Oxford: Oxford University Press, 2019. 13

Abrahám, Arpád, Cárceles Poveda, Eva, Liu, Yan, and Marimon, Ramon. On the optimal design of a financial stability fund. Working Paper, 2018. 107

Abreu, Dilip. On the theory of infinitely repeated games with discounting. *Econometrica*, 56: 383–396, 1988. 18

Acharya, Viral, Drechsler, Itamar, and Schnabl, Philipp. A pyrrhic victory? Bank bailouts and sovereign credit risk. *Journal of Finance*, 69(6):2689–2739, November 2014. 159

Aguiar, Mark, and Amador, Manuel. Growth in the shadow of expropriation. *Quarterly Journal of Economics*, 126:651–697, 2011. 34, 39, 40, 41, 44

———. Take the short route: How to repay and restructure sovereign debt with multiple maturities. *Working Paper* 19717, National Bureau of Economic Research, December 2013. 152

———. Sovereign debt. In *Handbook of International Economics Volume 4*, pp. 647–687. Amsterdam: North-Holland, 2014. 32

———. Fiscal policy in debt constrained economies. *Journal of Economic Theory*, 161:37–75, 2016. 38

———. A contraction for sovereign debt models. *Journal of Economic Theory*, 183:842–875, 2019. 32, 71, 76, 79

———. Self-fulfilling debt dilution: Maturity and multiplicity in debt models. *American Economic Review*, 110(9):2783–2818, September 2020. 50, 52, 57, 138, 139, 141–145, 151

———. Sovereign swaps and sovereign default: Fundamental versus confidence risk. *Working Paper*. 2021. 108, 152

Aguiar, Mark, Amador, Manuel, Farhi, Emmanuel, and Gopinath, Gita. Crisis and commitment: Inflation credibility and the vulnerability to sovereign debt crises. *Working Paper*, 2012. 50, 52, 57, 61, 100, 105, 106

———. Coordination and crisis in monetary unions. *Quarterly Journal of Economics*, 130(4): 1727–1779, 2015. 106

Aguiar, Mark, Amador, Manuel, and Fourakis, Stelios. On the welfare losses from external sovereign borrowing. *IMF Economic Review*, 68:163–194, 2020. 90, 151

Aguiar, Mark, Amador, Manuel, and Gopinath, Gita. Investment cycles and sovereign debt overhang. *Review of Economic Studies*, 76(1):1–31, January 2009. 34, 38

Aguiar, Mark, Amador, Manuel, Hopenhayn, Hugo, and Werning, Iván. Take the short route: Equilibrium default and debt maturity. *Econometrica*, 87(2):423–462, 2019a. 121, 124, 152

Aguiar, Mark, Chatterjee, Satyajit, Cole, Harold, and Stangebye, Zachary. Quantitative models of sovereign debt crises. In *Handbook of Macroeconomics Volume 2*, pp. 1697–1755. Amsterdam: Elsevier, 2016. 80

———. Self-fulfilling debt crises, revisited. *Working Paper*, 2019b. 4, 92, 101, 103

Aguiar, Mark, and Gopinath, Gita. Defaultable debt, interest rates, and the current account. *Journal of International Economics*, 69(1):64–83, 2006. 4, 45, 58, 66, 80, 81, 83

Aizenman, Joshua, and Lee, Jaewoo. International reserves: Precautionary versus mercantilist views, theory and evidence. *Open Economies Review*, 18(2):191–214, 2007. 153

Alburquerque, Rui, and Hopenhayn, Hugo. Optimal lending contracts and firm dynamics. *Review of Economic Studies*, 71:285–315, 2004. 34

Alesina, Alberto, Prati, Alessandro, and Tabellini, Guido. Public confidence and debt management: A model and a case study of italy. In Dornbusch, R. and Draghi, M., editors, *Public Debt Management: Theory and History*, pages 94–124. Cambridge: Cambridge University Press and CEPR, 1990. 92, 108

Alesina, Alberto, and Tabellini, Guido. A positive theory of fiscal deficits and government debt in a democracy. *Review of Economic Studies*, 57:403–414, 1990. 39

Alfaro, Laura, and Kanczuk, Fabio. Sovereign debt as a contingent claim: A quantitative approach. *Journal of International Economics*, 65(2):297–314, 2005. 7

———. Optimal reserve management and sovereign debt. *Journal of International Economics*, 77(1):23–36, February 2009. 153

———. Fiscal rules and sovereign default. *Working Paper* 23370, National Bureau of Economic Research, April 2017. 90

Alvarez, Fernando, and Jermann, Urban. Efficiency, equilibrium, and asset pricing with risk of default. *Econometrica*, 68:775–797, 2000. 17, 19

Amador, Manuel. *Essays in Macroeconomics and Political Economy*. PhD thesis, MIT, Cambridge, MA, 2003. 39

Amador, Manuel, and Phelan, Christopher. Reputation and soveregn default. *Working Paper*, University of Minnesota, August 2020. 7

Angeletos, George-Marios. Fiscal policy with non-contingent debt and the optimal maturity structure. *Quarterly Journal of Economics*, 117, 2002. 152

Araujo, Aloisio, Leon, Marcia, and Santos, Rafael. Welfare analysis of currency regimes with defaultable debts. *Journal of International Economics*, 89(1):143–153, 2013. 105

Arellano, Cristina. Default risk and income fluctuations in emerging economies. *American Economic Review*, 2008. 4, 45, 58, 66, 73, 80, 81, 83, 87, 89

Arellano, Cristina, Bai, Yan, and Bocola, Luigi. Sovereign default risk and firm heterogeneity. *Working Paper* 23314, National Bureau of Economic Research, 2017. 159

Arellano, Cristina, and Ramanarayanan, Ananth. Default and the maturity structure in sovereign bonds. *Journal of Political Economy*, 120:187–232, 2012. 9, 8, 130, 152

Arslanalp, Serkan, and Tsudo, Takahiro. *Tracking global demand for emerging market sovereign debt*. Washington, DC: IMF, 2014. 8

Asonuma, Tamon. Serial sovereign defaults and debt restructurings. *Working Paper*, IMF, March 2016. 7

Asonuma, Tamon, Chamon, Marcos, Erce, Aitor, and Sasahara, Akira. Costs of sovereign defaults: Restructuring strategies and the credit-investment channel. *Working Paper*, 2020. 159

Asonuma, Tamon, and Joo, Hyungseok. Sovereign debt restructurings: Delays in renegotiations and risk averse creditors. *Journal of the European Economic Association*, 18(5): 2394–2440, 2020. 159

Asonuma, Tamon, Niepelt, Dirk, and Ranciere, Romain. Sovereign bond prices, haircuts and maturity. *Working Paper* 23864, National Bureau of Economic Research, 2017. 123

Atkeson, Andrew. International borrowing with moral hazard and risk of repudiation. *Econometrica*, 59:1069–1089, 1991. 17

Auclert, Adrien, and Rognlie, Matthew. Unique equilibrium in the Eaton-Gersovitz model of sovereign debt. *Journal of Monetary Economics*, 84:134–146, 2016. 32, 71, 76, 79

Ayres, João, Navarro, Gaston, Nicolini, Juan Pablo, and Teles, Pedtro. Sovereign default: The role of expectations. *Working Paper*, 2015. 106

———. Sovereign default: The role of expectations. *Journal of Economic Theory*, 175:803–812, May 2018. 92

Azzimonti, Marina, Battaglini, Marco, and Coate, Stephen. The costs and benefits of balanced budget rules: Lessons from a political economy model of fiscal policy. *Journal of Public Economics*, 136:45–61, 2016. 90

Bacchetta, Philippe, Perazzi, Elena, and van Wincoop, Eric. Self-fulfilling debt crises: What can monetary policy do? *Journal of International Economics*, 110:119–134, January 2018. 106

Bai, Yan, and Zhang, Jing. Financial integration and international risk sharing. *Journal of International Economics*, 86(1):17–32, 2012a. 153

———. Duration of sovereign debt renegotiation. *Journal of International Economics*, 86(2): 252–268, March 2012b. 159

Baskaya, Yusuf Soner, and Kalemli-Ozcan, Sebnem. Sovereign risk and bank lending: Evidence from 1999 Turkish earthquake. *Working Paper* 22335, National Bureau of Economic Research, 2016. 159

Bassetto, Marco, and Galli, Carlo. Is inflation default? The role of information in debt crises. *American Economic Review*, 109(10):3556–3584, 2019. 105

Basu, Suman. Sovereign debt and domestic economic fragility. *Working Paper*, 2009. 159

Battaglini, Marco, and Coate, Stephen. A dynamic theory of public spending, taxation, and debt. *American Economic Review*, 98(1):201–236, March 2008. 39

Benjamin, David, and Wright, Mark. Recovery before redemption: A model of delays in sovereign debt renegotiations. *UCLA Working Paper*, 2008. 70, 159

Bhandari, Anmol, Evans, David, Golosov, Mikhail, and Sargent, Thomas J. The optimal maturity of government debt. *Working Paper*, 2019. 152

Bi, Ran. "Beneficial" delays in debt restructuring negotiations. *IMF Working Paper WP/08/38*, 2008. 159

Bianchi, Javier, Hatchondo, Juan Carlos, and Martinez, Leonardo. International reserves and rollover risk. *American Economic Review*, 108(9):2629–2670, 2018. 153

Bianchi, Javier, and Mondragon, Jorge. Monetary independence and rollover crises. *Working Paper* 25340, National Bureau of Economic Research, 2018. 105

Bizer, David S., and DeMarzo, Peter M. Sequential banking. *Journal of Political Economy*, 100: 41–61, 1992. 67

Bloise, Gaetano, Polemarchakis, Heraklis M., and Vailakis, Yiannis. Sovereign debt and incentives to default with uninsurable risk. *Warwick/CRETA Discussion Paper*, 2016. 32

———. Sustainable debt. *SSRN Electronic Journal*, 2018. 32

Bloise, Gaetano, and Vailakis, Yiannis. On sovereign default with time-varying interest rates. *Working Paper*, 2020. 79

Bocola, Luigi. The pass-through of sovereign risk. *Journal of Political Economy*, 124(4):879–926, 2016. 159

Bocola, Luigi, Bornstein, Gideon, and Dovis, Alessandro. Quantitative sovereign default models and the European debt crisis. *Journal of International Economics*, 118:20–30, 2019. 9

Bocola, Luigi, and Dovis, Alessandro. Self-fulfilling debt crises: A quantitative analysis. *American Economic Review*, 109(12):4343–4377, December 2019. 107, 130, 152

Bolton, Patrick, and Jeanne, Olivier. Sovereign default risk and bank fragility in financially integrated economies. *IMF Economic Review*, 59(2):162–194, 2011. 159

Borri, Nicola, and Verdelhan, Adrien. Sovereign risk premia. *MIT Sloan Working Paper*, 2011. 11

Broner, Fernando, Erce, Aitor, Martin, Alberto, and Ventura, Jaume. Sovereign debt markets in turbulent times: Creditor discrimination and crowding-out effects. *Journal of Monetary Economics*, 61:114–142, 2014. 28

Broner, Fernando, Lorenzoni, Guido, and Schmukler, Sergio. Why do emerging economies borrow short term? *Journal of the European Economics Association*, 11:67–100, 2013. 9, 130, 148

Broner, Fernando, Martin, Alberto, and Ventura, Jaume. Sovereign risk and secondary markets. *American Economic Review*, 100:1523–1555, 2010. 28

Brutti, Filippo. Sovereign defaults and liquidity crises. *Journal of International Economics*, 84(1): 65–72, May 2011. 159

Buera, Francisco, and Nicolini, Juan Pablo. Optimal maturity of government debt without state contingent bonds. *Journal of Monetary Economics*, 51(3):531–554, 2004. 152

Bulow, Jeremy, and Rogoff, Kenneth. Sovereign debt: Is to forgive to forget? *American Economic Review*, 79:43–50, 1989a. 79, 2, 14, 28, 32, 69, 79

———. A constant recontracting model of sovereign debt. *Journal of Political Economy*, 97: 155–178, 1989b. 70

———. Sovereign debt repurchases: No cure for overhang. *Quarterly Journal of Economics*, 106:1219–1235, 1991. 127

Burger, John D., and Warnock, Francis E. Foreign participation in local currency bond markets. *Review of Financial Economics*, 16(3):291–304, 2007. 8

Calvo, Guillermo. Servicing the public debt: The role of expectations. *American Economic Review*, 78:647–661, 1988. 92, 106, 108

Chamon, Marcos, Schumacher, Julian, and Trebesch, Christoph. Foreign-law bonds: Can they reduce sovereign borrowing costs? *Journal of International Economics*, 114:164–179, September 2018. 8

Chari, V. V., Dovis, Alessandro, and Kehoe, Patrick J. On the optimality of financial repression. *Journal of Political Economy*, 128(2):710–739, 2020. 159

Chari, V. V., and Kehoe, Patrick. Sustainable plans. *Journal of Political Economy*, 98:783–802, 1990. 18

Chari, V. V., and Kehoe, Patrick J. Sustainable plans and mutual default. *Review of Economic Studies*, 60(1):175–195, 1993. 18

Chatterjee, Satyajit, and Eyigungor, Burcu. Debt dilution and seniority in a model of default-able sovereign debt. *Federal Reserve Bank of Philadelphia Working Paper 12-14*, 2012a. 148, 80, 82, 86, 87, 108, 111, 146, 147, 153

———. Maturity, indebtedness, and default risk. *American Economic Review*, 102:2674–2699, 2012b. 5, 11

———. Endogenous political turnover and fluctuations in sovereign default risk. *Journal of International Economics*, 117:37–50, 2019. 89

Choi, S. J., Gulati, M., and Posner, E. A. Pricing terms in sovereign debt contracts: A Greek case study with implications for the European crisis resolution mechanism. *Capital Markets Law Journal*, 6(2):163–187, March 2011. 7

Cole, Harold L., Dow, James, and English, William B. Default, settlement, and signalling: Lending resumption in a reputational model of sovereign debt. *International Economic Review*, 36 (2):365–385, 1995. 7

Cole, Harold, and Kehoe, Timothy. Self-fulfilling debt crises. *Review of Economic Studies*, 67: 91–116, 2000. 100, 60, 95, 95, 100

Conesa, Juan Carlos, and Kehoe, Timothy J. Gambling for redemption and self-fulfilling debt crises. *Economic Theory*, 64(4):707–740, October 2017. 92

Cooper, Russell, and Nikolov, Kalin. Government debt and banking fragility: The spreading of strategic uncertainty. *International Economic Review*, 59(4):1905–1925, 2018. 159

Corsetti, Giancarlo, and Dedola, Luca. The mystery of the printing press: Monetary policy and self-fulfilling debt crises. *Journal of the European Economic Association*, 14(6):1329–1371, 2016. 105

Corsetti, Giancarlo, Kuester, Keith, Meier, André, and Müller, Gernot J. Sovereign risk and belief-driven fluctuations in the euro area. *Journal of Monetary Economics*, 61:53–73, 2014. 106

Cruces, Juan, and Trebesch, Christoph. Sovereign defaults: The price of haircuts. *CESIFO Working Paper 3604*, 2011. 7, 83

———. Sovereign defaults: The price of haircuts. *American Economic Journal: Macroeconomics*, 5:85–117, 2013. 11

Cuadra, Gabriel, and Sapriza, Horacio. Sovereign default, interest rates and political uncertainty in emerging markets. *Journal of International Economics*, 76:78–88, 2008. 89

Dechert, W. D. Lagrange multipliers in infinite horizon discrete time optimal control models. *Journal of Mathematical Economics*, 9:285–301, 1982. 20

D'Erasmo, Pablo. Government reputation and debt repayment in emerging economies. Working Paper, 2011. 7

Detragiache, Enrica. Rational liquidity crises in the sovereign debt market: In search of a theory. *Staff Papers (International Monetary Fund)*, 43(3):545–570, 1996. 92

Diamond, Douglas W., and Dybvig, Philip H. Bank runs, deposit insurance, and liquidity. *Journal of Political Economy*, 91(3):401–419, 1983. 107

Díaz-Cassou, Javier, Erce, Aitor, and Vázquez-Zamora, Juan J. The role of the IMF in recent sovereign debt restructurings: Implications for the policy of lending into arrears. Occasional Paper 0805, Banco de España, 2008. 127

Dovis, Alessandro. Efficient sovereign default. *Review of Economic Studies*, 86(1):282–312, 2019. 109, 152, 154

Drelichman, Mauricio, and Voth, Hans-Joachim. Lending to the borrower from hell: Debt and default in the age of Philip II. *Economic Journal*, 121(557):1205–1227, 2011. 13

Du, Wenxin, Pflueger, Carolin E., and Schreger, Jesse. Sovereign debt portfolios, bond risks, and the credibility of monetary policy. *Journal of Finance*, 75(6):3097–3138, 2020. 105

Du, Wenxin, and Schreger, Jesse. Sovereign risk, currency risk, and corporate balance sheets. *SSRN Electronic Journal*, 2016a. 8

———. Local currency sovereign risk. *Journal of Finance*, 71(3):1027–1070, 2016b. 105

Dvorkin, Maximiliano, Yurdagul, Emircan, Sapriza, Horacio, and Sanchez, Juan. Sovereign debt restructuring. *American Economic Journal: Macroeconomics*, 13:26–77, 2021. 127

Eaton, Jonathan, and Fernandez, Raquel. Sovereign debt. In *Handbook of International Economics Volume 3*, pp. 2031–2077. Amsterdam: North-Holland Elsevier, 1995. 32

Eaton, Jonathan, and Gersovitz, Mark. Debt with potential repudiation: Theoretical and empirical analysis. *Review of Economic Studies*, 48(2):289–309, 1981. 1, 2, 4, 12, 14, 17, 28, 45, 66

Egorov, Konstantin, and Fabinger, Michal. Reputational effects in sovereign default. SSRN Scholarly Paper ID 2724568, Social Science Research Network, Rochester, NY, January 2016. 7

Eichengreen, Barry, and Hausmann, Ricardo. Exchange rates and financial fragility. *Proceedings–Economic Policy Symposium–Jackson Hole*, pp. 329–368, 1999. 8

Engel, Charles, and Park, Jung Jae. Debauchery and original sin: The currency composition of sovereign debt. *Working Paper* 24671, National Bureau of Economic Research, 2018. 105

Erce, Aitor, and Mallucci, Enrico. Selective sovereign defaults. International Finance Discussion Paper 1239, Federal Reserve Board, 2018. 7

Esquivel, Carlos. The sovereign default risk of giant oil discoveries. *Working Paper*, University of Minnesota, August 2020. 153

Faraglia, Elisa, Marcet, Albert, Oikonomou, Rigas, and Scott, Andrew. Government debt management: The long and the short of it. *Review of Economic Studies*, 86(6):2554–2604, 2019. 152

Farhi, Emmanuel, and Tirole, Jean. Deadly embrace: Sovereign and financial balance sheets doom loops. *Review of Economic Studies*, 85(3):1781–1823, 2018. 159

Fernandez, Raquel, and Martin, Alberto. The long and the short of it: Sovereign debt crises and debt maturity. *UPF Working Paper 1459*, 2015. 152

Fernandez, Raquel, and Rosenthal, Robert. Strategic models of sovereign-debt renegotiations. *Review of Economic Studies*, 57:331–349, 1990. 70

Fleming, Wendell, and Soner, Halil Mete. *Controlled Markov processes and viscosity solutions*. New York: Springer, 2006. 50

Galli, Carlo. Self-fulfilling debt crises, fiscal policy and investment. *Working Paper*, 2019. 92

———. Inflation, default risk and nominal debt. https://carlogalli.github.io/files/Galli_JMP.pdf, 2020. 105

Gennaioli, Nicola, Martin, Alberto, and Rossi, Stefano. Sovereign default, domestic banks, and financial institutions. *Journal of Finance*, 69(2):819–866, March 2014. 159

Gordon, Grey, and Guerron-Quintana, Pablo A. Dynamics of investment, debt, and default. *Review of Economic Dynamics*, 28:71–95, 2018. 153

Gourinchas, Pierre-Olivier, and Jeanne, Olivier. Capital flows to developing countries: The allocation puzzle. *Review of Economic Studies*, 80:1484–1515, 2013. 34

Grossman, Herschel, and Van Huyck, John B. Sovereign debt as a contingent claim: Excusable default, repudiation, and reputation. *American Economic Review*, 78(5):1088–1097, 1988. 5, 154

Hall, George J., and Sargent, Thomas J. Fiscal discriminations in three wars. *Journal of Monetary Economics*, 61(C):148–166, 2014. 7

———. Complications for the United States from international credits: 1913–1940. In Norris, Era, editor, *Debt and Entanglements between the Wars*. International Monetary Fund, 2019. 7

Hall, George J., and Sargent, Thomas J. Debt and taxes in eight U.S. wars and two insurrections. *Working Paper* 27115, National Bureau of Economic Research, May 2020. 7

Hamann, Franz. Sovereign risk and macroeconomic fluctuations. *Banco de la Republica de Colombia Working Paper 225*, 2002. 45, 66

Harris, Milton, and Holmstrom, Bengt. A theory of wage dynamics. *Review of Economic Studies*, 49(3):315–333, 1982. 17

Hatchondo, Juan Carlos, and Martinez, Leonardo. Long-duration bonds and sovereign defaults. *Journal of International Economics*, 79:117–125, 2009. 111

Hatchondo, Juan Carlos, Martinez, Leonardo, and Padilla, César Sosa. Voluntary sovereign debt exchanges. *Journal of Monetary Economics*, 61:32–50, January 2014. 136

Hatchondo, Juan Carlos, Martinez, Leonardo, and Sapriza, Horacio. Heterogeneous borrowers in quantitative models of sovereign default. *International Economic Review*, 50:1129–1151, 2009. 89

Hatchondo, Juan Carlos, Martinez, Leonardo, and Sosa-Padilla, César. Debt dilution and sovereign default risk. *Journal of Political Economy*, 124(5):1383–1422, 2016. 108

Hatchondo, Juan Carlos, Roch, Francisco, and Martinez, Leonardo. Constrained efficient borrowing with sovereign default risk. *Working Paper*, 2019. 121

Hébert, Benjamin, and Schreger, Jesse. The costs of sovereign default: Evidence from Argentina. *American Economic Review*, 107(10):3119–3145, October 2017. 158

Holmstrom, Bengt. Equilibrium long-term labor contracts. *Quarterly Journal of Economics*, 98: 23, 1983. 22

Hur, Sewon, and Kondo, Illenin O. A theory of rollover risk, sudden stops, and foreign reserves. *Journal of International Economics*, 103(C):44–63, 2016. 153

Hur, Sewon, Kondo, Illenin, and Perri, Fabrizio. Real interest rates, inflation, and default. Staff Reports 574, Federal Reserve Bank of Minneapolis, 2018. 105

Jeske, Karsten. Private international debt with risk of repudiation. *Journal of Political Economy*, 114:576–593, 2006. 15

Kehoe, Patrick, and Perri, Fabrizio. International business cycles with endogenous incomplete markets. *Econometrica*, 70(3):907–928, 2002. 34

Kehoe, Patrick J., and Perri, Fabrizio. Competitive equilibria with limited enforcement. *Journal of Economic Theory*, 119(1):184–206, November 2004. 34

Kehoe, Timothy, and Levine, David. Debt-constrained asset markets. *Review of Economic Studies*, 60:865–888, 1993. 17

Kletzer, Kenneth, and Wright, Brian. Sovereign debt as intertemporal barter. *American Economic Review*, 90:621–639, 2000. 19, 27

Kocherlakota, Narayana. Implications of efficient risk sharing without commitment. *Review of Economic Studies*, 63:595–609, 1996. 17

Laibson, David. *Hyperbolic Discounting and Consumption*. PhD thesis, MIT, 1994. 40

Leland, Hayne. Bond prices, yield spreads, and optimal capital structure with default risk. *Working Paper* No. 240, IBER, University of California, Berkeley, 1994. 111

Lizarazo, Sandra Valentina. Default risk and risk averse international investors. *Journal of International Economics*, 89(2):317–330, March 2013. 11

Longstaff, Francis, Pan, Jun, Pedersen, Lasse, and Singleton, Kenneth. How sovereign is sovereign credit risk. *American Economic Journal: Macroeconomics*, 3:75–103, 2011. 12

Lorenzoni, Guido, and Werning, Iván. Slow moving debt crises. *American Economic Review*, 109 (9):3229–3263, 2019. 67, 92, 106, 145

Lucas, Robert. *Models of Business Cycles*. New York: Blackwell, 1987. 81

Luenberger, David G. *Optimization by Vector Space Methods*. New York: Wiley, 1969. 20

Mankiw, N. Gregory, Romer, David, and Weil, David N. A contribution to the empirics of economic growth. *Quarterly Journal of Economics*, 107(2):407–437, 1992. 43

Marcet, Albert, and Marimon, Ramon. Communication, commitment, and growth. *Journal of Economic Theory*, 58:219–249, 1992. 34

Mendoza, Enrique, and Yue, Vivian. A general equilibrium model of sovereign default and business cycles. *Quarterly Journal of Economics*, 127:889–946, 2012. 82

Meyer, Josefin, Reinhart, Carmen M., and Trebesch, Christoph. Sovereign bonds since Waterloo. *Working Paper* 25543, National Bureau of Economic Research, February 2019. 7, 9, 11

Mihalache, Gabriel. Sovereign default resolution through maturity extension. *Journal of International Economics*, 125C:103326, 2020. 127

Miranda-Agrippino, Silvia and Rey, Hélène. U.S. monetary policy and the global financial cycle. *Review of Economic Studies*, May 2020. 158

Muller, Andreas, Storesletten, Kjetil, and Zilibotti, Fabrizio. Sovereign debt and structural reforms. *American Economic Review*, 109(12):4220–4259, 2019. 17

Na, Seunghoon, Schmitt-Grohé, Stephanie, Uribe, Martin, and Yue, Vivian. The twin Ds: Optimal default and devaluation. *American Economic Review*, 108(7):1773–1819, 2018. 105

Neumeyer, Pablo, and Perri, Fabrizio. Business cycles in emerging economies: The role of interest rates. *Journal of Monetary Economics*, 52:345–380, 2005. 12

Niepelt, Dirk. Debt maturity without commitment. *Journal of Monetary Economics*, 68:S37–S54, 2014. 152

Nuño, Galo, and Thomas, Carlos. Monetary policy and sovereign debt vulnerability. *Documentos de trabajo/Banco de España*, 1517, 2015. 105

Ottonello, Pablo, and Perez, Diego J. The currency composition of sovereign debt. *American Economic Journal: Macroeconomics*, 11(3):174–208, July 2019. 105

Paluszynski, Radoslaw. Learning about debt crises. *Working Paper*, University of Houston, May 2019. 151

Pancrazi, Roberto, and Prosperi, Lorenzo. Transparency, political conflict, and debt. *Journal of International Economics*, 126:103331, 2020. 39

Park, Jung Jae. Sovereign default and capital accumulation. *Journal of International Economics*, 106:119–133, 2017. 153

Pekarski, Sergey, and Sokolova, Anna. Default costs and self-fulfilling fiscal limits in a small open economy. *Working Paper*, 2020. 92

Perez, Diego J. Sovereign debt maturity structure under asymmetric information. *Journal of International Economics*, 108:243–259, 2017. 7, 130

Perez, Diego. Sovereign debt, domestic banks and the provision of public liquidity. *Working Paper*, New York University, 2018. 159

Persson, Torsten, and Svensson, Lars. Why a stubborn conservative would run a deficit: Policy with time-inconsistent preferences. *Quarterly Journal of Economics*, 104:325–345, 1989. 39

Phan, Toan. A model of sovereign debt with private information. *Journal of Economic Dynamics and Control*, 83:1–17, 2017. 7

Pitchford, Rohan, and Wright, Mark L. J. Holdouts in sovereign debt restructuring: A theory of negotiation in a weak contractual environment. *Review of Economic Studies*, 79(2):812–837, 2012. 159

Pouzo, Demian, and Presno, Ignacio. Sovereign default risk and uncertainty premia. *American Economic Journal: Macroeconomics*, 8(3):230–266, July 2016. 11

Ray, Debraj. The time structure of self-enforcing agreements. *Econometrica*, 70(2):547–582, 2002. 23

Rebelo, Sergio, Wang, Neng, and Yang, Jinqiang. Rare disasters, financial development, and sovereign debt. *Working Paper*, Northwestern University, May 2019. 151

Reinhart, Carmen, and Rogoff, Kenneth. Serial default and the "paradox" of rich-to-poor capital flows. *American Economic Review*, 94:53–58, 2004. 9

———. *This Time Is Different: Eight Centuries of Financial Folly*. Princeton, NJ: Princeton University Press, 2009. 13

Reinhart, Carmen, Rogoff, Kenneth, and Savastano, Miguel. Debt intolerance. *Brookings Papers on Economic Activity*, 2003:1–74, 2003. 8, 39

Roldán-Peña, Jessica. Default risk and economic activity: A small open economy model with sovereign debt and default. *Working Paper* 2012-16, Banco de México, December 2012. 153

Rustichini, A. Lagrange multipliers in incentive-constrained problems. *Journal of Mathematical Economics*, 29:365–380, 1998. 20

Sachs, Jeffrey D. *Theoretical Issues in International Borrowing*. Number 54 in Princeton Studies in International Finance. Princeton University, July 1984. 92

Salomao, Juliana. Why do emerging economies accumulate debt and reserves? *Working Paper*, University of Minnesota, June 2013. 153

Salomao, Juliana. Sovereign debt renegotiation and credit default swaps. *Journal of Monetary Economics*, 90:50–63, October 2017. 12

Sánchez, Juan M., Sapriza, Horacio, and Yurdagul, Emircan. Sovereign default and maturity choice. *Journal of Monetary Economics*, 95:72–85, May 2018. 152

Sandleris, Guido. Sovereign defaults: Information, investment and credit. *Journal of International Economics*, 76:267–275, 2008. 7

Schlegl, Matthias, Trebesch, Christoph, and Wright, Mark. The seniority structure of sovereign debt. *NBER Working Paper 25793*, 2019. 6

Scholl, Almuth. The dynamics of sovereign default risk and political turnover. *Journal of International Economics*, 108:37–53, 2017. 89

Schumacher, Julian, Trebesch, Christoph, and Enderlein, Henrik. Sovereign defaults in court: The rise of creditor litigation 1976–2010. *SSRN Electronic Journal*, 2012. 7

Sosa-Padilla, Cesar. Sovereign defaults and banking crises. *Journal of Monetary Economics*, 99: 88–105, 2018. 159

Stangebye, Zachary R. Beliefs and long-maturity sovereign debt. *Journal of International Economics*, 127:103381, November 2020. 138

Stefanidis, Georgios. IMF lending in sovereign default. *Working Paper*, York University, January 2020. 127

Stefanidis, Georgios, and Paluszynski, Radoslaw. Borrowing into debt crises. *Working Paper*, York University, December 2020. 145

Sturzenegger, Federico, and Zettelmeyer, Jeromin. *Debt Defaults and Lessons from a Decade of Crises*. Cambridge, MA: MIT Press, 2007. 13

Sturzenegger, Federico, and Zettelmeyer, Jeromin. Haircuts: Estimating investor losses in sovereign debt restructurings, 1998–2005. *Journal of International Money and Finance*, 27: 780–805, 2008. 10

Sunder-Plassmann, Laura. Inflation, default and sovereign debt: The role of denomination and ownership. *Journal of International Economics*, p. 103393, 2020. 105

Thomas, Jonathan, and Worrall, Tim. Foreign direct investment and the risk of expropriation. *Review of Economic Studies*, 61(1):81–108, 1994. 34

Thomas, Jonathan, and Worrall, Timothy. Self-enforcing wage contracts. *Review of Economic Studies*, 55:541–553, 1988. 17

Tomz, Michael. *Reputation and International Cooperation: Sovereign Debt across Three Centuries*. Princeton, NJ: Princeton University Press, 2007. 13

Tomz, Michael, and Wright, Mark. Do countries default in bad times? *Journal of the European Economics Association*, 5:352–360, 2007. 9

———. Empirical research on sovereign debt and default. *Annual Reviews of Economics*, 5:247–272, 2013. 9

Tourre, Fabrice. A macro-finance approach to sovereign debt spreads and returns. *Working Paper*, 2017. 11

Trebesch, Christoph, and Zabel, Michael. The output costs of hard and soft sovereign default. *European Economic Review*, 92:416–432, 2017. 10

Uribe, Martin, and Schmitt-Grohé, Stephanie. *Open Economy Macroeconomics*. Princeton, NJ: Princeton University Press, 2017. 12

Uribe, Martin, and Yue, Vivian. Country spreads and emerging countries: Who drives whom? *Journal of International Economics*, 69:6–36, 2006. 12

Ventura, Jaume, and Voth, Hans-Joachim. Debt into growth: How sovereign debt accelerated the first Industrial Revolution. *Working Paper* 21280, National Bureau of Economic Research, 2015. 156

Worrall, Tim. Debt with potential repudiation. *European Economic Review*, 34:1099–1109, 1990. 17

Wright, Mark. Reptuations and sovereign debt. *Working Paper*, 2002. 19

Wright, M.L.J. Interpreting the pari passu clause in sovereign bond contracts: It is all Hebrew (and Aramaic) to me. *Capital Markets Law Journal*, 9(3):259–265, June 2014. 6

Yue, Vivian. Sovereign default and debt renegotiation. *Journal of International Economics*, 80: 176–187, 2010. 70

Zettelmeyer, Jeromin, Trebesch, Christoph, and Gulati, Mitu. The Greek debt restructuring: An autopsy. *Economic Policy*, 28(75):513–563, July 2013. 7

INDEX

Alfaro, Laura, 7, 90n11, 153

Arellano, Cristina, 159n4; incomplete markets and, 45, 58; long-term bonds and, 130n15, 152n35; maturity choice and, 8–9; one-period bond model and, 4, 66, 73, 80–83, 87, 89

Argentina, 5–6, 8, 11, 80, 82n8, 148n31, 157

Arrow-Debreu models, 16n2, 19n7

Auclert, Adrien, 76, 79

autarky: Bulow-Rogoff model and, 2, 28–32; deviation to, 17–18; Eaton-Gersovitz model and, 2, 69; limited commitment and, 17–18, 27–33, 154; one-period bond model and, 69–70, 73–74; payoff to government and, 17; punishment and, 2, 27, 29–32, 69–70, 73, 154; reputation and, 7

Ayres, João, 92n1, 106

Bacchetta, Philippe, 106

backloading, 2, 22, 33, 45, 51, 55

bank runs, 99, 107

Bellman equation: Hamilton-Jacobi-Bellman (HJB) equation, 50, 52, 56–57, 59, 112, 115–16, 119, 131, 139, 141–42; incomplete markets and, 50, 52, 56–57, 59; long-term bonds and, 112, 115–16, 119, 131, 139, 141–42, 146; one-period bond model and, 4, 75

Benjamin, David, 10, 70

Bianchi, Javier, 105n8, 153

Bizer, David S., 67

Bloise, Gaetano, 32, 79

Brady Plan, 5–6

Brazil, 8

break-even condition: competitive bond markets and, 3, 60; incomplete markets and, 59–63; long-term bonds and, 113–14, 120, 131, 141–42, 147; one-period bond model and, 68, 77; self-fulfilling debt crises and, 95–96, 99–100, 104

Broner, Fernando, 8–9, 28n10, 130n15, 148n31

Bulow, Jeremy: autarky and, 2, 28–32; buybacks and, 127; enforcing contracts and, 1; excusable default and, 5; limited commitment and, 2, 14, 28–32; long-term bonds and, 127; one-period bond model and, 69–70, 79; punishment and, 2, 32, 69, 79; self-enforcing constraints and, 30–32

buyback: holdouts and, 5, 120, 124–27; long-term bonds and, 13, 110, 120–30, 135, 144, 152; maturity choice and, 120–30; restructuring and, 120–30

Calvo, Guillermo, 92n1, 106, 108n12

capital flows, 3, 17n4, 34, 38

capital gains, 114, 126, 133

Chatterjee, Satyajit, 5; interest rate spreads and, 11; long-term bonds and, 111, 146–47, 148n31; maturity choice and, 8; one-period bond model and, 80–82, 86–87, 89n10; self-fulfilling debt crises and, 4, 92, 108n13

A NOTE ON THE TYPE

This book has been composed in Arno, an Old-style serif typeface in the classic Venetian tradition, designed by Robert Slimbach at Adobe.